WILL THE REVOLUTION SUCCEED?

WILL THE REVOLUTION SUCCEED?

Rebirth of the Radical Democrat

by Edward Schwartz

CRITERION BOOKS

Published by ABELARD-SCHUMAN LIMITED

LONDON • NEW YORK • TORONTO

Published in the United States by Abelard-Schuman Limited, New
York, New York.

Library of Congress Catalog Card Number 77–160104

ISBN   0 002 71855 X

Manufactured in the United States of America

CRITERION BOOKS are published by
ABELARD-SCHUMAN LIMITED, New York, N.Y. U.S.A.

LONDON	NEW YORK	TORONTO
Abelard-Schuman	Abelard-Schuman	Abelard-Schuman
Limited	Limited	Canada Limited
8 King St. WC2	257 Park Ave. So.	228 Yorkland Blvd.

An Intext Publisher

Printed in the United States of America

To the Memory of Addie Bridges

Contents

Acknowledgments

I acknowledge Professor John D. Lewis, Chairman of the Department of Government at Oberlin College, who in my junior year persuaded me that the study of political philosophy was far more relevant to the creation of social change than the study of anything else at Oberlin.

I acknowledge Wilson Carey McWilliams, a mentor, currently a Professor of Government at Livingston College in New Brunswick, New Jersey. There should be no reason for Mr. McWilliams to regret the publication of this book, inasmuch as its major arguments are based on *his* book—*The Idea of Fraternity in American Politics*—which, after 10 years in preparation, will be published by the University of California Press.

I acknowledge Edgar Z. Friedenberg whose *Coming of Age in America* and *Dignity of Youth and Other Atavisms* helped me put into words what I felt about the American system of education, and whose penetrating articles and stimulating conversations of the past three years helped me put into words what I feel about America.

I acknowledge John Schaar who helped me put into words what I felt about Edgar Friedenberg and W. Carey McWilliams.

I acknowledge three former high school English teachers—Mrs. Frances Bartlett, Mr. Frank Meyers, and Mr. John Cone—who helped me put into words what I felt.

Second, I must acknowledge those who have contributed to my efforts as a strategist.

I acknowledge Rennie Davis whose advice my freshman year at Oberlin was invalulable in showing me how to build political organizations and whose optimism in the face of extraordinary harassment has been a constant source of wonder.

I acknowledge D'Army Bailey, now a member of the Berkeley City Council, who in the summer of 1963 taught me what laying your body on the line for what you believed was all about.

I acknowledge Allard Lowenstein, the bum, who showed me that you could turn the entire country upside down if you knew what you were doing. In fact, I even have a recurrent dream—'my Allard Lowenstein dream'—in which I explain to him why I no longer agree with the strategy that he is pursuing. Yet I must admit, were there fifteen people like Allard Lowenstein trying to make the system work, the system still probably wouldn't work, but it surely would be phoning around for a repairman.

I acknowledge Michael Vozick whose friendship over the past three years has been the source of a delight as endless as our conversations about the appropriate posture for an American revolutionary. Our own posture tends to be supine; but when the last ding-dong of doom has clanged and faded from the last worthless rock hanging tideless in the last red and dying evening, even then there will still be one more sound: the two of us, having an argument.

I acknowledge Mary Lou Oates Palmer who showed me how a nice, sweet, retiring girl from Southern Philadelphia can browbeat the Associated Press, *the New York Times,* and the Columbia Broadcasting System with all its affiliated stations into covering a story.

I acknowledge Janet Berenson Sinburg, who showed me how a nice, sweet, retiring girl from Oregon can out-organize both Allard Lowenstein and Mary Lou Oates Palmer.

I acknowledge Margo Averill Neilson, who holds the world's record for the number of student body presidents persuaded by telephone to sign a petition in a single day.

I acknowledge J. Walton Senterfitt, who holds the NSA record for the largest pile of money hustled from the federal Government in a single year—above-board, anyway—but who left the racket to build a free school in California.

I acknowledge Al Milano, who showed me how an Italian boy from Brooklyn could keep an office with J. Walton Senterfitt, Margo Averill Neilson, Janet Berenson Simburg, Mary Lou Oates Palmer, Michael Vozick, and fifty other political freaks—including, as often as not, Allard Lowenstein—from exploding.

Finally, I acknowledge my wife, Jane Shull, who asked me not to, because all writers acknowledge their wives for being forbearing and stupid while they wrote their books. My wife was neither forbearing nor stupid while I wrote mine.

I acknowledge Nancy Schwartz, who will be pleasantly surprised to be acknowledged.

I acknowledge Robert Kenneth Carr, a former president of Oberlin College, who will be unpleasantly surprised to be acknowledged.

I acknowledge Bob Kuttner, Stu Rubinow, and Ann Gundersheimer in the hope that someday the troupe will perform again.

I acknowledge Cathy, Chris, Shelly, and Madeline in the hope that someday 247 will rise again.

I acknowledge John and Jeanne Lipsky, Don Shankman, Phil Furia, Bill Henderson, and Phil Singerman, in the hope that someday Keep Cottage will rise again.

I acknowledge Art Weiner, Al Handell, Julie Lokin, and Chuck and Rachelle Hollander for Sunday mornings at Hofburgs.

I acknowledge Gene Groves and Rick Stearns for the battle against the CIA; Michael Rossman, Mario Savio, Bettina Aptheker, and Frank Bardake for the battle of Berkeley; Paul Soglin for the battle of Wisconsin; Greg Movsesyian and David Hawk for the battle against the draft; Pat Roderick, Liz Tallon, Lois Balfour, and the entire Client-Oriented Caucus for the battle against the Massachusetts Department of Public Welfare; Larry Hirschhorn, Steve Arons, Rick and Barbara Yoder, and Neil and Paula Didriksen for the battle to build an Alliance for Radical Change; Teddy O' Toole and Dan McIntosh for the battle to save NSA; and Al and Ginny Record and Floyd and Carol Turner for the battle against destructive human relationships of every kind.

I acknowledge George McCray, Ellen Bulf, Randy Lee, Tina Walsh Milano, Norman Nexon, Lynn Liebermann, John Gage, Ann Beeler, Bill Callahan, and anyone else who has had to endure my smelly socks in a cooperative during the past six years, or to listen to my latest version of truth.

I acknowledge Marilyn Hornbeck, for smiling.

I acknowledge Nancy McWilliams, for laughing.

I acknowledge my mother and my late father, for caring.

Introduction

This is a book by a radical about America. It is also a book by an American about radicalism. Which precedes which? I can no longer be sure.

Since 1960, I have been involved in a variety of efforts to achieve change, ranging from participation in the Civil Rights Movement to extensive involvement in campaigns to reform the nation's colleges and universities, to more recent attempts to organize professionals in the welfare system on behalf of poor people's demands for adequate income. Radicalism for me has become more than a set of beliefs, it has become a career.

Always, however, I have felt a loyalty to the best traditions of this country, a by-product of a childhood spent in reading young people's books of American history. It is natural. My parents were not born in this country. My father is Canadian; my mother, a Russian whose family escaped the October Revolution when she was very young. For those of us who grew up in such homes, America has been a source of endless fascination. Since we cannot trace our lineage back to the Founding Fathers, we can say, "If we were alive then, we would have fought on the side of . . ." Fourth- and fifth-generation Americans, who are stuck with the mistakes of their grandparents, do not have such a luxury, and their sense of patriotism suffers for it.

Between 1966 and 1968, I served as a national officer of the National Student Association (NSA)—first, charged with administering its programs in educational change and community action, then, as its president. My concerns were straightforward enough. I felt that young people should gain increasing control over those decisions that affected them, both in the university and the society, that they should use their power to encourage social justice in the country as a whole. In this period, NSA helped popularize the slogan "student power," advising protests on over a hundred campuses. We assisted early efforts to involve "moderate" students in the anti-war movement. We helped lay the groundwork for the formation of a National Association of Black Students. We lent support to the Poor Peoples' Campaign. We initiated a law suit against General Lewis B. Hershey when he threatened to draft anyone who participated in a demonstration, and we encouraged resistance to the draft itself.

Yet even then, I was troubled. I was not convinced that my liberal friends could "make the system work" merely by devoting themselves to the McCarthy campaign and other movements within the framework of electoral politics. It seemed to me that the breakdown of politics reflected a much more serious breakdown in the social order, that the country needed a basic change in its values, in its institutions, and in the ways in which people lived their lives before many of its identifiable "problems" could be solved.

Nor, however, could I find much with which to identify in a New Left that, after such hopeful beginnings in the early sixties, was becoming little more than a cheering squad for foreign revolutions. I did not doubt that national leaders in agrarian countries of the Third World could inspire a spirit of solidarity and brotherhood in their societies, particularly in response to foreign invasion. Yet our battle was in the United States, an advanced industrial state in enormous confusion over the directions in which it was moving. The only lesson that the movements of the Third World might have taught us was that a successful revolutionary both had to identify both with the highest aspirations of his country and to display a sense of compassion for its citizens. The New Left was giving up on both assignments.

So after my term of office, I dropped out of the maelstrom of Washington, D.C., altogether—not so much out of despair as bewilderment. Why were things going so wrong? What in our ideology and our strategy was missing? Why did being an American now pose so many problems for a radical, and vice-versa? Was it simply the war in Vietnam, or were there deeper reasons that are rooted in our history as a people? And what about the people? Could they be won to our side, or were they lost, hopelessly, in W. H. Auden's words, to the "sufferings to which they are fairly accustomed?"

Pursuing these questions since then has not been enjoyable for me or for those around me. I returned to graduate school for one year—the Florence Heller School for Social Welfare at Brandeis —only to discover that what we were saying in NSA was accurate. Universities, even those that pretend to be "sympathetic," provide little help to those who are committed to creating social change. My work with organizations in the Boston area has proved little more fruitful. They, too, are not interested in moving beyond the established, and inadequate, formulas for "reform" that dominate the current scene.

Therefore, for the past nine months, I have kept to myself— reading, thinking, talking to a few close friends, and writing this book.

Do I pretend to speak for millions of people? No, I claim only to have tried to understand them, to report what I think I hear, and to make a few suggestions. Yet if this book does encourage people to rethink our situation, if it does contribute to breaking the political logjam in which we find ourselves, then it will have achieved its purpose. "In the deserts of the heart," wrote Auden in his elegy to Yeats, "Let the healing fountain start."

> *In the prison of his days*
> *Teach the free man how to praise.*

Edward Schwartz
Cambridge, Mass.
May, 1971

The horrors of our time fill our souls with reproach and everlasting shame. We have profaned the word of God, and we have given the wealth of our land, the ingenuity of our minds and the dear lives of our youth to tragedy and perdition. There never has been more reason for man to be ashamed than now. . . .

Let the blasphemy of our time not become an eternal scandal. Let future generations not loathe us for having failed to preserve what prophets and saints, martyrs and scholars have created in thousands of years. The apostles of force have shown that they are great in evil. Let us reveal that we can be as great in goodness. . . .

When Israel approached Sinai, God lifted up the mountain and held it over their heads, saying: "Either you accept the Torah or be crushed beneath the mountain."

The mountain of history is over our heads again. Shall we renew the covenant with God?

Abraham J. Heschel
Man's Quest for God

WILL THE REVOLUTION SUCCEED?

The Strategic Crisis

1 Will the revolution succeed?

The question certainly invites discussion. Indeed, there is a depressing regularity to it. In the fall, millions of students return to the nation's campuses after a quiet summer of recovery from the previous spring's rebellions. Pundits, politicians, academics, hold their breath. "Will this year be as stormy as the last?" they ask. "Has the rebellion finally subsided?" "Will more moderate young people assert themselves?" "Will the students recognize that they are generating massive repression?"

Then, relief—two weeks pass, and only three buildings are dynamited, clearly the work of "terrorists." Otherwise, the Establishment is optimistic. The Justice Department announces that its investigators, overt and covert, sense a new sobriety among young people, a recognition that previous radical tactics have failed. Local newspapers report similar comments from area campus administrators: "They missed a lot of work. They need to catch up." Others suggest that the appointment of several student leaders to faculty committees has heralded an "era of cooperation on our campus." Seymour Martin Lipset, eminent Harvard political sociologist, reiterates his biannual prediction that the "activist phase is over."

In the spring, however, all bets are off. In some years, it begins as a series of local confrontations that spread, intensify, and come to dominate the national scene. In others, an atrocity triggers it— a Cambodia, a Kent State. In still others, it is planned carefully, several months in advance—a national march, an event that sets the wheels in motion for local uprisings of every sort. Whatever the cause, it happens—convulsions everywhere, confounding the pundits, terrifying the people; until summer, that is, when the living is easier, and the cycle resumes.

It is a charade, isn't it? Some sort of Gilbert and Sullivan operetta in which we all play a part.

Yet the humor cannot conceal the main conclusion that we must draw from it. The radical movement, from its "New Politics" Right to its Maoist Left, faces a strategic crisis of major proportions.

At one point, the New Left thought of itself as nonideological, flexible, responsive, prepared to fight each travesty of justice as it appeared. Yet since 1965, it has revived virtually every ideology that has plagued radicalism since 1848. What happened?

At one point, the Movement was to be a vehicle for personal and social rejuvenation, an environment for development somehow healthier than that fostered elsewhere in the United States. Yet in the past decade we have seen the birth and death of a string of Movement operations; the disintegration of its driving force—the Students for a Democratic Society (SDS)—into eight mutually exclusive factions; and the conversion of most of its meetings into shouting matches. What happened?

At one point, the New Left talked of a society in which life and politics would be inseparable, in which all institutions would be involved in the formulation of common goals. Yet today radicals drive a wedge between their concerns and those that arouse the people. What happened?

Sheldon Wolin and John Schaar spell out the problem:[1]

> Over the first ten years, the New Left failed to create the new radical theory beyond both liberalism and socialism which the Port Huron Statement had called for. Although the New Left gradually had moved away from the single-issue, basically reformist outlook of the early sixties toward a general indictment of the system, that movement was not powered or accompanied by an increasingly coherent and comprehensive theory.

> Nor was the New Left able to develop a conception of political action coherent and effective enough, over the long pull, to sustain its members in a political vocation—to answer the question, "What does a radical look like in American politics, and how does he define himself in action which goes beyond the episodic and theatrical"

Many students telegraph their discontent as well.

What is missing now is *self*-confidence. A feeling pervades that even the language that the Left uses to describe the country has lost touch with what it is, with what it might be. Students are reluctant to continue traveling roads that have led to defeat in the past, yet they see no new ones to replace them. Hence, they withdraw, confining their complaints to intimate pot parties at which small groups of Jews contemplate the impending Nazi take-over.

Significantly, many Movement leaders themselves have grown concerned about the current status of the Left. A desire to undertake some "thinking and reading" was as much responsible for Sam Brown's leaving the Moratorium as were shifting public attitudes about the war.[2] In *The Trial*, Tom Hayden—a founder of the Students for a Democratic Society—calls for "more transformation of *white, male, middle-class attitudes*" among radicals and directs strong criticism at the Conspiracy itself:[3]

> *Our male chauvinism, elitism, and egoism were merely symptoms of the original problem—the Movement did not choose us to be its symbols; the press and government did. The entire process by which known leaders become known is almost fatally corrupting. Only males with driving egos have been able to "rise" in the Movement or the rock culture and be accepted by the media and dealt with seriously by the Establishment.*

At this point, the list of activists in relative seclusion, pondering the state of the world, would fill a year of *Newsweek* "Where Are They Now?" columns—ranging from Curtis Gans, former Staff Director of the McCarthy Campaign, to Mario Savio, main spokesman for the Free Speech Movement.

Everyone knows that a reversal of the Left's priorities is in order; everyone knows that with each abortive action, with each stultifying rally, with each half-cocked plan to save humanity with a weekend of marches, the chance of creating radical change grows dimmer.

Plus ça change, plus c'est la même chose.

Of course, there are activists who are attempting to propose alternatives. Some, like Sam Brown, insist that electoral politics is the answer, arguing that the election of "radical-liberal" candidates is an essential prerequisite to achieving what they perceive to be the major goals that the Movement has set for itself—an end to counterrevolutionary activity in the Third World; a reversal of national priorities from military to domestic programs. These are mediator-leaders trying to strike the classic American compromise by which liberals will move to the Left in exchange for which radicals will discard their disruptive tactics. Hence, they contend, the central problem lies in moderating the rhetoric, toning down the slogans, cooling off the demonstrations. In Brown's formulation, if there is a choice between John Lindsay's and Jerry Rubin's speaking at a rally—well, bring on the mayor! Not surprisingly, older liberals return the compliment with periodic speeches, editorials, and columns urging the young to heed their more "responsible" spokesmen.

A second alternative emerges in the writings of veteran activists of the New Left. Tom Hayden, for example, finds the sort of electoral campaigns in which Brown would have people engage to be a relatively ineffective vehicle for Movement politics. "The problem in this political strategy consistently," he writes in *The Trial*, "has been an over-reliance on politicians and an under-reliance on popular pressure. . . . The tragedy is that many young people who accept these notions of change are simply not confident of their own power . . . That power does not reside in their electoral potential but in their potential to disrupt the vital institutions containing them (the universities), to break the link between generations, to threaten the future stability of the country."[4]

Yet the tactical argument is merely a part of a broader strategic perspective, one that a number of students living in university communities take quite seriously. It is easy, indeed, for a resident of Berkeley, California, or Cambridge, Massachusetts, to believe, in Hayden's words, that "With the passage of time, with the further decay of the American empire, the discontent now felt most by youth will spread with them wherever they go to work or live. In the long run, then, the alienation of youth many become an alienation *of the whole people*.[5]

Thus, Hayden urges students and recent graduates to create "Free Territories"—large areas of the country that the Left would control. These, he contends, would serve as "utopian centers of new cultural experiment," "centers of internationalism," "centers of confrontation," "battlefronts inside the Mother Country," and "centers of survival and self-defense."[6] Ultimately, such territories would encompass areas of the United States so large that, in conjunction with revolutionary movements in the ghettos and the Third World, a "world-wide" confrontation between "the people and the pigs" could be effected with success.[7] An ingenious updating of Trotsky's strategy of "dual power," this image of Hayden's, with a rising class of the exploited young replacing the working class; a liberated university replacing liberated factories and cities —yet it has proponents.

A third alternative, dropping out of society altogether, has also attracted a growing number of converts, particularly as radical politics has come to seem so much a dead end. New advocates for "splitting," moreover, demand a far different life style than that projected by Haight-Ashbury a few years ago. "The life of the community," Ray Mungo, among the most prominent in this group, reports in *Famous Long Ago*, "the families building their new nation, is the only life on the planet now. Outside the door is adventure and beauty beyond description, but also danger. The dead bodies of our predecessors were stored in the barns till spring thawed out the land. Now the community can pray together for survival, and test its skills against the wild wrath of the heavens. . . . Here's the beginning of the "peace movement of the 70's, here's a clumsy attempt at self sufficiency, here's a bigger underground press than ever, for each hath one and is one . . ."[8]

The new commune-ists are nothing like the utopians of the past. As Mark Holloway suggests in his introduction to John Humphrey Noyes' *History of American Socialisms,* leaders of nineteenth-century communes possessed, "the absolute conviction that they and they alone had chosen the right path, and the ability to persuade others that this was so."[9] By contrast, Mungo asserts, "We're not trying to convince the world. The world has an energy of it's own, and we're only a tiny part of that."[10] Indeed, the mood here is less reform, reconstruction, than resignation. An older defender of the counterculture, Edgar Z. Friedenberg, expressed the sentiment well a few years ago. "Politics in our society," he observed, "demand that you have to deceive, flatter, and exploit weak, helpless, and often uncomprehending people in order to make out with them. . . . I do not think they can be remedied by application of the processes of reconstruction that have been built into it. Since revolution does not appeal to me on the basis of its previous record and is certainly not a responsibility to be imposed on the young, the alternative seems to me to be to emphasize private, personal, and particularistic relationships."[11]

Thus, the "drop-outs" seek intimacy and peace in harmony with nature. In return, they promise to live as good men and women, neither polluting nor destroying nor competing much for the dwindling supply of the world's resources. "We're only trying to change ourselves, what a preoccupation! But if we get better, I get better, you get better that's a tangible change, isn't it?"[12] Mungo's question may beg the central questions, but for him and those like him it is the only one worth asking.

Yet to a great many people, each of these alternatives begs the central questions. Nor do I refer to the ones who couldn't care less about radicals, the Movement, or anything to the Left of Robert McNamara. No, I mean those who are sympathetic to the Movement; who identify with the Conspiracy; who participate in the marches. I mean older people who are fed up with the state of the country, who understand that there must be a fundamental reconstruction of values, but who don't know how to go about effecting it. Both groups are confused by the various proposals, and they have good reason to be.

For example, anyone who engages in politics in this country

learns after a short time that the way to combat large institutions is to fight them at several points around the country. The Civil Rights Movement succeeded in this way, as did the numerous challenges against Dow Chemicals' manufacturing of napalm. The grape boycott, sponsored by the farm workers in California, operated on this principle as well. The strategy is essential, given the way in which national power disperses itself in the United States.

Thus, a Movement that hopes to succeed must prepare for long-range local organizing. Saul Alinsky is insistent on this point:[13]

> *The fundamental issue is how we go about building a national movement when so many of the present generation do not want to undergo the experience in time or detail of the organization of the parts, or of the local areas of organization. They want to jump right into a national organization. Either they do not want to do the tough and tedious job of building the parts, or are incapable of it, or it is a combination of both. Creative organizers are a rarity.*

Alinsky is not alone. One finds proponents of a sustained, localist approach among many groups on the Left.

Yet has the Movement responded effectively? Of course everyone pays lip service to "decentralization." "New Politics" liberals turn away from extravaganzas like the Moratorium to Congressional races, local elections, attempts to take over reform clubs. Hayden shifts from amassing people for national demonstrations back to the sort of base-building work he used to do in Newark— albeit, this time organizing young people into the "liberated area" of Berkeley. The New York "brain" of the Progressive Labor Party, true always to Mao, disperses a nervous system of cadres to various cities to build "support for the struggle" on campuses and in middle-class unions. The "street people" create collectives among themselves, broadening their base slightly by publishing newspapers and establishing consumer cooperatives for the purchase of food. Communes bring a new "element" to out-of-the-way-states like Vermont.

In practice, however, the behavior is quite different. Instead of *organizing* people locally in ways that give them a solid base from which to fight the establishment, radicals *mobilize* people for specific, one-shot actions designed to attract the attention of the media—just like the old days. It is ludicrous. A "revolutionary" who spends most of his time arguing that *real* decisions are made behind the scenes, beyond the scrutiny of the public, sees himself as Lenin the moment his name appears in the *New York Times*. The scene after campus demonstrations more resembles opening night on Broadway than a revolution, with the radicals huddled around the student union TV set watching for the 6:00 P.M. news like actors in Sardi's waiting for reviews. There is a difference between *power* and *attention,* but the Movement has not discovered it.

A Movement needs allies.

How many times have we heard the cry that the Left should build alliances with the poor, the blacks, the working people of the country?

Thus far it has been unable to do so.

Of course, in contrast to the late sixties, when SDS activists seemed to want to go it alone, every New Movement spokesman has a strategy for winning friends. "We have forgotten the working man," Sam Brown would say in campus appearances for Connecticut Senatorial candidate Joe Duffey, "whose real income has dropped every quarter since 1965. We must emphasize the economic effects of the war." Tom Hayden, while valuing alliances with Third World guerilla movements over those with the working class ("there comes a time when time is running out, when there can be no more waiting for the Silent Majority or the Working Class to be taking the stand which we have to take"[14]), argues that a coalition with black people is essential. "We need a nationwide 'political education' class or 'teach-in' as a tactic to create consciousness of this emerging domestic war against the Panthers," he writes. "Taking to the streets against racism and repression can be as important now as it was in the earlier phases of the anti-war movement."[15] Even Ray Mungo pays lip service to the problem of coalition-building— "Kiss your neighbor. . . ."[16] he tells us.

"Delivering," on these pledges, however, is proving difficult. Hayden himself understands well the difficulty of building alliances between white students and poor blacks. Whites "live better materially, never experience the daily crises that the Panthers do, never are repressed as severely as blacks," he acknowledges. "Even becoming 'more militant' than blacks cannot erase the color line: whites who try to act like John Brown are usually seen by blacks as manipulators who will not have to bear the consequences for whatever repression they bring down. . . . In political terms, this means that although whites can help the black struggle, they are inherently undependable."[17]

Yet even he is too gentle. He fails to make the point that blacks themselves make—that white radicals have yet to demonstrate a willingness and a capacity to organize their *own* communities around the issue of racism with anything approaching the energy and skill that they have brought to the anti-war movement. Lacklustre response to massacres at Orangeburg, South Carolina, in 1968 and Jackson State in 1970 are only flagrant examples. By and large, the students did not go "back to the suburbs" as Stokely

Carmichael asked. They went back to their universities and after a few months talked about the war—at the expense of the blacks. *Of course*, the blacks now resent them.

Radical attempts to create alliances with the working class have proved even less successful. The Boston experience is indicative. In the summer of 1969, the SDS sponsored a "work-in" in factories. It lasted no longer than the summer—less time than the brief periods that activists of the early sixties devoted to the South. During a strike against G.E. later that year, workers from one local plant ejected representatives from the Progressive Labor Party for distributing leaflets that attacked union leadership as "counter-revolutionary." Other radicals boasted of successful attempts at political education around the war and imperialism in factories without making any effort even to understand, let alone challenge, oppressive conditions affecting the workers themselves.

There is some humor in all of this, but much of it vanishes when one realizes that the young radicals have related to working people no more sympathetically than do their liberal parents. Though their "raps" have differed from those of the liberals who try to "civilize" the workers, they still have seen themselves as apostles of enlightenment with a peculiar mission to set those deluded saps straight about their oppression in terms that they simply *must* understand. Sadly, there is no precise word like "racism" to describe the prejudice that one class develops toward another. It would be appropriate here.

Yet the most critical need of a Movement—one demanded by everyone—is that it relate its general theories to the basic concerns of people as they live their lives.

For example, between 1966 and 1968, a small group of us branched away from the larger "Movement" to build a body of thought and action that became known as the Educational Reform Movement. Our main interest was in social change. Like other radicals of the period, we believed that society could not resolve its acknowledged political conflicts without a fundamental transformation of predominant institutions. Unlike them, however, we did not believe that merely talking about the Vietnam War, racism, and poverty was sufficient. One had to ask, we felt, "What is the nature of a country that enables Vietnams, racism, and poverty to develop?" Why was it, we inquired, that most citizens were unresponsive to the needs of the poor, indifferent to the demands of black people, and unconcerned about the suppression of revolutionary movements elsewhere in the world? The indifference struck as being as serious as the so-called problems themselves.

The questions pushed us to look at the processes of the society itself. Somehow, we found, the ingredients of what used to be called "politics" in the United States—that is, the debate surrounding public values and programs—had shifted to private corporations and bureaucracies that justified their decisions by reference to some mystical "role" that only they were fit to play. These institutions were interrelated—people moved from one to another—and inclusive. They performed virtually all social functions. To attack one was to threaten them all.

Moreover, higher education was a central cog in the wheel. Over time, it had become completely wedded to the process of production, explicitly through its reliance on industrial and government research grants for funding, implicitly through the structure of curriculum and courses. Universities trained students in styles of thought, behavior, and ideology appropriate to problem-solving—Jacques Ellul's notion of "technique": "the translation into action of man's concern to master things by means of reasons, to account for what is subconscious, make quantitative what is qualitative, make clear and precise the outlines of nature . . ."[18] That the product of the system was geared to meeting middle- and upper-class needs for private consumption, that its ethic sustained a competitive spirit that alienated men from one another, that the blind worship of production without regard for its uses was itself becoming a serious crisis in the growth of man—these were unimportant issues to most leaders of universities, as they became, in the approving words of Clark Kerr, the handmaidens of society.

Hence, we developed a major strategic proposition: If we could change patterns of educational institutions, then we could create new kinds of people who would rebel against other institutions as well. By encouraging communal values in the universities, we could project a model of a new kind of social order as a whole, with a drastically altered balance between public and private, competitive and cooperative values.

This proposition enabled us to address ourselves to the basic concerns of students' lives. We gained national attention by encouraging undergraduates to challenge the social relations, the power relations, between the various factions of campus governance—faculty, administration, trustees. We challenged grades, tests, credits, courses—all those arrangements that duplicated the competitive process of the corporation. We attacked the process, or lack of it, by which students determined their course of study as well as the curricula offered to students in making that determination. We attempted, in general, to open students to the notion that learning was self-development as much as the absorption of facts; that the creation of strong communities was the prerequisite to healthy personal growth; that a university in a world of revolution had to encourage action, experiment, conflict, not inhibit them.

And we succeeded. First, students obtained power in the decision-making processes of the campuses—a plank straight out of the original SDS platform. Then, they won a loosening of requirements and grading procedures. They began to develop their own courses and to formulate new methods of teaching. At a few institutions, they gained academic credit for direct work in the community. Most important, they legitimized the notion that a major institution *could* be changed if people worked at it—an important lesson to convey at a time when imparting a spirit of hope and confidence was becoming difficult.

Yet how did the rest of the Movement respond to these developments?

At best, radicals looked the other way, citing their own programs—all valuable, to be sure—as priorities. At worst, however, they attacked the campus efforts. The McCarthy kids, by and large, viewed them as "Mickey Mouse," certainly less interesting than electing a President of the United States. The "revolutionaries" saw little hope of changing higher education without overthrowing the system as a whole, even though they themselves were anxious to dramatize concrete connections that they were able to uncover between universities and the government. A few from both camps insisted that "university reform" was cooptive, that is, that it would satisfy students with a few minor changes in their courses when their angry involvement in a revolution was required.

The result was that the main body of radicals active in politics cut themselves off from an equally large number of students interested in education—to the detriment of both. Major campus upheavals like the Columbia strike showed the absurdity of the situation. The Left would sit in on a building, generally in support of two.or three specific demands relating to racism and the war. A large body of students, mostly irritated at general conditions of university life, would join them. Swiftly, the university would capitulate to the radicals' ultimatums—they tended to be symbolic, anyway—leaving only the broader institutional issues open for discussion. Instead of seizing leadership on these questions as well, however, the radicals would mumble something about "irrelevant nonsense," and leave the process of subsequent negotiations to the "moderates." Just as educational concerns had not polluted the political questions, so now, political concerns would not interfere with educational questions.

This was the state of a Movement that had begun as a search for what it called "integration of all areas of life."

"The role of the radical throughout the ages," writes Sidney Lens, "has been as antidote to privilege. Whatever his failings and ineptitudes, he has tried to repair the balance between those who have too much and those who have too little."[19]

The theme recurs again and again in radical writings. Thomas Paine tells the French Legislature in 1797 that, "when wealth and splendor, instead of fascinating the multitude, excite emotions of disgust . . . the case of property becomes critical, and it is only in a system of justice that the possessor can contemplate security."[20] Mark Twain, in his stirring defense of the Knights of Labor nearly 100 years later, contrasts the lot of the "few: the king, the capitalists, and a handful of other overseers and superintendents," with that of the "many—the workers; they that *make* the bread that the soft-handed and idle eat. . . . Why is it right that there is not fairer division of the spoils around?"[21] Agrarian Populists frequently see their world in terms of the "Goulds and Vanderbilts and Rockefellers," on the one hand, and "the industrial army, every man of which like the Saviour has no where to lay his head," on the other.[22] And today, of course, one thinks of the numerous indictments fashioned by urban blacks:

> *There is no need for anyone to be talking about a war on poverty, for instance, in the United States of America. What we need in the United States is a war . . . on the system that allows poverty to exist in the midst of all those riches.*[23]

> *The Nixon-Agnew-Mitchell administration—hand in hand with the Reagans, the Daleys, the Hoffmans, the Carswells, Rockefellers, Duponts, the Bank of America, and other exploiters—moves closer and closer to open fascism.*[24]

Those who see the world in terms of the privileged and the exploited, the haves and the have-nots, are special sorts of people. They are unpopular not because they want to be but because they have to be—because they respond to an exacting God who demands allegiance to justice regardless of the costs. In complacent times, the radical is a lonely prophet who perceives a horrible reality behind the illusions with which his fellow men and women have become too comfortable. In periods of crisis, the people ask him to translate their gnawing sense of wrong into an image of an alternative social order.

He raises expectations when others counsel patience, and in so doing increases their claims against himself. If he promises improvement, he must prove his ability to gain it. He must become an analyst, a philosopher, a strategist, a spokesman. He must excel both in virtue and talent, lest he lose either the admiration of the people, or their respect. If he is too kind, he is scorned. If he is too militant, he is hated. He has little room for error.

The radical concerns himself with *social* realities. He sees the world not merely in terms of the private destinies of people, but in terms of the relationships between them. When he works with the poor, he thinks of the rich, sipping crème de menthe from crystal glasses, oblivious to the suffering only miles from their homes. When he confronts the rich, he imagines the poor—their babies crying, the roaches crawling over their food. He explodes at what to "civilized" men seem "reasonable" remarks, because to the radical each off-hand comment about the "culturally deprived" or the "ignorant" is a slur on a friend, on someone whose experience he has shared.

The radical is concerned about *equality*, about erasing distinctions of rank, wealth, and power that enable some to live at the expense of others. In the eighteenth century, he points to man's natural state—the condition in which each of us enters the world —to justify his claim that social inequality is against the true interests of man. In the nineteenth century, he sees equality as the logical consequence of the unfolding of history, the kingdom that emerges when the oppressed finally triumph over their oppressors. In recent America, he demands equality as a right of citizenship; as a mandate of tradition; as the price of survival. Whatever his rationale, if privilege is vice to the radical, equality is the virtue to which it corresponds, the objective to which he commits his greatest energy.

Often, the radical is a *religious* person. American radicals, particularly, draw upon the teachings of traditional religion, even without wishing or intending it. One thinks of Eldridge Cleaver's embarrassed admission that his use of the term "Babylon" to describe America is the symbol of a decadent society found in Revelations. "*Fuck* the Bible. I don't want to peddle the Bible. But it comes out of the Bible anyway, out of Revelations."[25] Or Tom Hayden's parallel between the plight of the New Left and that of the early Christians: "Christ's very existence—the idea he embodied was sufficient to provoke the Establishment into violent overreaction."[26] Yet Cleaver and Hayden are hardly the first to invoke the Deity in defense of basic change. Thomas Paine found "freedom" "highly rated" in heaven,[27] and Mark Twain described the labor movement as "the only time in this world that the grace of God, King, was ever uttered when it was not a lie."[28] Eugene Debs, equated Christ with socialism:

> Jesus taught that the air and the sea and the sky and all the beauty and fullness thereof were for all the children of many; and that they should equally enjoy the riches of nature and dwell together in peace, and bear one another's burdens and love one another, and that is what socialism teaches and why the rich thieves who have laid hold of the earth and its bounties would crucify the Socialists as those robbers of the poor crucified Jesus two thousand years ago.[29]

And nowhere do the religious feelings of radicals emerge more insistently than when they discuss organized religion itself. "If Christ were here now," Mark Twain snarled around the turn of the century, "there is one thing he would *not* be—a Christian."[30] Yet even Twain has been matched more recently by Saul Alinsky, who explains in almost every speech why, "I never talk to a Catholic Priest, or a Protestant minister or a rabbi in terms of the Judeo-Christian ethic or the Ten Commandments or the Sermon on the Mount. . . . If I approached them in a moralistic way, it would be outside of their experience, because Christianity and Judeo-Christianity are outside of the experience of organized religion."[31]

The radical maintains an abiding distrust of hubris—man's pride, his quest for control over nature at the expense of his neighbor. Look, in every philosophy of the Left, for the apparatus that is supposed to tame man's lust for private gain. In the Anti-Federalists and Paine—indeed, through Jackson—it is the strength of the agrarian community against the government of kings, aristocrats, and bankers that guarantees humility and virtue. In the Workingmen's Parties, it is the might of the union against the industrial magnates. In the Populist Platform, it is the national government that must curtail the rampages of the plutocrats against the downtrodden masses of farmers and workers. Among the Marxists, it is the commitment to live in accordance with immutable laws of history, to the best of one's ability to understand them. Among the Leninists, Bolshevik or otherwise, it is the vanguard party that disciplines. Radicals debate furiously among themselves as to *which* of these means is best suited to curb avarice, yet the need for some mechanism, they do not dispute.

Nonetheless, radicals maintain faith in man's *potential* for good, for decency, if only institutions can be developed to encourage it. It is this faith that divides the radical from the conservative. The conservative lives either in a godless world, whose "natural laws" dictate the inevitable triumph of the strong over the weak, or a world whose god is so lofty, so magisterial, that it is foolish for men even to try to imitate his ways on earth. Each person is alone, locked irrevocably in a private self, which thwarts all efforts to help others in a useful way. The only promise that a community can make to its members is that of order; and, given the human condition, order must be enforced by weapons and arms.

By contrast, the radical seeks always to test what men might do *for* one another. The selfishness of men, their loneliness, is to him a challenge, not an excuse. "Is that *all* you can do?" he asks. "Can't you do more?" "How can we build a society that will help us *want* to do more for one another?" He poses Rousseau's question: "To find a form of association which may defend and protect with the whole force of the community the person and property of every associate, and by means of which each, coalescing with all, may nevertheless obey only himself, and remain as free as before?"[32] In other words, how can a citizen *insist* upon helping his community? How can he feel that he is free *only* when he is involved in a common enterprise with his brothers?

The radical believes in *power*—not the power of a king or a tyrant, who exalts himself above the people, but the power *of* a people to determine for itself the common laws under which it will live. "But let no man or combinations of men who ruthlessly exploit their fellow men," Alinsky writes, "assume because of the nobility and spiritual quality of the radical's hopes that he will not stand up for the fulfillment of his dreams, for . . . he carries within him the words of Jehova—'I will make my arrows drunken with blood, and my sword shall devour flesh from the blood of the slain and of the captives from the crushed head of the enemy.' "[33] "Black Power!" "Student Power!"—these are slogans of radical movements, whose tone and substance foretell of battles to change social relationships often "by any means necessary."

Yet to the radical, power is not an end, but the means, the essential means to the pursuit of *justice*. Again, one need look no further than the basic documents of Western culture to derive a conception of the just community that radicals seek. This community must encourage each citizen to discover that work to which he is suited. As Plato concluded, "Justice admittedly means that a man should possess and concern himself with what properly belongs to him."[34] Marx insisted that a decent society must provide appropriate rewards for its members' work. "From each according to his ability, to each according to his needs!"[35] The notion that a state must hold all its citizens accountable to standards of justice fills the Old Testament. "You shall do no injustice in judgment; you shall not be partial to the poor or defer to the great, but in righteousness shall you judge your neighbor."[36] And the contradiction between the pursuit of wealth and the pursuit of justice is a major theme of the New Testament. "No one can serve two masters: for either he will hate the one and love the other, or he will be devoted to the one and despise the other. You cannot serve God and mammon."[37]

Thus, regardless of the many disagreements among radicals throughout history and today—as to whether man is naturally evil or good; as to whether utopia is within his grasp or beyond it; as to whether morality is decreed by God, reason, or history; as to whether equality must be guaranteed by custom, government, or revolution—one vision united them: A world in which men care about one another as deeply as about themselves; in which differences of appearance, style, skill, and intellect become the sources of joy rather than fear; in which a common respect for justice overrides the war of all against all.

This is the dream of the radical, of the one who cries out against privilege.

Yet radicals are not perfect. They are human; therefore, they fail. Indeed, the very height of their aspirations make their imperfections seem all the more apparent. They misjudge themselves and those around them. They employ force at times when reason would do. They talk, sometimes, when nothing is needed at all. They can forget their dreams in their desire to win, or forget to win in their desire to dream. If at their best, they inspire millions to demand the best in themselves, at their worst, they alienate even their friends with slogans and worn-out manifestos.

And it is this side of the Left that we have seen in the past few years—the imperfect side—the side which loses confidence in the people to respond. Radicals, after all, are products of this society, the institutions of which devote far more energy to teaching techniques by which individuals might "make do" on their own than to give people the skills needed for effective political action. If young revolutionaries are dissatisfied with the world that they must enter, this does not mean that they are equipped to change it.

Thus, to ask, "Will the revolution succeed?" is to ask, "Can a radical movement revive?" Can the young people who fought successfully for social change in the sixties persuade their elders to join in a common effort to transform the country? Or will the journey end as Saul Alinsky fears it might?

> . . . we will see that the disillusionment, boredom, and sense of failure will finally fertilize a rationale of, "Well, I tried to fight this system, the establishment, I tried to do something but people won't listen and this whole goddamned system has just got to collapse of its own inner moral decay. There's no sense in my demonstrating and starving, so then. . . ." So then they get a job on Madison Avenue and at the ripe old age of twenty-eight are "elder statesmen" of their own fevered imaginations, ready to start reminiscing about, "their radical youth."[38]

The ingredients for a revival of the Left are all there—a reactionary, generally uninspiring President; a crisis in the economy; a *malaise* among the people about *all* parties, *all* movements, *all* political leaders; a sense even among so-called "moderates" that something has to happen to break the pattern that has brought violence from the few, apathy and cynicism from the many.

Moreover, there is an added ingredient. Jerry Rubin, notwithstanding, young people are growing up. Those of us who cut our political teeth in John Kennedy's 1960 Presidential campaign, who participated in Civil Rights demonstrations, who remember when there was neither an anti-war movement nor a phrase "student power," now are five, six, seven years out of undergraduate college. If we have not "liberated" any zones, we at least have remained active, some of us as professional radicals—organizing the poor, creating underground magazines and newspapers, opening coffee houses for GI's and drop-in centers for high school students; others of us, with advanced degrees, as radical professionals—using our skills to assist the various Left movements and causes, while challenging liberal dominance over the professional associations and the professions themselves. All of us see the task of developing a "conception of political action coherent and effective enough to sustain us in political vocation over the long pull," as being not simply the highest theoretical priority for the Movement, but the highest personal priority for ourselves.

The problem lies in pulling these ingredients together.

I want to explore the prospects for radicalism in the seventies. Specifically, I want to discuss what those who seek a revolution in this country might do to foment it.

In the next two chapters, I intend to explore the conditions that already have fostered radicalism in our society, particularly among young people. In so doing, I can draw a few conclusions about the process of radicalization itself—how it happens, what prerequisites must be met for it to occur.

I intend to examine today's crisis in both its theoretical and historical context. If neither liberalism nor socialism seem to fit the categories that the New Left has developed, then what *is* its set of fundamental beliefs and where do they come from?

Finally, I am going to talk about the problems of creating social change—in the university, through electoral politics, through organizing of communities and in existing institutions, and in the country as a whole.

The agenda is large, I admit, but at this point, it is the only one worth undertaking.

REFERENCES

1. Sheldon Wolin and John Schaar, *The Berkeley Rebellion and Beyond* (New York, *New York Review of Books,* Random House, 1970), p. 121.
2. Sentiments expressed in conversations in Joe Duffey's Campaign, February, 1970
3. Tom Hayden, *Trial* (New York; Holt, Rinehart, & Winston, 1970), pp. 109–11.
4. *Ibid.,* 137–38.
5. *Ibid.,* p. 155.
6. *Ibid.,* p. 163.
7. *Ibid.,* pp. 161–62.
8. Ray Mungo, *Famous Long Ago* (Boston, Beacon Press, 1970), pp. 197–201.
9. Mark Holloway, introduction. In John Humphrey Noyes, *History of American Socialisms* (New York, Dover, 1966), p. vi.
10. Mungo, *op. cit.,* p. 196.
11. Edgar Z. Friedenberg, *Dignity of Youth and Other Atavisms* (Boston, Beacon Press, 1965), *Preface,* p. 17.
12. Mungo, *op. cit.,* p. 202.
13. Saul Alinsky, *Reveille for Radicals* (New York, Vintage, 1969), p. 226.
14. Tom Hayden, *op. cit.,* p. 145–46
15. *Ibid.,* p. 225
16. Ray Mungo, *op. cit.,* p. 202.
17. Tom Hayden, *op. cit.,* pp. 109–111.
18. Jacques Ellul, *The Technological Society* (New York, Random House, 1964) p. 43.
19. Sidney Lens, *Radicalism in America* (New York, Thomas Y. Crowell Co., 1969), p. 1.
20. Thomas Paine, "Agrarian Justice," in John Dos Passos, *The Living Thoughts of Tom Paine* (Greenwich, Conn., Premier, 1961), p. 148.
21. Quoted in Philip S. Foner, *Mark Twain: Social Critic* (New York, International Publishers, 1966), p. 168.
22. Lorenzo Lewelling, "Speech at Huron Place, July 26, 1894." In George B. Tindall, *A Populist Reader* (New York, Harper, 1966), p. 158.
23. Lee Lockwood, *Conversation with Eldridge Cleaver* (New York, Delta, 1970), p. 64.
24. Bobby Seale, *Sieze the Time* (New York, Vintage, 1970), p. 428.
25. Lee Lockwood, *op. cit.,* p. 53.
26. Tom Hayden, *op. cit.,* p. 42.

27. Thomas Paine, *American Crisis*, in Dos Passos, *op. cit.*, p. 81.
28. Foner, *op. cit.*, p. 173.
29. Quoted in James Weinstein, *The Decline of American Socialism: 1912–25* (New York, Vintage, 1967) p. 21.
30. Foner, *op. cit.*, p. 53.
31. Alinsky, *op. cit.*, p. x21
32. Jean Jacques Rousseau, *The Social Contract* (New York, Washington Square Press, 1967), pp. 17–18.
33. Alinsky, *op. cit.*, p. 18.
34. Plato, *Republic*, ed. Francis Donald Cornford (New York, Oxford, 1945), Chap. XII:IV, 433, p. 128.
35. Karl Marx, *Critique of the Gotha Program*, in Lewis Feuer, *Marx and Engels: Basic Writings in Politics & Philosophy* (New York, Anchor, 1959), p. 119.
36. Leviticus, 22:32.
37. Matthew, 7:5.
38. Saul Alinsky, *op. cit.*, p. 232.

Daddy, Where
Do Radicals
Come From?

2 In the first chapter, I sketched out a few central concerns of radicalism: privilege; social relationships; equality; duty; justice. How do young people develop such concerns in our society? Before we can examine what they might do, we must understand who they are. We must ask, "Why do the young *become* radical?"

There have been a number of theories to explain it. One that held sway in the early sixties argued that radical children merely were the offspring of radical parents. Those who held this view contended that although the fifties provided little opportunity for dissent, Old Left activists did not relinquish their views, they merely went underground. By the sixties, their militant sons and daughters had grown up, fully prepared to begin where mother and father left off. Some people in the Movement itself accepted this analysis and suggested that radical ancestry become a criterion for inviting people to conferences, until, as W. Carey McWilliams put it, "they began to sound suspiciously like refugees from the British aristocracy." To this day, there are those who contend that the only *real* radicals—reliable, trustworthy, and all that—are those who gained their political education around the breakfast table.

A second hypothesis became popular among conservatives, social scientists, and members of the American Psychiatric Association. Briefly, it stated that young radicals were little more than father-haters, displacing hostility toward an authoritarian or a rejecting male parent onto any other authority figure that got in its way. Lewis Feuer's *Conflict of Generations* was the major testament to this theology, examining the atrocities of student protests all over the world in more than five hundred action-packed pages. Feuer found a positive quality here and there—idealism, social concern, energy—and an issue or two that prompted the uprisings at specific periods. Sometimes, a rebellion was even justified, though rarely the one that actually happened. Most often, however, whatever good the revolutions produced was secondary to the violence, the destructiveness, the explosive power that they unleashed in their wake. History was irrelevant to this process, merely a backdrop against which the young would re-enact the oedipal saga in all its horror. Left unchecked, Feuer warned, it could destroy the world.

By far, however, the most penetrating of these analyses, and one that refuted both the "red-diaper baby" and the "radical rebel" theory in its text, was provided by Dr. Kenneth Keniston, psychologist at Yale University. In the summer of 1967, he undertook a study of participants in Vietnam Summer—the three-month canvassing drive against the war involving a number of student radicals—aimed specifically at exploring how their attitudes had evolved. He conducted interviews with students, examining family background, education, experience within the Movement itself. He probed unusual areas. What were the activists' first memories? their sense of historical movement? their experience with violence? He talked with them both during and after the summer project, hoping to compare perspectives on their work. The conclusions that he reached, reported in a book entitled *Young Radicals,* soon became part of the conventional wisdom about the student left.

Keniston's main proposition was that radicalization occurred not so much in the home as in society as a whole. Parents, to be sure, played an important role. For the most part, they were liberals living in the affluent suburbs who inculcated values into their children that they themselves frequently ignored. As Keniston's subjects put it, "On the one hand, the father was portrayed as highly ethical, intellectual, strong, principled, honest, politically involved, and idealistic. But on the other hand, this same father in other contexts was seen as unsuccessful, acquiescent, weak or inadequate."[1] Yet although the "formal values" of parents (their views on social and political matters) conflicted with those of their children, the "core values" ("basic assumptions concerning desirable human relationships, feelings and motives") remained the same. "The great majority of these radicals' parents currently applaud, approve, or accept their activities. . . ."[2]

The country was somewhat less enthusiastic about them, however. Indeed, Keniston continued, it was not until the young confronted society that they even realized the disparity between their parents' ideals and behavior. "These young men and women took affluence and opportunity for granted, so it rarely occurred to them to feel guilty about something that had always been a fact of their lives."[3] Therefore, they became "angry and indignant upon realizing that their own good fortune was not shared, their disillusion when the social myth they had believed began to seem false, and their indignation when they 'really' understood that the benefits they had experienced had not been extended to others."[4]

They learned that the mild hypocrisy of their parents was merely a symptom of the massive hypocrisy of the system as a whole:

> In most societies . . . there occurs what can be called the institutionaliza-
> tion of hypocrisy. Children and adolescents routinely learn when it is
> 'reasonable' to expect that the values parents profess will be imple-
> mented in their behavior, and when it is not reasonable . . . In time of
> rapid social change and value change, the institutionalization of hy-
> pocrisy tends to break down . . . The universal gap between principle
> and practice appears without disguise . . . What is special about the
> present situation of rapid value change is, first, that parents themselves
> tend to have two conflicting sets of values, one related to the experience
> of their childhood; the other to the ideologies and principles acquired
> in their adulthood; and, second, that no stable institutions or rules for
> defining hypocrisy out of existence have yet been fully developed.[5]

In the home, at least, young radicals had been able to debate matters. Elsewhere, they encountered administrators who refused to discuss grievances with them, politicians who dodged questions, bureaucrats who hid behind their "authority" rather than defend a position, and reactionaries who attacked their motives. Their anger intensified.

Finally, they entered the Movement itself. There, they met others who shared their beliefs; experienced the strain of attempt-ing to achieve change on a continuing basis; encountered older radicals with well-thought-out social philosophies; and, in general, gained support for the transition into politics that they wanted to make. Over a period of time, they came to see society in a new way, and, in so doing, committed themselves to a long-term effort to change minds and rebuild institutions. Again, their family back-ground helped rather than hurt, for it gave them the confidence to believe that they *could* make a difference. Yet they were deter-mined to go beyond what their parents, and other parents like them, had been willing to do themselves.

Young Radicals was a marked advance in the study of the Move-ment. Although an examination of the psychology of the New Left, it explored other aspects as well—ideology, structure, style, cen-tral concerns. It pointed to a continuity between the values of the young and traditional American values, as espoused by their par-ents. It emphasized the complexity of forces that contributed to shaping youth consciousness—mass affluence, democratic homes, social inequities, the demands of politics itself—rather than over-emphasizing any one of them, such as "the breakdown of authority" or, conversely, "the repressive nature of modern society." It characterized the Movement as a search for justice rather than a collection of specific campaigns, and, at several points, urged that the public judge Movement demands only in the context of that search. Most important, it caught something of the *flavor* of the Movement—the exuberance as well as the strains.

The book was not without its limitations, however. Radicalism is an exacting philosophy in all its forms, and radicals themselves are troublesome people. They do not merely *talk* about values that their societies believe, they insist upon them, they demand them, until the people change or drive the radicals away. The only popular campaign of a radical is his last one.

Yet Keniston was optimistic; he felt that America could handle the changes that the students were demanding. Hence, he was so anxious to make the public *like* "these young people," to "understand them," that he blinded himself to the deep disaffection that their Movement represented. When the disenchantment became apparent, when the radicals really became *radical*—sitting in, trashing, shouting down speakers—every element of Keniston's argument—the role of the family; the encounter with institutions; the quality of the Movement itself—came to seem inadequate.

"*I* taught him those values?" one heard a parent say, particularly after the riots started. "Well, perhaps. We *did* emphasize a concern for people in our home. But we encouraged other attitudes as well: intellectual curiousity, for example, and tolerance for differing points of view. He never reads anymore, and he grows so angry at us when we disagree with him that he won't even talk to us.

"And if he doesn't feel estranged from us, why is he so reluctant to come home? Keniston might say that he's upset that we don't do more politically, but this has been going on long before he got involved in politics. In high school, he was knocking everything about this town—the people, the values, the spirit. He was *always* angry, always criticizing something. Oh, I wouldn't say that he's just using politics as an excuse—he obviously takes them quite seriously and works hard at them. But it's wrong to say that he *became* a radical by working for the Movement. Somehow, before, for reasons which we don't understand, he always *was* radical, and this New Left just taught him to express it in political terms."

The parent's concerns were well taken. *Young Radicals* tried so hard to affirm the continuity of values between the generations that it minimized the enormous areas of conflict between them. To say, "Where father and son part company, as the son sees it, is that father's actions are not based on his perceptions,"[6] is to dismiss casually a dynamic that has contributed to, if not world revolution, at least a few patricides. Indeed, the notion that parents can transmit a sense of "duty" is a strange one in an age in which people are assumed only to act out of narrow self-interest. No doubt this was happening in the homes which Keniston examined, but he should not have taken the achievement so lightly.

His discussion of the students' encounters with the system was equally vague. "They were shocked to learn," he contends, "that their affluence was not equally shared." Why? What value contributed to provoking the shock? "The system was hypocritical," they found. In relation to what? "The institutions did not live up to their principles." In what way? Did they require revolutionary confrontations, or merely reforms? What did the young radicals think? How would they respond if a particular tactic failed? What was their *basic* concern, the point at which they would draw a line? Keniston never answered any of these questions.

Finally, Keniston painted a somewhat confusing picture of the Movement itself. He talked of its aversion to violence, an outgrowth of life in the nuclear era, and he cited activists' ability to control rage as one of the strengths that enabled them to cope with the frustrations of Movement work. Subsequently, however, many young people began to regret their reluctance to employ violence and to argue that it was indispensable to the pursuit of change. What value assumed priority? He discussed the Movement's emphasis on honesty, and its demand that "Movement people" live honestly as well. Within months of the study, however, it became commonplace to say that a radical would lie to the police or to the FBI investigating a crime. Which value assumed priority? He described the sense of flux among radicals, their constant motion from coast to coast, their willingness to experiment, their eagerness to test experiences of all kinds. Shortly thereafter, however, the expression "get it together," implying stability, rootedness, coherence, became fashionable on the Left. Which value assumed priority?

Thus, if Keniston produced the *best* analysis of the process of radicalization, it still was not good enough. Indeed, at this point, it should serve more as an outline of basic elements than as a coherent description of how they fit together. We must return to his propositions—that radicals acquire a sense of obligation in the home; that they are aroused to action by a perception of injustices in the society as a whole; that their commitment is strengthened by the Movement itself—and examine them in greater detail. If there are to be new radicals, there must be better understanding of how the old ones came about.

First, let us look at the family.

American parents, particularly those who grew up in the thirties and early forties, live, as Keniston suggested, in a state of ambivalence between two worlds. The one is the world of poverty, in which a closely knit family struggles to survive in the face of overwhelming material hardship, but sustains itself through shared work, common observance of religious customs, and a pattern of social occasions that draw relatives together. The other is the world of moderate affluence in which sticking together is no longer essential to survival and in which the rituals of traditional religious and social life cease to convey any special meaning.

The contrasts between these worlds is striking. During the Depression, a family was something of a clan, with hordes of aunts, uncles, cousins, all living within reasonable proximity to one another, exchanging gossip about the job, the weather, the news, the children, and each other. Today, parents are lucky if their kids come home for Christmas. The traditional home was as much an enterprise as a household. Sons helped out in the store; daughters cooked. Everyone cleaned, shopped, and took out the garbage. Today, the father commutes, the dish washer does the dishes, and mother spends three evenings a week telling her boys to clean up their rooms-which-look-like-a-bunch-of-pig-sties. In the thirties—so the story goes—children used to walk eight miles through driving snow to get to an ill-heated classroom in which a 90-year old Latin teacher drilled "amo-amas-amat-amamus-amatis-amant" into their tormented brains until they wanted to scream. Today, a car pool escorts the suburban 12-year-old to a glass high school where, at least once a week, he joins his classmates in the auditorium for a pep rally, a play, or a lecture from a noted doctor on, "Sex, Drugs, and Teen-Agers—Do the Three Go Together?"

Parents insist that things are better now, that they would never return to that earlier life, but not without some misgivings. They complain about the rat race to one another, to their friends, and they devour books like *Future Shock* or *The Greening of America* that describe it. They think of themselves as practical people, but when they discuss their youth, the word "dreams" pops up— dreams not simply that food would be on the table, not simply that heat would filter from the basement to the rooms of the house, but that a shared sense of human kindness could be brought to *all* the world, the world of bigotry, tyranny and war, as well as their own. Indeed, when they talk of their past, their spirits seem to rise, their imagery becomes clearer, even their eyes glow more than usual.

Moreover, when they return to the present, they speak of "coping" with their new security rather than enjoying it. Some writers, like Daniel Bell or Irving Kristol, choose to ignore the anxieties of the modern era, hearing only praise for the material improvements without taking seriously the complaints that usually accompanies them. Others, like Charles Reich, see only a technological

wasteland—a corporate parking lot that has paved over our traditions, our ideals, and our inner selves to a point almost beyond
resistance. Most people, however, are caught between the image
of progress and the vision of despair, and it is the uncertainty that
makes life so difficult to handle.

Nor is the there any one response. As Alvin Touffler has demonstrated, each social group develops its own mechanisms to cope
with "future shock." For our purposes, I must examine three—
lower-middle class, ethnic, and suburbanite. Then, I will explore
the ways in which each of these groups transmit their anxieties to
their children.

LOWER-MIDDLE CLASS

These are, specifically, small real estate operators, gas station
attendants, salesmen—all those who have gambled on the Horatio
Alger myth, and lost. Edgar Z. Friedenberg has referred to such
people as the *ressentient*. Eight years before the term "silent
majority" became fashionable, he described it.

> *Those social groups are most prone to* ressentiment *whose members are
> especially subjected to frustration in their position in life, but who feel
> so impotent that they do not dare to get consciously angry and rebel
> and hit back, or strike out themselves against the actual source of their
> frustration. Generally, they dare not even recognize it. Instead they
> identify with and accommodate to the very individuals or social forces
> undermining their position, and whose strength they tend to admire
> and exaggerate. By thus exercising their impotence, they increase it;
> what a less threatened individual would have felt as rage becomes
> resentment, then a kind of small-shopkeeper's fearful and self-pitying
> distrust, and finally, perhaps, merely an unconscious predisposition to
> sanctimonious spitefulness.*

If there is a "Consciousness I" in America, it is the *ressentient*
who possesses it. He is, indeed, rooted in the small town and the
style of life that it represents. Moreover, he seeks the perpetuation
of a specific *role* within the town as, for example, the owner of the
main store, the banker, the chairman of the Chamber of Commerce. *He* would be no Richard Corey, who one evening put a
bullet through his head, despite his respected position. No, he
would be responsible—a man of property, an Elk, a delegate to the
Republican National Convention.

Yet he cannot. He might possess the skill to rise to a reasonable
economic level, even to attain something of the position that he
seeks, but who cares? Rockefeller, Howard Hughes, Henry Ford
—these are the men of corporate power in our society, next to
whom the small-town merchant is nowhere. Indeed, if he wants

real stature, he cannot go it alone; he must join a "team." Even those in second- and third-level positions in large corporations earn more money than he does.

Wedded to the hopes of an earlier period, however, he cannot make the adjustment. Instead, as Friedenberg suggests, his illusions of power increase in direct porportion to the level of his impotence. "We must not imagine Howard Hughes and H. L. Hunt in isolation," he tells himself. "They are *generals*, commanding a large army" in which he is an important soldier. "I will defend them and myself against all invaders—domestic or foreign —regardless of the consequences." Even in the atheistic world of today, people have to stand for *something*, don't they? Why not for the virtues that made this country what it is—courage, strength, individual initiative? That's the trouble with things now. Everything's gotten so soft. . . ." Gradually, he loses his grip on life itself. A few such people occasionally do reach positions of power in the United States—even as high as the Vice-Presidency. The example speaks for itself.

URBAN ETHNIC

Often lumped in the phrase "Silent Majority" along with *ressentient* is the white unionist, the urban ethnic, the Americanized immigrant. Charles Reich makes this mistake in *The Greening of America*, dismissing anyone born before 1930 as "Consciousness I." He, along with many others, commits an injustice. While Nelson Rockefeller's grandfather was turning oil into gold, the immigrant's grandfather was manning the sweatshops and the factories. While Spiro T. Agnew was learning a bastardized version of the King's English so as to impress intellectuals with his erudition, this fellow was struggling to master a few words of Italian or Yiddish for fear that they might get lost in the Melting Pot. As Richard Nixon keeps discovering, for all *his* encomiums to the lonely road from rags to riches, the workers still go out on strike.

Yet they, too, are torn. During the New Deal, their parents demanded not so much "success" as what the black movement seeks today—a route to affluence that did not require that they disregard their religion, leave their communities, sacrifice their local customs in order to survive. If Horatio Alger said "aspire," the Church countered with, "It's easier for a camel to pass through the eye of a needle than for a rich man to enter the Kingdom of Heaven." If the WASP establishment intoned, "*Make* something of yourselves," the union leaders shot back, "The *common* man— the *working* man—*he*'s the strength of the country." Hence, these "common" people tried to strike a balance—to keep up with the Joneses, but not too far ahead of them—to maintain a decent standard of living without indulging themselves. Moreover, as the country prospered, they thought they had succeeded.

Not for long, however. "I resigned from the Urban Coalition," a New York labor leader snorts, "after I discovered it was a Protestant plot. 'Give a damn, you Catholic construction workers. Move over and make room for blacks.' And then they say, 'Give a damn, you Jewish teachers, in Shanker's union. Move over and make room for blacks.' Great. But do you ever hear them say. 'Hey, fat cats, give up your oil depletion allowances so we can build up some housing with the taxes?' It is a plot, for God's sake, aimed at the Catholic construction unions and the Jewish teachers' unions so that we don't mess around with the oil depletion allowance."

The 'limousine liberals' add insult to injury. "You're a racist," they shout, when it is the wealthy suburbanite who often leads the campaigns against welfare, open housing, and urban development about which liberals complain. "You're uncouth," the intellectuals insist, when only a few years earlier immigrant folk communities had been "romantic," part of the "charm" of pluralism. "You're backward," the ad agencies imply, with commercials that depict working men as hopelessly confused (for not having discovered the new . . .) and their wives as pedestrian mannequins. Once it was supposed to be the "common people" who, despite their lack of wealth and education, were the "repository of enduring values."

Thus, they, too, become *ressentient*, though less in the spirit of losing a game than of watching the rules change at the moment of victory. Their culture is under fire from the Left, which used to support them; their economic security is being undermined by the Right. If early in life they were militant, now they appear to have acquired a neurotic attachment to the Joint Chiefs of Staff. The image is unfair, incomplete, but they don't know how to change it. Even their own spokesmen betray them either by channeling their frustrations into cries for "law and order" against the blacks and the young or by denying that they experience any problems at all. So they talk to interviewers from national magazines; demand higher wages from their employers; and wait, hoping that someday people will understand.

SUBURBANITE

The dilemma that the working-class ethnics face now is merely the other side of the quandry that a third group—their cousins in the suburbs—experienced fifteen years ago. These are the ones who converted forests, marshes, and hills surrounding the cities into "metropolitan areas"; who bought into the middle-level corporate society that permits little room for expression of distinctive values and styles; who hoped that a much higher standard of living would compensate for separation from family, friends, and traditional patterns of life. Government helped by providing low-interest loans for the construction of middle-income houses. Businesses helped by informally encouraging employees to move where top executives lived. Yet the lure was there without these incentives —air, land, gardening, good schools for the kids—the up-to-date version of an American Eden that settlers have pursued since the Founding.

It was Eden, that is, until they got there. The movies of the fifties, the ones that dominate late-night television, tell the story —'hard-driving-:young'-executive-stops-at-nothing-for-success-which-he-finds-meaningless-without-love.' The lead character always grows up poor; struggles through school; attends college on scholarship; and justifies every manipulation, every maneuver by asserting, "I never had anything; I was always the underdog." His wife more often than not tries to reason with him. "I don't know what's come over him. He wasn't like this when we were married." Failing, she moves out with the children. Then, suddenly, a trip to Christmas past, a visit from sister, a glance through an old scrapbook, and he sees himself as he is—prominent, prosperous, but alienated from all that really matters.

Obviously, such pictures are caricatures, but different only in degree, not in kind, from the reality to which they attest. If in the movies the husband stops at nothing to "better himself," in the suburbs, he is uncertain—he asks his family, his friends, before he takes off in a new direction. If in the films, the wife is impotent, in the suburbs, she often is at least somewhat effective in puncturing her husband's dreams of empire and glory. If in the movies, the hero requires a catharsis to regain his past, in real life, the past intrudes more regularly in the form of a sister who never left the city or a cousin who invites everyone to Thanksgiving Dinner once a year, or of a funeral of a life-long friend that reminds him that "this, too, will pass."

Yet the basic tensions—between power and virtue; between success and stability; between egoism and love—are there. If the suburbanite is indeed more "open" to new experiences, to new ideas, it is because a "receptive" posture is his only protection against the uncertainty that he feels about himself. "So I *am* making money," he muses. "That doesn't mean I've become selfish and narrow. No, in fact, now I can concern myself with the *broader* questions of war and peace, of social justice, of education. I can read, travel, widen my horizons. That makes it worthwhile, doesn't it?" He opposes the War, admires the Panthers, stands on long lines to see the latest Godard or Andy Warhol flick. Yet when blacks ask to move into the neighborhood, or when the city to which he commutes threatens to tax suburbanites for essential services, he resists, certain that if *he* earned his success by hard work and enterprise, others must do so as well. Saul Alinsky described this fellow over twenty-five years ago. He is "Mr. But."

Three distinctive types—the lower-middle class *ressentient;* the ethnic, the suburbanite—not inclusive, to be sure, are nevertheless exemplary of those caught in the bind between an old world and the new one. They hardly are united. The *ressentient* votes for Richard Nixon "despite the concessions that he makes to the liberals." The ethnic threatens Wallace up to the elections, then supports the Democratic ticket. The suburbanite backs McCarthy. Often, they not only argue with one another, they hate one another. Yet they share one worry in common—their kids.

Indeed, expressing anxieties about the young is often the only way in which they can express the tensions surrounding their own lives. Each group hopes that its children will fulfill the dreams that they themselves could not realize. For the *ressentient,* it is success; for the ethnic, it is peace and respectability; for the suburbanite, it is a balance between talent and virtue. The young respond, but in ways that their parents do not anticipate.

One does not need much imagination to picture the way in which a lower-middle class parent would handle his child. The young demand consistency, coherence, perfection, and when they do not find it, they want to know why. The questions that they ask are precisely those which the *ressentient* is afraid to answer:

"Daddy, what do you do?"

"Why?"

"Daddy, can we go to Florida this winter? Johnny is?"

"No."

He cuts the kid off, tells him to go do his homework, anything to get him off his back. "Why is he always hanging around the kitchen?" he demands of his wife. "Doesn't he have anything *constructive* to do?"

At the same time the parent also expects perfection. "My kid's going to be a *success,* " the father tells himself. "*He's* not going to end up like me." If the kid brings home a bad report card or a complaint of bad behavior, there's hell to pay. "How can you do this to me? After all I've worked and slaved for you!" No achievement is good enough. "Only a B? Why not an A?" No one else can be better. "Why can't you be like Billy Windmiller? Now *there's* someone who knows what he's doing?" If there is permissiveness in America, it is not in homes such as these. No battle is harder for a child than the one against a fractured illusion, against a hope gone sour.

Moreover, such a child can never win. Even if he does fulfill the ambitions of his father—Harvard Business School, a high-paying managerial job at 26, a vice-presidency at 40—he is always haunted by the feeling that his accomplishments are insufficient. A moment of self-recognition, and the whole world crumbles around him. "The Machine Begins to Self-Destruct," Charles Reich entitles a chapter in *The Greening of America*,[8] and at least one manifestation of the erosion has become commonplace—the man who, without warning, gives up status, career, job, to work among the poor or to build a farm in the woods. As Reich points out, the dismal reality of corporate life finally destroys the illusion that success, American-style, can bring happiness along with it.

When the illusion crumbles as early as college, it becomes what Reich identifies as a "conversion":[9]

> What happens is simply this: in a brief span of months, a student, seemingly conventional in every way, changes his haircut, his clothes, his habits, his interests, his political attitudes, his way of relating to other people, in short, his whole way of life. He has "converted" to a new consciousness. The contrast between well-groomed freshman pictures and the same individuals in person a year later tells the tale. The clean-cut, hard-working, model young man who despises radicals and hippies can become one himself with breathtaking suddenness.

Reich implies that the "conversion" is the route by which *every* young person rejects society—an inference from Yale, perhaps, but wrong when applied universally. He also suggests that the "conversion" marks the *final* step to radicalism, a proposition so misguided, yet so central to the thesis of his book, that it demands a rebuttal at a point farther along in this analysis.

Among children of the *ressentient*, however—"star athlete, an honor student, the small-town high school boy with the American Legion scholarship"[10]—it is clear that a decisive break with the past, borne of an understanding that what the family wants is not worth having, *is* the most common route to the Left. Moreover, the form that the rebellion takes does approximate the patterns that Reich describes: "hippy" life-styles; draft resistance; gentleness—all the qualities suppressed in the world of competition and climbing. The parents of course, grow furious, some even disowning their children until they "come around." Yet it doesn't work. The "children" have disowned themselves and become adults.

For the ethnic, child-raising poses different problems. If the *ressentient* wants a son or daughter to "make it" to the elevated conference rooms of capitalism, the urban immigrant expects his youngsters to stay, to preserve the community, to lend it the dignity that it deserves. Yet he knows that his hopes are not shared by the rest of the country. There are no decent jobs where he lives. His neighborhood is falling apart. The mayor is trying to attract the rich to other areas of town to improve the tax base by building expensive urban-renewal projects that destroy his homes. Moreover, the governor is cutting a swath around his district with an expressway to make commuting more convenient for suburbanites. *He* may see a value to the traditions that his parents tried to preserve, but nobody else does, and his children cannot help but understand this.

Thus, in the absence of the carrot, the parent resorts to the stick. When *he* was young, people helped out around the house, so he establishes a stern roster of duties. When *he* was young, school encouraged order, discipline, respect, so the neighborhood school in working-class areas becomes a prison whose function is to terrorize more than teach. *He* felt a responsibility to remain in his place of birth, so although his kids go to college, they attend the local college or the state university, within easy traveling distance of home. The patterns of the past remain, but without any warmth and support to give them meaning.

Despite the insularity of the working-class community, however, the kids find ways of resisting. To be sure, they cannot undergo a "conversion" à la their *ressentient* counterparts at Yale. As a group of students protesting restrictive dress codes in a Boston high school discovered, the principal has a powerful weapon. He can ask the parents for assistance, and they will arrive in person to bring their errant children into line. Nor does the long arm of familial law contract when the child receives his secondary-school diploma. Nothing is more difficult than fomenting a revolt at a University located in a community whose voters are alumni and parents of the current student generation. Such is the nature of the colleges that sons and daughters of working people often attend.

Yet there are forms of rebellion that even parents cannot control. Residents of Cambridge, Massachusetts, discovered one in the summer of 1970. The local Chamber of Commerce sponsored a series of rock concerts that brought top-name artists to Harvard Stadium at reasonable prices, as a way of providing young people with something to do during the week. "Summerthing" it was called, and it succeeded beyond wildest expectations. On three separate occasions, a riot nearly erupted, either as a result of fighting between warring groups of kids or as a response to sporadic incidents of purse-snatching. By the end of July, one didn't have to be a "rock" fan to know that a concert was underway. He merely had to stand in Harvard Square, some distance from the Stadium, until an emissary from the assembled platoon of policemen told him to get-the-hell-home-the-kids-were-coming-out. If he valued the contours of his scalp, he got.

Taking drugs has become an attractive option. To be sure, hard narcotics *always* were available in working-class neighborhoods, particularly in those penetrated by organized crime. Suffice it to say the "Problem" has grown since the late sixties. Nor is the popularity of marijuana at elite colleges and universities the major cause. No, the greatest propagator of drugs, say organizers who talk to working-class young people, is the army, where the kids learn how to use them. If, in 1945, GI's gave chocolate bars to children in liberated areas of Europe, today they bring "joints" to the unliberated zones of the United States. The response here is equally warm.

Finally, the reaction can take political forms. Following a rally against the war in 1970, for example, a group of local revolutionaries calling themselves the "Bobby Seale Brigade" paraded off the Boston Common along Massachusetts Avenue toward the Cambridge police station near Harvard Square where a large contingent of "street people" and neighborhood kids significantly joined them. At first, the encounter proceeded along lines that have become all too familiar: Kid screams, "Pig"; pig screams, "Get back"; kid throws can; pig swings club; kids charge; pigs charge; kids, pigs, all together in one big asphyxiating cloud of tear gas. In this case, however, the locals—who were watching from the sidelines—got into the swing of things. They threw rocks, bottles, sticks. They broke windows; they beat up bystanders; they turned over cars. They set fires. Then, they disappeared. The next morning, spectators told one another, "It's funny. The students started it, but the 'street kids' did most of the damage." No one could understand it.

The revolt of working-class young people, when it bursts to the surface, is by far the most violent of any that the country experiences, so much so, in fact, that some radicals interested in "reaching" them have urged collegiate trashing as a way by which students can win their respect. Of course, this proposal misses the point entirely. The volatility of the immigrants' children is not a cause but a symptom of their discontent, an expression of the enormous anger that builds up inside people who *know* that the country is depriving the communities in which they live of needed resources and, more important, respect; who *know* that the enemy is out there in the suburbs; but who have yet to determine an appropriate response to the situation. Heaven help the "limousine liberals" when they do.

The suburbanites show us yet a third technique by which parents can inflict their own anxieties upon their children. It is as if for thirty years they have been holding their breath hoping that through exhortation, discussion, and threats, they could sustain a morality that only austerity has been able to foster in the past. "He'll never starve, and we'll see him through college," they say, but their sense of pride coexists with a lingering fear that maybe he *should* have to struggle for something, that maybe life has been *too* easy for him. Unlike their own parents to whom the law was the law, they want to "treat him with respect—reason with him —try to make him come to his own conclusions," but they fear spoiling him. They want him to "*make* something of his opportunity—to be motivated"—but they are unsure as to how to contribute to the process.

Hence, as in other areas of their lives, they equivocate. "These young men and women took affluence and opportunity for granted," Keniston wrote, but he saw only one side of the picture. No one who grows up in the suburbs takes *anything* for granted because the moment he does, somebody says, "The trouble with you is, you take things for granted." He leaves the lights on his room. "What? You think we're made of money. You take things for granted." He comes home late from a party. "Boy, do you take things for granted. You just *assume* you can stay out all night and somebody's going to leave the door unlocked so that you can get in." He forgets to send a thank-you note for a gift. "Haven't you got *any* sense of decency at all? Do you take *everything* for granted?" When one day he strikes back—"Well, why *shouldn't* I take things for granted. I grew up here, didn't I?"—the parent unleashes the most devastating weapon of them all: self-efface-ment. "You're right, John. It's not your fault. We *spoiled* you. We never had your opportunities when we were young, so it's just *natural* that we should indulge you a little bit. But try to look at it from *our* point of view." How can he fight back?

Religious observance becomes a major source of strain. The conflict is particularly acute in Jewish homes where not only are parents trying to preserve the customs of their childhood, but the traditions of two thousand years, the identity of a persecuted people, the theology that lies at the root of Western civilization. "You cannot escape your identity," they insist as they drive to the County Municipal Auditorium to accomodate overflow, once-a-year crowds, all converging in the latest Oldsmobiles. "The German Jews tried to assimilate, and look what happened to them," they continue at a brief reception after the service, as two men discuss the wonderful new short skirts that *all* the women are wearing. "Besides," they conclude, "Even if you don't understand it now, someday you will learn to appreciate it," while behind them a couple speculates as to whether they will attend the observance next year.

So, kicking and screaming, the kid attends Sunday School—at least until 13, when an enormous Bar Mitzvah party proves the strain to have been a worthwhile business investment. At this point, he knows a little bit of the Bible, a little bit of Hebrew, a little bit about the B'nai B'rith, a little bit about Israel; but most of all, as Philip Roth might put it, he knows that like Jack Benny, Jacob Javits, Arthur Goldberg, and the local butcher he is Jewish, that he has a *tradition*—which *means* something—that people won't always *accept* him because he's Jewish, but that he shouldn't care because he should be *proud* of his heritage. Of course, he doesn't know *what* his Christian friends believe—most of them seem to be facing the same problems in relation to church—and his Jewish friends buy Christmas trees in late December, but who is he to argue with two thousand years, the German Jews, and his grandfather? Someday, it might even make sense.

Mostly, however, suburbanites paint a picture of their past that can only create tension. "Why are we Democrats?" the child asks as an election approaches.

"Because the Democrats are the party of the poor and the working people."

"Well, we're not poor, are we?"

"No, but we used to be, and there still are many people who are."

"What was it like to be poor?"

"Oh, it was very hard. People stood in bread lines for food, thousands had no jobs. Your father and I lived above a store, in one room, while he worked as a copy boy at the *World Telegram*."

The image sticks. There they were, his poor parents, huddled together in one little room—hungry, destitute, struggling for survival. How awful it must have been. They still remember it. They still vote for the Democratic Party because Franklin Delano Roosevelt brought them out of a Depression. They still identify with *that* experience and not the affluence around them. *His* childhood is nothing like that. He won't remember it thirty years from now, and tell it to his kids as an object lesson in human perserverence. All he has to face is an occasional problem in getting to school every morning. "Why couldn't *I* have been poor," he complains to himself, "so *I* could go through something difficult and painful, too."

He takes it out on his community. To this day, I imagine there is a substantial group of kids in Scarsdale, New York, where I grew up, who refuse to admit that they live there. One learns elaborate techniques. "Where do you live?" somebody asks.

"Uh . . . New York,"

"The City?" "No, just outside . . ."

"Long Island?"

"No, it's a small town in Westchester County."

"Oh, which one? I know several places out there."

"Scarsdale."

If he says, "I *never* would have guessed it," you heave a sigh of relief, knowing that you've made the right impression. If, however, he snorts, "*Oh*, one of *those*," you're finished. No amount of explaining, excusing, effacing, can undo the damage.

The result is that the suburban child enters the world *looking* for something that might justify his existence. Keniston suggests that he experiences "anger and indignation" more than guilt, and, to a point, this is true. After all, he did not choose to grow up in the suburbs; it just happened that way. Yet his past is still a burden from which he must wrest himself. If his parents had wondered, "How can we 'make it' without sacrificing our values?" he wonders, "Must I give up my wealth and security to live up to my principles?" If his parents sought to preserve the faith of the fathers, he awaits the creation of a new faith, something that can withstand materialism better than the available models. If his parents sought to lift themselves from a "lower" class, he attempts to transcend class, to envisage a world *without* class, and to confront the system that perpetuates it.

His parents approve, provided, of course, he finishes school, remains polite, *does* something with his life, and doesn't talk too much about redistribution of income.

Thus, each group—the *ressentient*, the ethnic, and the suburbanite—experiences tensions that, if telegraphed to the young, may move them to the Left. The *ressentient* parent may encourage humility and a sensitivity to injustice merely by pressing too hard in the opposite direction. The worker's heritage may inspire his son or daughter to fight for the community that he is losing, albeit after a period of some confusion. The suburbanite may transmit a hatred of privilege to his children by warning them constantly against abusing it. All search for a world between present and past; radicalization begins when they demand it.

REFERENCES

1. Kenneth Keniston, *Young Radicals* (New York, Harcourt, Brace, & World, 1968), p. 55.
2. *Ibid.*, pp. 112–13
3. *Ibid.*, p. 132
4. *Ibid.*, p. 131
5. *Ibid.*, p. 238.
6. *Ibid.*, p. 59
7. Edgar Z. Friedenberg, "The Gifted Student and His Enemies," in *Dignity of Youth and Other Atavisms* (Boston, Beacon, 1965), pp. 120–121,
8. Charles A. Reich, *The Greening of America* (New York, Random House, 1970), pp. 189–216)
9. *Ibid.*, pp. 223–224.
10. *Ibid.*, pp 224.

The Transition—
Apertura
à Sinistra

3 As Keniston suggests, the transition between uncertainty and radicalism occurs as the young person confronts society. It is in this context that the observation, "The family is losing its ability to guide the young," or the corresponding parental cry of bewilderment, "*I* never taught him those things," is perfectly reasonable. Parents exercise influence, to be sure, but the tensions that they themselves experience make impossible their providing for a clear sense of direction for their child. An 18-year-old leaves for work or college more with a set of questions than a handbook of rules. If the poles of the debate in his home set limits to his inquiry, the space between the poles provides a considerable amount of latitude for choice. He must resolve these conflicts, as he interacts with others, in terms that make sense to him.

Moreover, the transition is neither automatic nor easy. To be sure, there are some who think it is. Between 1966 and 1968, a few university radicals, who themselves had become "revolutionaries" only after several years of observing or participating in the Movement, concluded that dedicated insurgents could spring, full-blown, from the aftermath of a police riot. This was the "disillusionment" theory of change, and it accounted for more than one campus upheaval. The idea was to program a situation whereby the administration would lose its cool, call the police, bust heads, and show the college to be little better than the U.S. government in its handling of social and political crises. If the radicals had predicted the response that the power structure would make, the argument went, the student body would rally behind its leadership.

The revolutionaries were correct on every point but one. After the demonstrations, after the takeovers, after the police, after the riots, after the disillusionment, the students did not rally around the radicals; they created their own structures of representation and leadership. They did not adopt the platform of the Left; they evolved their own demands. How many times did the pattern repeat itself—Columbia, Wisconsin, Harvard? Reporters needed only to fill in the spaces left blank for the name of the university, for the story was essentially the same. "Damnit," the radicals would cry in disgust. "we're forgetting the original issues. The war, racism—what happened to them?" All we're discussing are the police and civil liberties and university structure."

The radicals had not read Marx:[1]

> But the democrat, because he represents the petty bourgeoisie, that is, a transition class, in which the interests of two classes are simultaneously mutually blunted, imagines himself elevated above class antagonism generally. The democrats conceded that a privileged class confronts them, but they, along with all the rest of the nation, form the people. What they represent is the people's rights; what interests them is the people's interests. Accordingly, when a struggle is impending, they do not need to examine the interests and positions of the different classes. They do not need to weigh their own resources too critically. They have merely to give the signal and the people, with all its inexhaustible resources will fall upon the oppressors.

Nor had they read Engels:[2]

> The time of surprise attacks, of revolutions carried through by small conscious minorities at the head of unconscious masses, is past. Where it is a question of a complete transformation of the social organization, the masses themselves must also be in it, must themselves already have grasped what is at stake, what they are going in for (body and soul). The history of the last fifty years has taught us that. But in order that the masses understand what is to be done, long persistent work is required. . . .

Instead, they assumed that an unorganized body of young people—uneasy about its class poition, perhaps, but hardly prepared to renounce it—would speak in the name of black people or Vietnamese people at the mere discovery that a progressive administrator would become a general if his office were ransacked. Such innocence—as if the students themselves were a full-blown proletariat! No, without an intensive period in which the ambivalent undergraduates could come to grips with alternatives, with different ways of living, with new patterns of response to conditions that they perceived to be unjust, they remained as their parents had been: liberals committed to openness, to reason, to persuasion as a way of settling disputes in the absence of clear guidelines for the settlements themselves. Therefore, when the Left demonstrated that a university president could become a bad liberal—unreasonable, lawless, violent—the students simply proved that they could become good liberals. They took it upon themselves to restore the rules, and to enforce them, even against the radicals. Although the revolution had undertaken to "liberate" the university from procedures that obscured its real functions, it ended up encouraging a plethora of new rules, new committees, new procedures. By attempting a short-cut, the Left got cut short, and it had only its theories to blame.

Liberal commentators who want to believe that there is an easy route to justice fare little better. Charles Reich is a prime example. "Consciousness III," he writes in *The Greening of America*, "says for the present, all that is necessary to describe the new society is to describe a new way of life. When we have outlined a different way of life, we have said all that we can meaningfully say about the future. This is not avoiding the hard questions. The hard questions—if by what is meant political and economic organization—are insignificant, even irrelevant."[3]

Sheer nonsense! In the world of the young, the realization that contemporary institutions ignore basic personal and social needs lends itself to a painful search for alternatives appropriate to meeting them. In the world of Mr. Reich, the "conversion" from "false" to "true" consciousness—from a belief that economic abundance can solve all problems to an understanding that it cannot—*ends* the search, or at least, makes it easy. "But the whole Corporate State rests upon nothing but consciousness," he writes. "When consciousness changes, its soldiers will refuse to fight, its police will rebel, its bureaucrats will stop their work, its jailers will open the bars, nothing can stop the power of consciousness."[4]

In the world of the young, millions of people live at subsistence levels without food, clothing, shelter. An uncomfortable proportion of these people live in the United States. In the world of Reich, "everyone's economic interests are or can be satisfied" without difficulty[5] and a civil rights movement against privilege is an "older form of revolution"[6] rendered somehow irrelevant to the modern age.

In the world of the young, a contradiction between perceived obligation and private feelings lends itself to an intense struggle to reconcile the two. The current battle of young men against their own male chauvinism is a good example. In the world of Reich, however, "to observe duties toward others, after the feelings are gone, is no virtue and may even be a crime . . . It is equally wrong to alter oneself for someone else's sake."[7]

Reich's book is riddled with contradictions, implicit and explicit. Reich expends long paragraphs in an almost defiant assertion of the "radical subjectivity" of the personal "self" that "Consciousness III" seeks to recover—only to describe the "recovery of self" among black people as a "search for one's origins and uniqueness,"[8] that is, a search for a reality defined by history and society independent of the individual. For more than 150 pages, he regales us with the horrors of the technological state: its ability to trample culture, work, love, play, life itself, beneath its feet. Yet it turns out that the liberating Consciousness III "could only have come into existence given today's technology."[8] Reich dismisses the "Consciousness I" of America's past as selfish, parochial, and aggressive, yet elsewhere he asserts: "The 'average man' is descended from people who had the capacity to put community ahead of their own immediate wants. The oldtime peasant had very real capacity for a non-material existence."[9] These are just samples.

His facts concerning the youth movement are often wrong. Take the following passage:[10]

> It is commonly believed that the confrontation resulted from "activism" and "militancy" by the students, who appeared to be following a pattern of making demands and then devising a strategy to get the demands met. But is this an accurate description of what was happening? Most of the Consciousness III people are notably unaggressive, nonviolent, uninterested in the political game, absorbed by their new culture and its possibilities, and mainly ask to be left alone. . . . it was the State which had the aggressive role.

Was it? Where was Mr. Reich in 1960 when young people were demanding that the State override local segregation statutes and ordinances in the South—fully eight years before the apolitical, "please-let-me-alone-I've-got-more-beautiful-things-to-do" Consciousness III emerged? Where was he in 1964 when Mario Savio's sit-in against discrimination in a newspaper owned by William Knowland *prompted* the Berkeley administration to revoke access to the "strip" along Telegraph Avenue for political recruiting? Where was he in 1965 when SDS *initiated* a march against the Vietnam War on behalf of the Vietnamese, at least two years before the draft even *affected* large numbers of college students? Where was he during these critical points in the growth of the youth movement? Commuting from Cambridge to Yale, waiting for a revelation?

No, Charles Reich turns the youth movement on its head. The option that he describes as a "high" form of Consciousness is precisely the one from which most young people—even those he thinks he describes—are trying to *escape*—a private existence in communion with the fruits of privilege, rationalizing a callous dismissal of the starvation of two thirds of the world's population, the poverty that paralyzes 20 percent of the people of the United States, the brutality of the U.S. government against insurgents here and elsewhere by saying, "All those things would go away if people would just learn to love and trust one another."

Timothy Leary told people to "turn on," only to end up in Algeria with Eldridge Cleaver. Jerry Rubin warns the Yippies against noninvolement in politics at every one of his frequent happenings. Abbie Hoffman raises money for the Panther Defense Fund in the name of the "Woodstock Nation;" and on Mr. Reich's own campus, Yale, no more than two months after he must have completed *The Greening of America*, young people from all over the East Coast converged to protest the trial of Bobby Seale. No, the broad movement of this decade among the young has not been from protest to personal levitation; it has been, with only a few interruptions, in the opposite direction.

The process of radicalization, then, has borne little relationship to the prevailing theories surrounding it. To speak of radicalism simply as an outgrowth of "disillusionment" with the country doesn't make sense. Students responded to developments in the sixties more with a set of hunches about America than with a clearly formulated philosophy as to what it was and what it could be. Further, the outlines of whatever social theory did emerge coalesced only after several years of sifting out primary concerns —equality, obligation, world survival—from the maze of conflicting values—equality vs. liberty; obligation vs. escape; world survival vs. domestic comfort—with which the young had wrestled. To become a radical was not merely to decide "that the system had failed;" it was to conclude that the moral stance from which one said, "The system has failed," was the only one worth taking.

Nor could this stance be characterized merely as "expressiveness," the attempt to "liberate" the self from oppressive institutions. Surely, an emphasis on the emotions, on sexuality, was an important aspect of the politics of the new generation, but it was only an aspect. The desire to feel was part of a deeper desire to *respond*—to remain sensitive to inequities rather than to maintain a "rational detachment" from them which made morality impossible. Even the best known proponent of the revolution-as-liberation-of-the-shackled-psyche-from-the-state theory, Herbert Marcuse, defined the freedom that would emerge in the new order as the "capacity to share." Thus, the central demand was for a society that would help men determine their *common* objectives, that would encourage citizens to do that which they should do. If a respect for the emotions was an ingredient necessary to such a system, as Rousseau had argued it would be in the eighteenth century, it was hardly sufficient. Significantly, all the heroes of the various factions of the youth movement—the Kennedys, Gene McCarthy, Martin Luther King, Malcolm X, Eldridge Cleaver, C. Wright Mills, Noam Chomsky, Herbert Marcuse— were admired not so much for their passions, or even for their faculties as creators, but for their ability to focus their talents in socially useful directions.

Therefore, we must develop our own framework to describe how radicalization can occur. An analysis of the past decade suggests that eight elements are essential:

1. The person must develop goals that are neither within his grasp nor measurable in material terms, i.e., "the idea of the true and the beautiful."

2. The person must develop a sense of self-interest by experiencing treatment himself that he perceives to be unjust.

3. The person must develop a sense of the common interest. He must face a challenge from another exploited, oppressed, mistreated individual or group that he join it in a common search for justice.

4. The person must sense that such a life is legitimate. He must understand those elements in his heritage that support the ideal of justice that he might try to realize.

5. The person must sense that such a life is possible. He must come into contact with experienced radicals who serve as models for his development and growth.

6. The person must sense that such a life is natural, that it can bring him closer to people, not farther away from them, that he will derive more from experience, not less from it.

7. The person must understand that such a life can be difficult. He must undergo experiences that test his committment to the new kinds of objectives that he is pursuing.

8. The person must realize that such a life must be shared. He must find people who will hold him and one another accountable to their own best intentions.

Yet such principles will have little meaning unless applied. I want first to examine the impact of three major events of the sixties on the youth movement: Kennedy's election; the Civil Rights Movement; and the Vietnam War. From there, I will discuss techniques by which youth organizers sustained the involvement of students in the campaigns of the past decade. Finally, returning to the eight basic elements, I will explore why radicalism has grown among young suburbanities while remaining latent in other segments of the youth population, and make some concluding points about radicalization itself.

KENNEDY

Even during the Kennedy administration, radicals were discovering that the promise of a 'New Frontier" outstripped its programs by several speeches. The President's unwillingness to press for Civil Rights legislation until forced by events to do so; the fervent anti-Communist rhetoric that dominated the early days of his adminstration; his expansion of the military budget; the Bay of Pigs debacle; his ineffectiveness at persuading Congress to adopt much of his legislative program; his emphasis on the style and process of government, often at the expense of its substance—such shortcomings were the subject of more than one article written during the early sixties.

Since then, moreover, the Left has added to the list: Kennedy's support of the Diem regime in South Vietnam; his underestimation of the need for a fundamental realignment of social and political power throughout Latin America before the meager economic assitance offered by the United States could begin to make a difference; his willingness to permit industry to control regulatory agencies created to control industry; his reliance on the "corporate liberal"—the clinical, human computer who reduces questions of fundamental moral significance to a ledger sheet of "options," "assets," and "liabilities"—to formulate key policies and programs. The litany is a long one, and if one still remembers Camelot with nostalgic affection, at least some of the luster has faded with time.

Nonetheless, credit is due where it is due. The "New Frontier" was as central to reviving a radical movement in this country as the radical movement has been in exposing its deficiencies. Nor do the usual adjectives—"idealistic," "energetic," "youthful"—explain the precise impact that the President had on the young, or at least on the sons and daughters of the suburbs. His central contribution lay in bringing to politics a set of concerns that meshed easily with those the new generation had come to develop. Three themes come to mind: politics as principle; principle as obligation; obligation as survival.

In general, the route away from a view of life that promised only a war of all against all demanded the invocation of higher principles that would force people into common activity with their fellows. As Wilson Carey McWilliams has put it:[11]

A physical barrier prevents sensation from ever being common. Ideas and values, conceived abstractly, are not subject to the same limitation. Moreover, if values and purposes free men from dependence on others, they equally free them from a neurotic anxiety regarding others. In-

deed, any close bond between them depends on values; on the capacity to attach worth to a particular human being because of the qualities he possesses or arouses in the self.

The classics understood this human need and, therefore, in contrast to materialistic formulations of government, devised an "alternate course: the quest for abstract values, the idea of the true and the beautiful which, lacking the limitation of space, could be shared in ways that material goods could not."[12] Yet, for a number of reasons, modern society had ignored this lesson that the Greeks just took for granted:[13]

> *It is the logic of modern society that it reverses the natural order of things: that it places a premium on men who can send the intellect out into the world of events and concentrate the emotions within the mind and self. The process which makes possible an abundance which might permit all men the life of the mind makes it likely that few men will avail themselves of the opportunity.*

Consequently, politics had become little more than bartering for a few pieces of the pie; the pursuit of justice had entailed little more than a general acceptance of a few "rules of the game."

Kennedy, however, attempted to reintroduce the classical notions about governance into the modern state and to revise the nation's outlook on politics itself. The New Frontier was not "a set of promises—it is a set of challenges. It sums up not what I intend to *offer* the American people, but what I intend to *ask* of them."[14] His inaugural observed "not a victory of party, but a celebration of freedom," and it called not for a war against the "enemy," but for a "struggle against the common enemies of man: tyranny, poverty, disease and war itself."[15] Civil Rights was" 'a moral issue as old as the scriptures . . . as clear as the American Constitution.' "[16] He told the United Nations, "But man does not live by bread alone, and members of this organization are committed by the Charter to promote and respect human rights."[17]

Moreover, all men shared an *obligation* to pursue these higher standards, to wrestle with these complicated matters of principle. Nowhere was this theme clearer than in the inaugural address. "With a good conscience our only sure reward, with history the final judge of our deeds, let us go forth to lead the land we love, asking His blessing and His help, but knowing that here on earth God's work must truly be our own."[18] Yet it recurred again and again:

> *It would be easier to shrink back from that frontier, to look to the safe mediocrity of the past. . . . But I believe the times demand invention, innovation, imagination, decision. I am asking each of you to be new pioneers on that new frontier. . . .*[19]

This race is a contest between the comfortable and the concerned, between those who believe that we should rest and lie at anchor and drift, and between those who want to move this country forward in the 60's.[20]

It is not enough to pin the blame on others, to say this is a problem of one section of the country or another, or deplore the facts that we face. A great change is at hand, and our task, our obligation is to make that revolution, that change peaceful and constructive for all. Those who do nothing are inviting shame as well as violence.[21]

Finally, in the thermonuclear age, fulfilling one's duties to a higher, Divine standard of justice was not merely the prerequisite to virtue but a condition of national and international survival. "The world has been close to war before," Kennedy noted in his acceptance speech, "but now man, who has survived all previous threats to his existence, has taken into his mortal hands the power to exterminate the entire species some seven times over."[22] "In the long history of the world," he reiterated in his inaugural address, "only a few generations have been granted the role of defending freedom in its hour of maximum danger. I do not shrink from this responsibility; I welcome it."[23] Ultimately, as he warned the United Nations:[24]

. . . a nuclear disaster, spread by wind and water and fear, could well engulf the great and the small, the rich and the poor, the committed and the uncommitted alike. Mankind must put an end to war—or war will put an end to mankind. . . . Let us call a truce to terror.

The vision of hell itself was no more terrifying than the image of World War III that penetrated national consciousness during the Kennedy years, a grim reminder that the fire next time might not have to appear as a celestial lightning bolt.

Kennedy never lived long enough for his new approach to politics to take hold among the people as a whole. Certainly, the outpouring of grief following the assassination suggested that he had made some steps in the right direction, but the state of his legislative program in November, 1963, attested to how far he had yet to travel. No doubt, it seemed strange to a nation of the poor and the recently poor to hear that they had to give to their society as well as to take from it.

Among young people, however, the Kennedy philosphy made a considerable amount of sense. As we have seen, they, too, sought a set of principles that transcended the material goals of their parents. Prior to the sixties, the only outlets for such needs had been provided in programs in the arts and humanitites offered by suburban high schools. It was, thus, not uncommon for secondary school students of the late fifties to be as versed in O'Neill, Hem-

ingway, Faulkner, and Tennessee Williams—not to mention Jack
Kerouac, Allen Ginsberg, and Gregory Corso—as students today
are familiar with Eldridge Cleaver and Malcolm X. Yet Kennedy
pointed to a new set of challenges for one's burgeoning creativity:
the prospect of influencing the course of history and society as a
whole. Given that this alternative involved action as well as
thought, it had enormous appeal.

The notion of principle as obligation also fit well into the lessons
that suburban kids were learning. Lest the point be lost, Democratic parents would make it for their youngsters. "You see, it's like
Roosevelt. Kennedy's an enemy of his class. Instead of defending
the rich, he's working for the poor and the people. You should not
take such things lightly." Indeed, it was Kennedy's wealth that
made possible his political virtues. "He's got nothing to gain from
being a politician, so he *can* look after the country's needs." This
point was somewhat contradictory, perhaps, but at 17, who knew
from logic? Indeed, how could a bored, indulged, underdirected,
guilt-ridden adolescent from Shaker Heights, Ohio, *resist* this image of a self-sacrificing aristocratic, attuned always to the interests
of his countrymen? Someday, he, too, would be a great moral
leader.

Finally, Kennedy's emphasis on the quest for survival struck a
responsive chord. On its face, one would think the opposite—that
the children of affluence would be entrapped in the illusion of
eternal beauty and youth. Such was not the case, however. If the
young were unconcerned about the physical death, they were
obsessed with the prospects of spiritual death, for it was constantly
being predicted for them, their generation, and the country. The
notion of obligation as survival hit the mood precisely, and they
responded.

Thus, the three themes—politics as principle; principle as obligation; obligation as survival—became fundamental laws of the
politics of youth that were destined to appear and to reappear in
a variety of forms as the sixties unfolded.

THE CIVIL RIGHTS MOVEMENT

The Civil Rights Movement provided the direct link between
the personal and the political needed to sustain continuing social
action. After all, following the 1960 campaign, one could only
observe developments in the Kennedy administration. The Peace
Corps had yet to evolve, and even when it did, its recruitment was
limited. Thus, the main difference between a young Kennedy
supporter and his friends was merely that he read the *New York
Times* every day—a major breakaway from the fifties, but hardly
the foundations of a revolution.

Yet what could one say to a high school student in Georgia who was willing to risk beatings and jail in order to pursue justice? How could one respond to a 15-year-old girl in Alabama who would endure the hostility of an all-white classroom to fulfill her commitment to equality? Where did the child of the suburbs "fit into" the evolving struggle for freedom?

Note that I use the terms "justice," "equality," and "freedom," instead of "black people," for in the early periods such words were the magnets that attracted the participation of Northern whites more than a rhetoric that asked the sons of wealth to help the children of the poor out of their misery. However misguided, white youth saw the Civil Rights Movement as being little different from the struggle in which they were engaging. The blacks were young, at least the ones who protested. They, too, had been taught standards of citizenship that they were prevented from fulfilling. They, too, were proving that one could make sacrifices for fundamental beliefs. Perhaps black people *were* trying to redress economic, social, and political grievances against society; they also were becoming the vanguard of a battle for a new America, one that would infuse the future with the highest aspirations of the past. "We are not free until *all* people are free," the speakers cried, and everywhere, students responded.

Such recruits learned quickly, however, that a commitment to principle was not enough. Young blacks were not merely cardboard figures in a morality play marked "Liberty and justice for all." They were human beings. If they were espousing an attractive philosophy in the course of their campaigns, this was incidental to the constellation of thoughts, emotions, and actions that gave the philosophy meaning. "We were so intent on transforming Mississippi in a summer," Paul Cowan recalls of the Mississippi Summer Project of 1964, "that we were unable to relate to its people as human beings."[25]

Moreover, the situation of the blacks *was* different, and the whites had to come to terms with the distinctions. Cowan is particularly incisive on this point:[26]

> So: if we had to judge black activists we must be very careful: to understand them within the context of their own culture and traditions, and not condemn them because they failed to be the ideal citizens of our imagined utopias. . . . We needed to rid ourselves of the double standards on which so many of our opinions were based. Our job was to transform the America that had provided us the wealth and freedom to roam the streets of the world seeking to do good—that America whose history most black people saw as the embodiment of violence and evil.

More than one activist discovered after only short periods of time that if his work elicited the appreciation of the local community occasionally, it did not always win its undying friendship and understanding.

Indeed, because the plight of the blacks was unique, their attitude toward the hazards inherent in nonviolent protests differed from that of the whites as well. The blacks always were matter-of-fact about confrontations, viewing them as just another aspect of the work that they were trying to accomplish. "We've got nothing to lose," they would say, "because your people have taken everything else away. We'll march tomorrow because we've *got* to march, because it's the only way to get the job done. If you want to join us, fine—we need your help. But we're *going*—with you or without you—and there'll be no more debate about it." Thus, the meeting would end, or shift to details of the attack.

By contrast, the whites showed uneasiness in various ways. At one extreme were those to whom a jail sentence was a red badge of moral, intellectual, and social excellence, according its possessor unlimited authority and wisdom. "Have *you* been in jail?" they would ask new arrivals. "Well you don't know what it's all about until you have." At the other extreme were those to whom each new protest, even a mild one, appeared a major step toward disaster. "It's *insane*," they would say. "We're all going to get *murdered* for no good reason at all." There was more in common between these two groups than either would have cared to admit, but, under the circumstances, they argued rather than commiserated. It was amusing, indeed, the accolades heaped on these affluent young people who "risked jobs, security, and life itself for something in which they believed," when they themselves found heroism difficult to handle. Only the blacks held them together.

Yet one cannot overestimate the impact that the Civil Rights Movement had on the white movement as a whole. First, it dramatized that the choices one had to make were never clear. If, on television, the battles between restaurant owners and the sit-inners, between the sherriffs and the Freedom Riders, seemed open-and-shut, in reality they represented a complicated matrix of calculations. "What if the press ignores us?" people asked beforehand. "What if they arrest us with little violence?" "What if we lose in court?" Again, to blacks and to a few whites, these issues resolved themselves—you had to try. Yet for every protest that succeeded in the sixties, ten failed—victims of bad timing, bad weather, bad judgment, or all three. People just learned to live with uncertainty.

Further, the blacks emphasized the social context within which moral decisions had to be made. A revealing incident in Cowan's *Making of an Un-American* was common:[27]

Though the movement talked proudly about its belief in "one man, one vote," we had discovered that the slate of local people who were supposed to represent the Freedom Democratic Party at the Democratic Convention in Atlantic City had been chosen by a group of SNCC workers, including Papa Doc, the night before the state convention in Jackson. The organization decided which local people should be rewarded for their loyalty and then rigged the convention accordingly. They were afraid that too many middle-class Negroes would be nominated in an open convention, for it was clear that many of the poor blacks with whom we worked still accepted most of the ideas of representation and respectability that they learned from their segregated society.

Although later generations would come to see the necessity of such "riggings" to redress social and economic imbalances created over three centuries, at the time they seemed "distressingly hypocritical" and to contradict Cowan's belief that, "white volunteers were working in Mississippi to help make America a more democratic country." Robert Moses, director of SNCC, cut him short:[28]

I think a lot of people here know more about democracy in the country that killed President Kennedy than most of you who have lived in the North. They haven't studied it in universities, like many of you, but they've seen how the American system works on them. All their lives they've been made to suffer in the name of democracy. So many terrible things have been justified by that word. . . . The convention in Jackson would not be one of the first I would criticize.

The lesson was no more complicated than Eldridge Cleaver's observation a few years later. "What seems irrational to the Mother Country may seem rational to the colony." But most young whites had to learn the hard way.

Basically the black revolution was teaching students about the class structure of American society and their own relationship to it. At first, the realization that an underclass still existed came as a relief to the suburban refugees—a reprieve from a life that seemed to pose no meaningful challenges. The more the "invisible men" revealed their essential humanness, however—their resentment, their anger, their bitterness, their pride; the more their tactics threatened violence and destruction; the more their platforms demanded a fundamental realignment of power and wealth in all institutions—including the universities that white activists attended—the more the students had to face the question that had paralyzed their parents years before: "What are you willing to lose for what you believe?"

And this question got to the heart of the matter because it brought the abstraction, "obligation," down to its human dimension—loyalty. "You're with us?" blacks challenged. "by *any* means necessary?" Whites equivocated. "You see—you're *not* with us!" "What did it mean," white students asked one another, "to be loyal to blacks?" "Did one do *anything* they wanted, or did one argue?" "Should you argue in private meetings and remain silent in public, or could you attack the blacks in public, too, in the style of older liberals?" And, beneath it all, "We're *not* racist, damn it! We want to help, but they won't let us!"

Many undergraduates withdrew from the Movement, bewildered and angry over the new militancy among their former allies. "I was hurt by the hatred that blacks were beginning to express toward people like me who had worked for years to achieve integration," Cowan admits. "I could accept the cultural explanations for their efforts to rid their organizations of whites, but no rational argument really healed the pain of the personal attacks."[29] Malcolm X and Stokely Carmichael urged them to go back to their *own* communities, but in a real sense, this was impossible. Young whites *had* no communities. They felt only an abstract connection with their past, only disaffection with the present. If the blacks were not to be the future, then what hope was there for them? What would be their heritage, their style, their language? What would be their demands, their institutions, their vision? Those who couldn't answer just stopped asking, hoping, as their parents had hoped, that someone else would straighten things out.

Yet a few remained and learned. They learned that the principles guiding relationships with blacks were no different from those governing bonds between friends. Friends defended each other, even as they argued to the death. Friends respected mutual weakness, even as they made demands on one another almost beyond mutual fulfillment. Friends set limits to their relationships, even as they subjected each boundary to continual assault. While most whites were asking, "Why don't the blacks like us?" these few were wondering, "Why don't we like ourselves?" "Be true to your conviction!" those who were leaving the Movement urged. "What convictions survive," the few asked, "without others with whom to share them?" They were becoming radicals.

VIETNAM

The war reinforced these lessons and taught new ones. First, it added an international dimension to the problem of privilege. No longer could the radicals view themselves simply as the children of an upper class under attack from the poor; they were the elite of an overgrown empire whose industries held controlling interest in underdeveloped countries throughout the world. The word "imperialism" crept back into the language, as the Left made building an anti-imperialist movement within the United States its number-one priority. Top Movement leaders established direct communications with leaders of the National Liberation Front.

Vietnam complicated the Movement's efforts to determine its true loyalties. Presumably, one could persuade students to support the Vietnamese revolution, but what about blacks and working people? Should a radical divorce himself from struggles in the United States if they threatened to isolate him from an identification with revolutions elsewhere? Conversely, should organizers of the poor attempt to recruit them into the anti-war movement? If efforts to end the war failed, what were anti-war forces obliged to do to express their opposition? Was this a Nuremberg situation? What, indeed, did it mean to be "loyal" to the National Liberation Front—a group that wisely refrained from offering tactical advice to its American allies but that thereby permitted the use of every sort of tactic in its name?

Questions of patriotism arose. During the Civil Rights Movement, one could say, "I am loyal to the principles of the Declaration of Independence and the Constitution as distinguished from the practices of our government." But could one make such a statement in relation to a war? What was the relationship between democratic principles and foreign policy? The sordid side of American history burst to the surface. Instead of the continuing march toward that equality which De Tocqueville had described a century earlier, which liberal historians had tried to read into the modern era as well, the Left saw only an unbroken string of atrocities—against Indians, against blacks, against Latin Americans, against immigrants, against Japanese, and against the Vietnamese. "Alienation is fighting a war and hoping the other side will win," the Oakland 9 proclaimed in the course of their trial for organizing resistance to the draft. If once they had lost their past, radicals now were losing their country.

The war shifted the Movement's attitudes toward violence, creating what Wilson Carey McWilliams called a "crisis of illegitimacy."[30]

> *Rarely have concerned and apparently sincere men classified so many of their own actions as legitimate. Police officers find it legitimate to hold target practice with a college dormitory or the home of a radical as the mark; radicals regard bank burning as a legitimate form of protest and show but slight uneasiness over the manufacture and use of what were once called "infernal machines."* . . .
>
> *Ours could be called, more accurately, a "crisis of illegitimacy," a decline in the conviction that some actions are impermissible, for one's*

self as well as for others. Lacking the secure expectation that their political opponents will feel morally restricted in their choice of means, men are forced and permitted to reject such limitations on themselves.

Yet more than Hammurabi's Code was involved. One became violent to assert the primacy of a social morality over personal morality,—to say, "We are a class whose interests are being trampled, and our ethical assumptions spring from our consciousness as part of the class, not as individuals." One was violent because revolutions were violent, and that is what the Vietnamese were fighting.

Indeed, a few in the Movement raised the specter of violent revolution within the United States itself. In response to social democrats who were arguing that the U.S. economy did not depend on investments elsewhere in the world, (that, therefore, an effective liberal coalition could bring imperialism under control), radicals pointed to powerful oil lobbies dependent on supplies from the Middle East and to corporations that would define their overseas investments as top priorities as examples of political interests that could gain military support for counter-revolutionary activities. Insurgent movements in the Third World could fight off a U.S. attack for a while, they argued, but such movements needed help. It was the obligation of revolutionaries in the United States to provide it.

Thus, the central themes—equality, obligation, social justice— remained the same; but in the atmosphere of war and international upheaval, the confidence that they could be realized easily did not.

Picture it—
.
Two-thirds of the nations demanding the wealth of the remaining one-third.

An uncontrolled population explosion.

A mass of citizens in the developed word so accustomed to its comforts, earned over fifty years of hard work, as to be incapable of relinquishing them.

An ecology losing the capacity to absorb the technological growth that might feed the world's people without a redistribution of its wealth.

A nuclear capability within reach of any government that wanted it.

Could such a world survive?

Were people in the wealthy nations even aware of the impending crisis?

Were so-called "reformers" attuned to the sacrifices that the rich countries would have to make?
Or was the answer to be more Vietnams, more Dominican Republics, more Czechoslovakias and Polands? Was it to be an international empire carved out by the United States and the Soviet Union, administered without regard for the real needs of humanity and protected by thermonuclear bombs?

Yes, even the configurations remained the same—politics as principle; principle as obligation; obligation was survival. Yet where once there was optimism, now there was uncertainty; where once there was hope, now there was despair.

ORGANIZERS

Of course, events alone did not organize the Movement. People did. At every point, there were specific individuals and groups who took it upon themselves to interpret national trends, to plan strategies, to win support for new assaults upon the establishment. Nor was there anything conspiratorial about the process. Most major campaigns evolved out of conferences that radical organizations sponsored during the summer; many were reported in the newspapers before they occurred. To announce a year of demonstrations against military recruiters, to project a national campaign for student power, was as much a part of the Movement style as the open-ended meetings that planned such activities.

Moreover, the position that the white Left frequently assumed —that of a support group for movements spearheaded by blacks or Third World insurgents—lent itself to a certain kind of leader. Frequently, he was a cross-cultural mediator more than a spokesman, a person who could bridge gaps between different kinds of people and who could convey to both sides of an alliance the sense that each understood the other, that each respected the other, that each would be reliable over the long pull. The trip to Atlanta, the fact-finding journey to Vietnam—these were not fringe benefits that radical organizers received as reward for services rendered. They were the activities from which the organizers derived their legitimacy as strategists. Northern students obtained first-hand information about the sit-in movement in the early sixties not from Bob Moses of SNCC but from Tom Hayden and Paul Potter. Radicals related to the National Liberation Front not directly through Vietnamese representatives but indirectly through Rennie Davis and others. Thus, if the central problem of the youth movement was to transcend its class position, it accepted as leaders those with a demonstrated capacity to do so.

Movement organizers rarely fit the popular stereotypes surrounding them. Newspaper photographers worked hard to catch radicals in their nastiest, meanest, sloppiest moments, and once such pictures existed, they ran over and over again. Indeed, eventually they did find counterparts in reality, as younger militants sought to imitate the models that the media had created. Yet any resemblance between the caricatures that snarled at nervous readers of the *Chicago Tribune* and the most effective spokesmen for the Left was purely coincidental.

As mediators who had to cope with a variety of delicate situations, radical organizers by and large tended to be soft-spoken. There were exceptions, to be sure: Abbie Hoffman and Jerry Rubin; Mario Savio; Carl Ogelsby. Yet these were atypical. Until the Conspiracy trials, Rennie Davis rarely addressed public gatherings. Tom Hayden absorbed people more with the quality of his rhetoric than its volume. One often had to strain to hear people like Paul Potter, Nick Eagelson, Greg Calvert, Clark Kissinger— all leaders of SDS at some point in the sixties. And David Harris employed *sotto voce* deliberately, as a technique, forcing his audience to remain absolutely quiet until he had finished.

They maintained a sense of irony. A presentation by Rennie Davis to a meeting of the Oberlin Alumni Association in Boston comes to mind. "How do you face the prospect of a long jail sentence?" someone asked.

"Well, I don't know," he replied straightforwardly. "In some ways it might be better. When you've been forced to move from place to place because the police keep raiding the apartments where you're staying; when you've thought that a patrol captain had decided finally to pull the trigger of the gun which he was holding to your head, then jail doesn't seem so horrible. Who knows? Maybe jail will be the best place to stay over the next two years."

After a moment of uneasy silence, the discussion shifted to another topic.

Effective radicals were patient. It often came out in question-and-answer sessions.

"Where do you get your money?" an angry listener would inquire.

"Well, part of it comes from speeches like this one, and part of it comes from royalties on my books. Besides, we don't make a great deal of money."

"What are you people *for*, anyway?"

"I tried to explain that in my speech. I said that we're for a withdrawal of American troops from Indochina, for a fundamental redistribution of wealth in this country, for the creation of structures throughout the United States to enable people to exercise democratic control over the decisions which affect their lives. We're for juries which are chosen from the communities in which the defendent lives—juries of his peers. Shall I go on? What are *you* for?"

"Do you support the bombings and violence as tactics to get what you want?"

"Well, again, I tried to get into that in my speech. I don't think that anyone *likes* bombings or violence, but when a Movement has succeeded in persuading the majority of the people that a policy's wrong, but the policy continues, then it's natural that some will use violent tactics."

"Yes, but these people don't seem to be *for* anything. All they try to do is destroy, without putting anything in its place."

"Well, perhaps I didn't make myself clear. The Movement does have several constructive proposals—some of which the people even have supported. Yet, again, as I tried to point out, the government. . . ."

Always, at the end of such a session someone would approach the speaker—a sympathizer, to be sure—and say, "Boy are you patient! That was an unbelievable audience!" Yet headlines the following morning would read, "Militant Supports Violence: Says Tactics 'natural.' " And so it went.

Finally, radical organizers knew when to be reasonable. Tom Hayden was a master at this. "I see no reason why we shouldn't accept the support of Kingman Brewster in the fight to save Bobby Seale," he told an audience in New Haven in May 1970. "If the President of Yale wants to project himself as the Left wing of the ruling class, that's his business—and if we do our work, his support can only help us." Doubtless, many of those who joined the ensuing round of applause were thinking, "Gee, I didn't know that Hayden was so flexible in his thinking," yet this was precisely the response that the speaker had hoped to arouse. If, later, he had felt obliged to urge more militant action, he would have been in a much better position to do so.

Even these strengths were unequal to the tasks of mediation and leadership in the Movement, however. An organizer had to possess a kind of personal magnetism that could draw people together. The popular word, of course, is *charisma*, but there is, perhaps, too much mysticism associated with this term for it to be applicable here. Radical organizers didn't just "have it" at birth; they acquired "it" in the course of their development; they cultivated it in the course of their work.

They were intense. Perhaps all of them did not spend thirty minutes in meditation before every public appearance, as did David Harris, but each one in some way conducted a private war between his work and his life, between his thought and his practice, between his obligations and his needs. If radicals appeared to have discovered a "higher self" within them, it was because the nature of their goals demanded it. Unlike other people, they did not give themselves the luxury of saying, "Well, that's just the way things are, I guess." They had to devote complete attention to being themselves what they would have had others become.

In organizing, they sought less to persuade people than to engage them; less to convince them of an answer than to impress upon them the importance of the question, "What kind of system is it that allows 'good' men to make those kinds of decisions?" Paul Potter demanded at the first national march against the Vietnam War in 1965, "What kind of system is it that justifies the U.S. or any country seizing the destinies of the Vietnamese people and using them callously for our own purpose?[31] Carl Ogelsby resumed the theme the following year, identifying the system as that of "corporate liberalism":[32]

> *It performs for the corporate state a function quite like what the Church once performed for the feudal state. It seeks to justify its burdens and protect it from change. As the Church exaggerated this office in the Inquisition, so with liberalism in the McCarthy time—which, if it was a reactionary phenomenon, was still made possible by our anti-Communist corporate liberalism.*

He, too, saw the situation as a challenge, however:[33]

> *Let me speak directly to humanist liberals. If my facts are wrong, I will soon be corrected. But if they are right, then you may face a crisis of conscience. Corporatism or humanism: which? For it has come to that. Will you let your dreams be used? Will you be a grudging apologist for the corporate state? Or will you help to try change it—not in the name of this or that blueprint or 'ism,' but in the name of simple human decency and democracy and the vision that wise and brave men saw in the time of our own revolution?*

Always pose the right question, the radical said, for without it, the right answer could never come.

The radical organizer maintained a sense of assurance while taking enormous risks. The draft resister was a prime example. "This is the way I have chosen to live," he explained. "I understand what it entails, but I still feel that it is preferable to other courses of action which I might have taken." No, he wouldn't urge anyone else to do what he has done—each person must make up his own mind. At least, however, he hopes that people will work against the war in some capacity.

"How can he talk about this so calmly?" anxious students asked themselves during the presentation. "He's going to spend the next five years in jail." By disobeying a law for his principles—without fanfare, without fear, without regret—the resister had opened up the possibility that anyone could adhere to his beliefs if he took them seriously enough. Now the listener was on the defensive. "What *am* I doing against the war," he wondered. "Would *I* serve in the army if drafted?" The following weekend, he would leaflet the neighborhood for a local peace organization. The resister had succeeded.

Thus, radical organizers mediated between conflicting groups, won new recruits to the Movement, conveyed an overall sense of direction not so much by what they said or by what they did as by what they were. Every aspect of their behavior suggested: "There is no door that opens automatically to the Promised Land; we must begin to seek it for ourselves, in the way we live our lives, and in what we demand from our institutions." They were insistent, moreover, that neither individuals acting alone nor groups pursuing private interests on their own could create a just world, for they understood that justice, by definition, is a standard governing *relationships* between people and groups.

Indeed, this latter view pointed to the peculiar role that the organizer played. While the average man, even within the Movement, attempted to secure what was *his,* the organizer attempted to strengthen what was *theirs.* Whether negotiating an agreement between the SDS and the Panthers, between the Mobilization Committee and the National Liberation Front, his impact was the same. By exuding a sense of optimism about an alliance, by making his life available to its growth, he hoped that eventually the alliance would develop a sense of pride in what it could accomplish and would gain a sense of confidence in itself.

Having assessed the impact of events and organizers, we may see the ways in which they filled the prerequisites of radicalization for young suburbanites.

1. The person must develop goals that are neither within his grasp nor measurable in material terms.

From their parents and schools, the young people learned the importance of pursuing the "higher things" made possible by their affluence, even as they were being condemned because their parents had become rich. Kennedy's emphasis on "excellence" in all things reinforced the lessons of the home.

2. The person must develop a sense of *self*-interest by experiencing treatment himself that he perceives to be unjust.

The young themselves felt implicated in the spate of indictments of suburbia that appeared in the late fifties, reinforcing their parents complaints that "they took things for granted." Being blamed for having grown up in a world that they did not make they felt to be terribly unjust.

3. The person must develop a sense of the *common* interest.

Their sense of personal injustice, in turn, made it possible for them to respond to challenges posed by Kennedy, blacks, and later by Vietnamese to pursue standards of justice in a nationwide, then worldwide struggle for the common good.

4. The person must sense that such a life is *legitimate*.

Kennedy made it seem that only such a life was legitimate for a person of reasonable comfort. The blacks appealed constantly to sections of the Declaration of Independence and the Constitution, as well as to central tenets of the Judeo-Christian tradition. Finding common ground with the Vietnamese proved more difficult. Indeed, the anti-war movement was harder to mobilize than either support for the Kennedy Campaign or recruits to the Civil Rights Movement had been. Yet, eventually, more than one student was proud to point out that the preamble of the North Vietnamese Constitution quoted the American Declaration of Independence.

5. The person must sense that such a life is *possible*.

Movement organizers constantly dramatized ways in which people could live at the cutting edge of change without either starving or falling apart.

6. The person must sense that such a life is *natural*.

In early periods of the Movement, the young boasted of the new people whom they were meeting; their confrontations with "average" citizens in door-to-door canvasses; their sustained involvement with the poor. One measure of the decline of the Movement in the late sixties, in fact, was the extent to which it failed to fulfill this prerequisite—by asking people to choose between the world as most people saw it and the world as the Left made it out to be.

7. The person must understand that such a life can be difficult.

The grind of both the Civil Rights Movement and the anti-war effort showed many young people how difficult the pursuit of change could be. Each confrontation became the source of new debates over appropriate strategies and tactics for change.

8. The person must realize that such a life must be *shared*.

New recruits to the Movement discovered quickly that they needed help: friends who would support them through periods of tension and uncertainty; teachers who would help them determine what to do. An important element in the cry for "community" was a quest for a larger conversation among people concerning what social change really meant.

Yet why did the same events *not* generate movements among the *ressentient* and the urban ethnics? Again, the theory is helpful in showing which prerequisites were missing for each group.

The emphasis in lower-middle class families on material standards and popularity rather than on abstract standards of excellence made it difficult for their children to imagine that any world is worth seeking other than the one that exists. Thus, even when a lingering respect for the Judeo-Christian tradition did override their lust for power, creating a "conversion," they lacked confidence that arousing people, exciting them to demand social change would produce any useful result. Indeed, they often felt that such efforts would merely replace one form of manipulation with another, for they could not distinguish between different goals. So they assumed a "hippie" stance in the belief that at least they could try not to harm anyone, even if they couldn't help them. Only a strong jolt from another group and a good deal of sympathetic guidance would have moved the *ressentient* from this position. In the sixties, neither was forthcoming.

For the young ethnic, the problem was somewhat different. He, at least, had experienced the frustration of pursuing unrealizable ideals: "duty," "loyalty," "integrity". Even if the goals came wrapped in a book of rules on how to achieve them, their invocation gave him some sense of a world beyond his grasp that he had to try to emulate to obtain salvation, regardless of the cost. Moreover, society was making it hard for him to pursue these ideals by depriving his communities of resources; and this filled him with a deep sense of personal injustice—the sort that his parents projected into anger at flag-burnings and the elimination of prayers in public schools—but that he often took out on the symbols of the rich.

The other elements were missing, however. The one group that could have challenged him to join in a common fight, the blacks, failed to do so, and white organizers who might have made the connections between the groups failed as well. While the young ethnic's appreciation of traditions was strong, he saw them more as the backbone of existing institutions than as a framework within which to justify their continuing renewal. Surely, traditions did not legitimize revolution in his eyes. Most important, he had no sense that a radical's life was possible. There were none of "his" people in the new movements who could translate the Left's rhetoric into language that he could understand and trust. Thus, he confined his rebellion to street corners.

Yet beyond the usefulness of any specific application of the theory, its underlying proposition is the important one: The creation of radicals is not a task to be left to either spring frolics or even to summer vacations in Biloxi. It is the exacting job of persuading a person that he has no choice but to seek a world in which man's higest moral standards are infused into the patterns of his life. Of course, disillusionment is essential. The person must be disabused of his belief that humanity requires only tinkering to correct itself. Of course, expressiveness and creativity are essential. Without them, who can conceive of the alternatives upon which change depends? These are the raw materials, however, not the process itself.

The process is that which tells the poor that they are right to complain; which tells the rich that they have reason to worry; which tells both that they must confront one another. Given the nature of man and of the systems that he creates, such lessons are the hardest to learn. He who would teach them, then, must appreciate what they mean and how they appear in a thousand different tongues. Only then might he make them understood. Only then might the people want to understand them.

REFERENCES

1. Karl Marx, *The 18th Brumaire of Louis Bonaparte* (New York, International Publishers, 1963), p. 54.
2. Fredrich Engels, Introduction, Karl Marx, *Class Struggles in France; 1848-1850* (New York, International Publishers, 1964).
3. Charles A. Reich, *The Greening of America* (New York, Random House, 1970), pp. 356-357.
4. *Ibid.*, p. 342.
5. *Ibid.*, p. 309.
6. *Ibid.*, p. 312.
7. *Ibid.*, p. 228–229.
8. *Ibid.*, p. 353.
9. *Ibid.*, p. 284–285.
10. *Ibid.*, pp. 320–321.
11. Wilson Carey McWilliams, *The Idea of Fraternity in American Politics* unpub. doctoral dissertation, p. 52. A revised version of this thesis is to appear fall, 1971, published by the University of California Press.
12. *Ibid.*, p. 52.
13. *Ibid.*, p. 133.
14. John F. Kennedy, "Acceptance Speech," Democratic Party Nomination, in Arthur Schlesinger Jr., *A Thousand Days* (New York, Fawcett, 1965), p. 64.
15. John F. Kennedy, "Inaugural Address," Jan. 20, 1961, in Houston Peterson, *A Treasury of the World's Great Speeches* (New York, Simon and Schuster, 1967), p. 832.
16. Quoted in Schlesinger, *op. cit.*, p. 880.
17. Quoted in Peterson, *op. cit.*, p. 842.

18. *Ibid.*, p. 832.
19. Schlesinger, *op. cit.*, p. 64.
20. *Ibid.*, p. 76.
21. Kennedy, "Civil Rights Address," June 11, 1963, in Albert P. Blaustein and Robert L. Zangrando, *Civil Rights and the American Negro* (New York, Trident, 1968), p. 484.
22. Quoted in Schlesinger, *op. cit.*, p. 64.
23. Quoted in Peterson, *op. cit.*, p. 832.
24. Quoted in Schlesinger, *op. cit.*, p. 448.
25. Paul Cowan, *The Making of an Un-American* (New York, Viking, 1970), p. 32.
26. *Ibid.*, p. 48.
27. *Ibid.*, p. 47.
28. *Ibid.*, p. 48.
29. *Ibid.*, p. 62.
30. Wilson Carey McWilliams, "*On Political Illegitimacy,*" (Unpublished manuscript.)
31. Paul Potter, "The Incredible War," in Massimo Teodori, *The New Left: A Documentary History* (New York, Bobbs-Merrill, 1969), p. 248.
32. Carl Ogelsby, "Trapped in a System," *Ibid.*, p. 187.
33. *Ibid.*, p. 187.

The Search
for Justice

4 Radicals always face enormous problems in trying to achieve their objectives. The established institutions resist them. The people are afraid to support them. Even their own followers, promising more than they deliver, tend to be unreliable. If there are rewards to being a radical, comfort is not among them.

Yet today's radicals—the spokesmen for a New Left—have developed a new problem, one that compounds all the others. They don't know who they are.

They are not liberals. The liberal view is that the average man is practical—his capacity for idealism is limited. He thinks only of his pocketbook, how he might obtain the fruits of the very system that the radical has rejected. An American is not evil, says the liberal. He will respond to appeals for change if they are made properly. Yet he is not perfect, either. If he is forced to do more than he wants to do, he will fight back ferociously. The liberal, thus, assumes the burden of persuading the "haves" to make sacrifices voluntarily in order to avoid a revolution from the "have-nots," while he urges the "have-nots" to work within the system. In no way do today's revolutionaries, with their principled opposition to "imperialism, racism, militarism, and sexism," approve of such a program.

Nor is the New Left an offshoot of Marxism. To be sure, some of its leaders agree with the predictions that Marx made in *The German Ideology* concerning the way in which a capitalistic system would evolve. Marx did foresee, they point out, that capitalism would be able to operate at high levels of production; he even foresaw that it would create a higher standard of living for the poor. What he also said, however, was that people would lose control over the work in the process. They would be locked away in factories and offices, performing jobs that demanded little of their talents, energy, or skill, while a small number of corporate executives would wield more and more power over the system as a whole. The masses would want to share in the creation of a decent society, but they would find no way of doing so. Even economic growth would come to seem oppressive. The more the corporations showed themselves capable of producing, the more the average citizen would want to tell the corporations what to produce. At some point—alienated, furious, desperate to reassert themselves—the people would revolt.

Some in the Movement insist that this sort of revolution is in the making today. Yet on major questions of ideology and organization, the New Left and Marx have little in common.

Marx was insensitive to the problems of building socialism in a large country. Indeed, he hoped that the Communist revolution would unite workers throughout the world.

Contemporary revolutionaries tend to be localists whose concern for decentralization in politics is as genuine as their demand for a redistribution of the wealth. Indeed, many contend that in a country of this size nationalization of industry will fail without local structures of self-government through which the people can exercise political control over the bureaucracy that would result.

Marx viewed primitive, agrarian cultures as "regressive"! He insisted upon the assimilation of the farmers and nationalities into the industrial system.

The New Left is concerned that these distinctive cultures of the world be preserved. The uprooting of the American Indian; the assimilation of the immigrants and the blacks; the destruction of the villages of the Vietnamese—these horrify young people as much as the exploitation of working people in the factories or the failure of private enterprise to respond to the crisis of the cities.

Marx contended that utopia lay at the end of history.

The New Left rejects the myth of a future utopia. Try, today, even to talk to the young revolutionary of the "kingdom of freedom," that Marx envisaged, where workers "hunt in the morning, fish in the afternoon, rear cattle in the evening, criticize after dinner."[1] He will say, "Fine. Provided the Bomb doesn't kill us all first."

Marx derided idealism as "mystification"; emotionalism as "unscientific." The New Left speaks constantly of ideals, fundamental values, and the capacity to feel.

Therefore, when someone today asks a radical, "What are you?" the radical is often incapable of answering. He is neither a liberal nor a Marxist. He seems to have no tradition behind him.

The New Left *is* the product of a tradition, however—an important one. To understand this, we first must get a clear picture of what its broad perspectives are.

Fundamentally, the radicals are engaged in a search for justice. The word means more to them than "fairness in dealings," or "giving each person his due." It is an ideal; a goal. Theirs is the vision of Plato's *Republic*—of a community in which each citizen could find the role to which he was best suited; of a system that would sustain a balance between its various needs; of a society in which there would be a correspondence between what a person wanted to do, what he was able to do, and what he had to do.

Indeed, the plea of the New Left is that everyone join in the search for justice—that people become involved, engaged, committed to what it means. Radicals realize that no social system can achieve absolute justice any more than an individual in relatively good shape can remove the viruses that circulate throughout his blood stream. Yet they contend that societies can try to live up to their principles, just as individuals can pay attention to their health. Were people in our society to do so, they say, the country would not tolerate any number of existing conditions: racism and sexism; the cultural, economic, and military exploitation of the Third World by the United States government and private industry; harassment of those who seek social change by the FBI and the Army. The people would demand an end to such inequities as surely as they now demand an end to the Indochina War.

It is from this perspective that radicals shout "power to the people." They sense that people are powerless to pursue justice through existing institutions. As John Schaar expressed it to a seminar examining the problems of social change,[2]

> *Wherever you hear this basic theme of powerlessness. . . . The manifestations of it are many. There are many, many ways of responding to powerlessness. But somehow you hear it from more and more quarters, to compress it desperately. We also seem to be caught in a system of logic and structures which don't need us and which in effect are superfluous and cannot change. Apparently, what's powerless is man and the human claim.*

Radicals seek power, then, not as an end in itself, but in order to do what is right.

It is the quest for power to achieve justice, finally, that has driven the radicals to build a movement. The Movement is, in effect, the New Left's answer to the age-old question of organizing: How can people get together to achieve their collective aims? It provides a base—a mechanism that lends coherence, continuity, and a sense of direction to the lives of its participants. If existing institutions thwart the pursuit of justice, say the radicals, then the movement will confront them, create alternatives to them, even destroy them until the pursuit of justice can be revived.

Indeed, their strong emphasis on morality, their insistence on "living up to our ideals," suggests that the radicals' search for justice is almost religious in nature. They would be reluctant to admit this, of course, but the parallels between their own view of human life and the view fostered by many of the world's religions is striking.

At the heart of all religious conceptions of justice is an image of a community in which virtue is man's highest value, in which he is willing to relegate all other concerns to its pursuit, and from which he derives that satisfaction that comes from the disciplined pursuit of the moral life. Within traditional theology the image is the Kingdom of Heaven; within Christian socialism, the image is "utopia."

Yet the form that the ideal takes is less significant than its purpose: to serve as the measure of all human aspirations for moral excellence and to inspire the pursuit of justice as an end in itself. "There can be no liberty without virtue,"[3] Jean Jacques Rousseau insisted in *A Discourse on Political Economy*. Later, in *The Social Contract*, he argued that there could be no democracy without virtue as well. In more recent times, Martin Buber has distinguished utopian socialism in its refusal to "believe that in our reliance on the future 'leap' we have to do now the direct opposite of what we are striving for; it believes rather that we must create here and now the space *now* possible for the thing which we are striving, so that it may come to fulfillment then!"[4] There are important differences between Rousseau and Buber, but none so critical as what unites them: the belief that there is no road to goodness other than that which is paved with a concern for what goodness means.

At the same time, those who adhere to a religious conception of justice understand that human beings are weak, that they need help in realizing their ideals. For this reason, proponents of religious justice pay special attention to the ways in which a country defines and structures itself.

They respect traditions. The demands of justice are uncertain; history at least suggests how people fulfilled them in the past. Organized religions are well-known to speak in the name of their traditions, but it happens as well when a radical commits himself to the ideal of a cooperative or socialist society. Suddenly, he asks, "What does this mean? Who has helped to define socialism before me?" He reads Marx, Engels, Lenin, Trotsky. He might examine the arguments of their opponents within the socialist tradition—Fourier, Owen, Proudhon, La Salle, Landauer. He relates interpretations and interpolations of socialism to earlier treatises on "What Is to Be Done?" At meetings, he debates among friends whether Lenin would have continued his loosening of restrictions over the Soviet Union had he lived. One's obligations are never clear, but they become slightly clearer when precedent can be invoked as a guide.

Proponents of religious justice support strong governments, that hold citizens accountable to their ideals. They have no confidence that people, left to their own devices, will do what they ought to do. As Rousseau put it,[5]

> We find in history a thousand examples of pusillanimous or ambitious rulers, who were ruined by their slackness or their pride; not one who suffered for having been strictly just. But we ought not to confound negligence with moderation or clemency with weakness. To be just, it is necessary to be severe; to permit vice, when one has the right and power to suppress it, is to be oneself vicious. It is not enough to say to citizens, be good; they must be taught to be so.

Yet in the religious view, the strong exercise of authority is neither viewed an end in itself nor the means to force people into a blind acceptance of rituals without meaning. It is, rather, intertwined with the idea of the quest, the search for something beyond the self to which one owes allegience, the attempt to achieve moral and spiritual excellence. In athletics, for example, we admire the strong coach who pushes his men to the limit in order to bring out the best in them. In music, we understand that a conducter might demand that his orchestra rehearse several hours a day, going over the same passages again and again, in order to achieve the most beautiful sound of which it is capable. So it must be, say philosophers like Plato and Rousseau, for those who aspire to build just societies. They need strong leaders who themselves are engaged in a strenuous pursuit of the Good, who both inspire excellence by example and who push people to live up to the highest vision of what they might be.

Even as they insist on public authority, however, the religious strategy for justice encourages the formation of small communities through which people can discuss with one another their fears, doubts, and anxieties about pursuing their highest goals. Indeed, among the organized religions, one can almost formulate a Law of the Inverse Relationship Between Orthodoxy and Size. The harder a theology assumes the achievement of a moral life to be, the greater its efforts to involve members in intimate discussion groups, informal social gatherings, and classes in religious education. Orthodox synagogues in Judaism, for example, tend to be small, communal, decentralized, demanding extensive contact among those who enter it, in sharp contrast with the relatively impersonal services of reform congregations, often conducted in huge auditoriums. Similar comparisons could be made among the various Christian denominations.

Political theorists attuned to the problems of justice have insisted upon small communities as well. In the *Laws,* Plato suggests that states limit their size to 5,040 citizens. Throughout his writings, Rousseau contends that, "generally speaking, a small state is strong in proportion than a great one."[6] Martin Buber argues that "an association based on community of views and aspirations" cannot satisfy the "eternal human need" that gives rise to the demand for socialism, "the need of man to feel his own house in a room in some great, all-embracing structure in which he is at home." "The only thing which does that," he notes, "is an association which makes for communal living."[7] Whenever philosophers have assumed that the good life involves a difficult struggle, they have advised the construction of local institutions to help people along the way.

Thus, even though they avoid the various organized religions, the radicals of the New Left pay great attention to the religious instinct itself. They set exacting ideals for themselves and admire leaders who demand sacrifices in the name of the higher justice which they are trying to pursue. They speak bitterly of the failure of the United States to honor its own basic documents: the Declaration of Independence, the Constitution, and the Bill of Rights. And they organize themselves into "collectives," small groups that enable them to discuss personal problems, ideological differences, and strategic plans among people whom they trust. That is what justice requires.

The demand for religious justice establishes the framework from which radicals indict modern society. Indeed, the New Left has come to the point of rethinking the questions that perplexed political philosophers at the dawn of industrialization itself.

In 1749, Rousseau, then thirty-seven years old and known primarily as a composer, noticed a poster announcing the annual essay contest for scholars and intellectuals sponsored by the French Academy of Dijon. The question posed by the Academy was straightforward enough: "Has the progress of the arts and sciences tended to the purification or to the corruption of morality?" The preferred answer was no less clear than if the B'nai B'rith today were to ask its members, "Has the establishment of the state of Israel contributed to the purification or to the corruption of the Jews?"

Defiantly, Rousseau chose to argue the negative side of the case. "Our minds have been corrupted in proportion as the arts and sciences have improved," he charged, in language that present-day readers of underground newspapers will find familiar.[8]

As the conveniences of life increase, as the arts are brought to perfection, and luxury spreads, true courage flags, the virtues disappear, and all this is due to the effect of the sciences and of those acts which are exercised in the privacy of man's dwellings.... Even from our infancy an absurd system of education serves to adorn our wit and corrupt our judgment. We see, on every side, huge institutions, where our youth are educated at great expense, and instructed in everything but their duty. Your children will be ignorant of their own language, when they can talk others which are not spoken anywhere. They will be able to compose verses which they can hardly understand ... but magnanimity, equity, temperance, and courage will be words of which they know not the meaning ... Whence arise all those abuses, unless it be from that fatal inequality introduced among men by the difference of talents and cheapening of virtue? ... The question is no longer whether a man is honest but whether he is clever.

Ironically, the response to Rousseau's blast merely confirmed it. He won the Academy's contest for the style of his essay, even though its substance shocked "right-thinking" people all over Europe.

Rousseau was writing about the French Enlightenment, but radicals have come to the same conclusions about the major assumptions of society today. Not only do they question capitalism; they question any "ism" that argues that political and economic justice is unimportant until the conquest of nature has been completed. They challenge the Enlightenment itself. We must examine why.

At the heart of the Enlightenment conception of justice is the image of progress, of the inexorable movement of history that both determines man's conceptions of the Good and presumably enhances them. The Enlightenment looks forward to that day in the future when man, through a supreme exercise of intellect, will have freed enough resources from nature to provide for every human need; will have developed enough understanding of the biological, mental, and social forces affecting man to permit cure of almost every ailment; and will have learned enough from his past experience to temper his "bad" instincts and cultivate his "good" ones. Whether man believes in absolute, divine justice is irrelevant to this process. Man will be served best, says the Enlightenment, by developing knowledge about himself and the world. If he does so, goodness will take care of itself.

In the Enlightenment strategy for justice, society gears itself to expanding its productive capabilities. People accord allegience not to political leaders, or to moral philosophers, but to technicians, those who can "get the job done" most efficiently. Frank E. Manuel's summary of the writings of St. Simon—the French

Utopian Socialist who predicted with approval the directions that technological societies would take—is an apt characterization of the position of the Enlightenment as a whole on the problem of authority in a state:[9]

> *It was to the interest of the non-propertied class to accept a position subordinate to scientists and property holders and to subscribe to the international scientific fund because in science lay the sole prospect of the amelioration of their condition. If the elect of humanity, the scientists were universally acclaimed the foremost men in the world, then the most elemental drives for human action would be transformed, the rich and the mighty of the earth would forsake their struggles for power and glory and seek prestige in good works in order to win the greater glory.*

What is the role of traditions in such a scheme? The answer is, "not much." Indeed, there is a danger in doting on the past. If next year brings progress, why concern oneself with the one just completed? Of what relevance can the debates of ancient philosophers be to an age in whose grasp is the solution of all of man's problems: how to eradicate hunger, how to bring peace, how to create a good life throughout the nations of the world? Man must look ahead, not behind. His uncertainty about the future is naïve, frivolous, immature. He should absorb the new developments as they come and make the most of them, shedding his earlier "life-styles" and moral systems wherever appropriate. All things are technologically possible if man would just learn to accept the judgments of technology.

Finally, where the religious strategy for justice demands a small community within which people can share their aspirations for excellence with one another, the Enlightenment strategy requires the entire universe—any place that promises to provide a shred of knowledge, constructive or destructive, to an ignorant world. The Enlightenment man is the one who pledges allegiance to no flag, ascribes loyalty to no community or group, adheres to no fixed system. He is where the smart ones are—the brilliant technicians, the incisive analysts, the keen wits. Someday, he tells himself, everyone will be rich enough, keen enough, secure enough to live as he does. Why try to build utopias in out-of-the-way places in the wilderness based on foolish abstractions like the "just life"? Why even remain in one city in a futile effort to reconstruct its moral and social environment? Prepare for the universal existence, says the Enlightenment where, in splendid abundance, human beings can merely escape anything that grows the least bit unpleasant or difficult.

The radicals point out that Modern America has adopted virtually every element of this strategy. Every institution is designed to train people to work within existing bureaucracies that, in turn, are mandated to keep the productive machinery moving at all costs. To hold such institutions accountable to any higher moral standard is to invite ridicule, scorn, and contempt.

Yet the radicals resist. They believe that the pursuit of justice must become man's primary concern.

Like the prophets, they condemn society not so much for sin as for blasphemy, for the belief that power and profit and goods will bring salvation cheaply.

The worship of power, profit, and goods will not bring salvation cheaply, they say.

It will bring only the destruction of us all.

In many ways it is not surprising that the United States has generated a radical movement of idealists in the sixties and seventies. Indeed, a look at American history reveals an interesting fact: *Religious justice was the central demand of virtually every major radical movement in the United States throughout the nineteenth century. It was central to the philosophy of the American democrat.*

One would never know this from reading most contemporary accounts of the country's past, of course. These generally argue that early American society was merely agrarian, idyllic in its way but hopelessly backward in every important respect. The farmers were uneducated, locked to the land, deprived of all the benefits that "broad" understanding might have given them. After the Civil War, they were no match for the "Robber Barons" who were concentrating wealth in their own hands. The poor people who fought back—the early labor organizations, the Populist Party, the immigrant machines—were trying to stop Progress at a time when the people wanted to move forward. Thus it is only in the twentieth century, with mass education, that "enlightened" liberalism has shown the nation that a government can and should help those who "cannot help themselves."

The analysis ignores several points:

1. People were farmers in early America not simply because they enjoyed the occupation but because the occupation fostered religious values that they shared. The real "founding fathers" of the country were the Puritans who landed at Plymouth Rock in 1620. The Massachusetts Bay Colony that they established was to be a "city on a hill" bound by common theology and dedicated to the pursuit of spiritual excellence. Even after the Puritans had receded in importance, even after their descendants had become part of the commercial establishment, the ideals that had inspired them became part of the American dream.

2. The democrats in the nineteenth century—the farmers, the

immigrants, the small shopkeepers—also fought to preserve a society that they felt would be conducive to the search for justice. They hoped that America would evolve into a confederation of small communities, each sending representatives to a national government that would use its authority to preserve relative equality between rich and poor. Even when the Robber Barons, the capitalists, did begin to take over the country after the Civil War, the farmers attempted to decentralize and diffuse the pattern of economic development rather than nationalize and control it as an end in itself. They always feared, in effect, that in a country of this size people would lose control of a technology that reached continental proportions.

3. Liberals were never reliable allies of the democrats in these battles. It was liberalism in the early part of the nineteenth century that encouraged the poor to believe that America's large tracts of uninhabited land made conflict between farmers and commercial interests unnecessary. It was liberalism that tried to persuade the poor in the last half of the nineteenth century that industrialism could be modified if only they would accept it. It has been the liberals in the twentieth century whose reforms have made it virtually impossible for the democratic tradition to reassert itself.

Therefore, given that the broad movement of history in this country has been from a theocracy, with a deep fear that commercialism would pervert society, to a liberal state that insists that utopianism will destroy it, we must ask whether the transition has fulfilled the vision that the democrats were pursuing. First, I want to examine the roots of the religious justice in which the democrats believed—the theology developed in the seventeenth century by the Puritans of the Massachusetts Bay Colony. From there, I want to show how the poor farmers and working people attempted to apply these principles to the social and political conflicts of the late eighteenth and early nineteenth centuries. Then I want to review the manner in which liberals modified the programs of the democrats, rendering them useless in the effort to bring industrialism under control. Finally, I will return to the question of whether modern society has met the demands that the democrats were making, and, if not, why the New Left has found it so difficult to respond.

I. ROUND ONE—THE PURITANS VS. CAPITALISM

Religious justice in America beings with the Puritans. They were our first settlers; their attitudes toward man and society survived long after their own writings had been forgotten. Modern critics, of course, say that they were pietistic, cruel, obsessed with sex and other forms of private decadence; or, sometimes, that they were responsible for the growth of *laissez-faire* capitalism. Max Weber tells us that the Puritans' doctrine of "free will" led to the doctrine of "rugged individualism"; that their insistence that each person develop some sort of "calling" led to the notion that each person had to work no matter what the work entailed; that their hatred of "self-indulgence" led to the idea that savings might be used for investments for the future.

Yet the charges are unfair. The private morality about which the Puritans were concerned was only part of their effort to cultivate a strong standard of *public* morality in their settlements—what we would call "standards of citizenship." They may have permitted capitalism to develop, but they were not pleased with its results. In fact, throughout the seventeenth century they even imposed penalties against those who used their wealth to exploit others. What the Puritans did bequeath to later generations of Americans was an ethic quite distinct from what we call the "Protestant Ethic." They warned that the pursuit of power would lead to corruption. They urged that the pursuit of justice become man's only true mission in life. To understand this we must examine the earliest doctrines of the Puritans, how their leaders did respond to the growth of capitalism in their colonies, and the ways in which their beliefs became incorporated into American political thought.

The late Perry Miller[10]—the historian who has given us the most complete account of the colonial experience—tells us that the Puritans were driven by

> the Augustinian strain of Piety, [that] flows from man's desire to transcend the self, to open channels for the influx of an energy which pervades the world, but with which he himself is inadequately supplied. It takes flight from the realization that natural man, standing alone in the universe, is not only minute and insignificant, but completely out of touch with justice and beauty. It cries out for forgiveness of the sins by which he has cut himself off from full and joyous participation ... It draws sustenance from the moments of exaltation in which glimpses of the original happiness are attained, a bliss, which, though seen but faintly extinguishes by contrast all other delights.

The goal, then was to achieve "regeneration ... a way in which supernal beauty could be carried across the gulf of separation."

The Puritans' settlements were hardly libertarian. The Magistrates believed that people had to help one another if they hoped to attain the salvation that God offered them. "Wee must be knitt together in this work as one man," noted John Winthrop. "Society in all sorts of humane affaires is better than Solitariness." Therefore, they formulated a Covenant, a secular replica of the Covenant between God and man in the persons of Abraham and Christ, whereby a settler was asked to "bind and ingage himself to each member of the society to promote the good of the whole." The colonist would exercise his free will in agreeing to this covenant. He would be held accountable only to its terms. "New England leaders did not come before the people as conquerors or dictators," Miller observes, "but as judges. They did not sentence any offender for a crime which he could not help committing." Nonetheless, the Magistrates would be able to punish citizens for "wilful refusal to do what they had promised and were thoroughly competent to perform." Thus, "by the terms of the compact a Christian people were committed to walking before God in active holiness and positive fulfillment of His commands, and the government was to see that they kept their word."[11]

The "calling," the "work" that Puritans demanded was a symbol of each person's obligation to the common pursuit of justice as well. No Puritan would have said, as is implied today, that *any* work could meet the Divine requirements. Within the Puritan's community, all work had to be devoted to the pursuit of spiritual goals. "Work" toward the pusuit of private goals was to be condemned. "If thou has two thousands to spend, yet if thou has not a calling *tending to the publique good* (italics mine), thou art an uncleane beast." As Miller points out, "All labor, no matter how homely or hazardous, is a worship of God *provided it is done in the proper frame of mind.*"[12]

Finally, the Puritan's insistence on "self-discipline" had nothing to do with the notions of efficiency in commerce and "moderation" in politics with which it would later become associated. Its intent, rather, was to limit the private pursuit of power and wealth. As Miller suggests,[13]

> *Contractual theory was pointing toward liberalism and individualism, permitting a difference of power and riches to different abilities and opportunities without regard for the welfare of the race, but Puritanism was still unready to give up the belief that no man should become more honorable or wealthy than another, "out of any perticuler and singuler respect to himself but for the glory of the Creater and the Common Good of the Createure, man."*

Thus, although the Puritans did believe in "free will," a "calling," and "self-restraint," the doctrines were integrally related to their religious mission. The city of man would disintegrate, they believed, unless governed in accordance with the teachings of God. Such teachings demanded fraternity, not liberty; work for the good of the community, not work as an end in itself; restraint in the acquisition of wealth, not simply in its use. Their aim was not so much to destroy "passions" as to direct them toward a quest for salvation in heaven and justice on earth.

Indeed, the so-called "Protestant Ethic" of capitalism emerged not because of the Puritans but in spite of them. If Cotton Mather[14] could assert, "It was a melancholy fact that rich men have always eaten up the estates of poor men by oppression, and even Christian men, if they be not the more watchfull will be so eaten up with their businesses as they have no leisure to feed on the Lord,"[14] in the seventeenth century, at least the Magistrates could practice what he preached. "In 1639," Miller notes,[15] "John Cotton condemned as a 'false principle' the assertion that 'a man might sell as dear as he can, and buy as cheap as he can, and Mr. Robert Keayne was fined 200 pounds by the General Court and admonished by the Church of Boston for making a profit of six-pence or more in the 14 shilling."

Unfortunately, strict enforcement of the rules did not last long. Life in the colony grew more and more complex. Its population grew. Its economy expanded. Britain discovered new ways to exploit it. Under the circumstances, the settlers discovered new ways to exploit one another. Ralph Nader would have found the following commercial practices difficult to handle:[16]

> The fish is naught; the Tar has undue mixtures; there is Dirt & Stone instead of Turpentine; there are thick Layes of Salt instead of other things that should be there; The Cheese is not made as t'is affirm'd to be; the Liquor is not for the Quantity or quality as was agreed for; the Wood is not of the Dimensions that are promised unto the Purchaser; or, perhaps, there was a Trespass in the place of cutting it; the Hay does not hold out Weight by a abundance; the Lumber has a false number upon it; or, the Bundles are not as Good within as they are Without.

How could Cotton Mather, who uncovered them, deal with them?

The Bible itself provided only uncertain guidelines for the New World. It may have warned that a plush life would tempt man with corruption; it also suggested that the good life would yield prosperity. When Israel adhered to the teachings of the Lord, did it not prosper? As Miller notes,[17] "The New England clergy could not demand that the people stay poor, for their economic opportunities were specifically opened by the providence of God; on the other hand, they could not quietly acquiesce to letting New England go the way of all flesh."

Thus, by 1700, when the Magistrates found themselves faced with precisely the situation that they had tried to prevent: The rich were getting richer, while the poor weren't getting anything at all. They were in no position to do much about it. In 1715, John

Wise, an early eighteenth-century liberal, proposed the creation of a bank to extend credit and paper money to poor people on easy terms. There were inequalities among the settlers; this was a way to erase them. The Covenant itself demanded as much. "It is hardly possible to uphold Equality when there is no Common Medium known and allowed to be as a Rule or Mesure," Wise asserted. The conflict represented, Miller notes, "a new frame of reference . . . within which for the first time colonial thinking adopted—and clearly expressed—what were to become classic counters for the American mind: debtor against creditor, farmer against merchant, poor against rich."[19]

To the Magistrates, however, the plan spelled Armageddon. Their indecision, perhaps, had permitted the emergence of a few capitalists, but they would be damned, quite literally, if they let the sickness spread. Inequality or no, with a Bank, speculation would be unstoppable. It would create "a Gulph of Misery by Stock-jobbing." It was "The Philosopher's Stone" whose clients would find themselves "Bubbled Borrowers."[20] Wise died before his plan got off the ground.

From that point forward, however, the influence of the Puritans could only decline. Indeed, having lost the ability to impose penalties upon the commercial elite, the Magistrates came to seem more and more hypocritical in demanding abstinence from the poor. It was not long before they, too, faced the cry of "privilege" that the farmers and workingmen had begun to raise against all those who were unresponsive to their interests. By the end of the American Revolution, David Ramsay,[21] a historian of the period, had to write:

> In consequence of the War, the institutions of religion have been de-
> ranged, the public worship of Deity suspended and a great number of
> the inhabitants deprived of the ordinary means of obtaining religious
> knowledge . . . which tames the fierceness and softens the rudeness of
> human passions . . . From the diminution of their number, and the
> penury to which they have been subjected, civil government has lost
> many of the advantages derived from that useful order of men.

Nonetheless, the legacy that the Puritans bequeathed to America was quite different from that which is attributed to them in the standard textbooks. What they really fostered was a deep fear of the corruptibility of man; a respect for the nation's natural environment; and, in general, a concern that the people live up to high moral principles. No other ideology fostered these assumptions in the eighteenth century—at least none with which Americans were particularly familiar. Yet for years, spokesmen on both sides of the political fence made constant reference to them.

Politicians outdid one another in their pronouncements on the corruptibility of man. "The latent causes of faction are thus sown into the nature of man," wrote James Madison in his famous *Federalist 10.* "It is vain to say that enlightened statesmen will be able to adjust to these clashing interests and render them all subservient."[22] Timothy Dwight, an early President of Yale, warned his brethren that, "without religion we may possibly retain the freedom of savages, bears, and wolves; but not the freedom of New England. If our religion were gone, our state of society would perish with it; and nothing would be left worth defending." And years later, after the democrats had triumphed over the commercial classes, James Kent[24] predicted: "We are going to destruction . . . All checks and balances and institutions in this country are threatened with destruction from the ascendency of the democracy of numbers and radicalism, and the horrible doctrine and influence of Jacksonism."

Nor were the poor people in early America particularly rosy in *their* view of human nature. A political scientist recently has described the democrats who opposed ratification of the United States Constitution as "Men of Little Faith,"[25] a label easily justified by charges such as these:[26]

> *(Some disreputable characters) are endeavoring by all the arts of insinuation and influence to betray the people of the United States into an acceptance of a most complicated system of government; marked on the one side with the* dark secret *and profound* intrigues *of the statesman, long practised in the purlieus of despotism and on the other, with the ideal projects of young ambition, and with its wings just expanded to soar the summit. . . .*

Within two years of George Washington's administration the people were referring to the major leaders of Congress as a "corrupt squadron" owing to a scandal surrounding the First National Bank.[27] By Andrew Jackson's day, in 1840, the National Bank had become, "one of the fruits of a system at war with the genius of all our institutions . . . the means by whose silent and secret operation a control would be exercised by the few over the political conduct of the many . . ."[28]

Early Americans balanced these attacks against one another, however, with a unanimous vote of confidence in the country's natural environment. John Jay, a Federalist (his main contribution to the *Federalist Papers* was to assure the democrats that a foreign attack would result from their proposals) proclaimed, "It has often given me pleasure to observe that independent America was not composed of detached and distant territories, but that one connected, fertile widespreading country was the portion of western sons of liberty."[29] Thomas Paine, a democrat (upon return to the United States from France, he referred to the Federalists as "men in the government hostile to the representative system"[30]) explained to Europe that the American Indian showed none "of those spectacles of human misery and poverty and want present to our eyes in all the towns and street of Europe," because he had "ten times the quantity of land to range over to procure himself sustenance, than would support him in a civilized state, where the earth is cultivated."[31] One cannot read early American history, in fact, without concluding that he who owned the land seemed to own something of the spirit of the nation as well.

Yet the critical legacy of the Puritans was religious justice itself, the idea that man had to govern his life by a divinely inspired set of principles. As Alexis De Tocqueville[32] noted in 1840:

> If the mind of the Americans were free from all hindrances, they would shortly become the most daring innovators and the most persistant disputants in the world. But the revolutionists of America are obliged to profess an ostensible respect for Christian morality and equity, which does not permit them to violate the laws that oppose their designs; nor would they find it easy to surmount the scruples of their partisans even if they were able to get over their own. Hitherto no one in the United States has dared to advance the maxim that everything is permissable for the interests of society, an impious adage which seems to have been invented in an age of freedom to shelter all future tyrants. Thus, while the law permits the Americans to do what they please, religion prevents them from conceiving and forbids them to commit, what is rash or unjust.

The Enlightenment might come to America, but in a harness that only a theological heritage could have fashioned.

II. THE AMERICAN DEMOCRAT

It was the farmer, the worker, the independent entrepreneur —the American democrat—who made, however, the major case for religious justice after the demise of the Puritans in the Eighteenth century. There was some irony in this, or course. The Puritans had feared democracy. They had opposed demands to institute democratic procedures in the Church, arguing that a congregation would fail to make the right choices if given the opportunity to vote on everything. Only those who had devoted their lives to the study of Scripture could promote adherence to God's will.

Further, after the American Revolution, ministers themselves often did not live up to religious teachings. Their reaction to Alexander Hamilton—George Washington's Secretary of the Treasury —was indicative.Albert Fried[33] notes:

> For Hamilton, the twin ideals of national unity and prosperity were bound up with the fortune of the nascent class of bankers, merchants, and manufacturers. These entrepreneurs, he thought, carried the future

in their hands . . . The rise of industry, he believed would destroy the economic base of American democracy and create a centralized, hierarchical society in which power, resting on wealth, would be exercised responsibly.

When Hamilton proposed to add the church to this elite through the formation of a Christian Constitutional Society in 1800, the clergy was more than willing to go along. "The sons and daughters of the Winthrops, Nortons, Dudleys, Saltonstalls, Bradstreets," Perry Miller tells us, had become "less the dedicated leaders of a religious movement and more a closed corporation of monopolists . . . the clergy no less than the merchants were a vested interest —which was not what the founders had intended."[35]

Yet the agrarian democrat had a mind of his own, one quite resistant to the doctrines of an establishment of this kind. As Henry Mumford Parkes suggests, he, too, was religious. Parke writes:[36]

Evangelists soon went to work in the Mississippi Valley and made it the most religious part of America. The inhabitants of the Valley responded quickly to the more emotional forms of religious appeal, of the type that had originated with the Great Awakening and been systematized by Jonathan Edwards, and the power of the churches was established through a series of violent and hysterical revivals.

Moreover, Western religion was "similar to that of the New England Puritans and the Southern Scotch-Irish . . . It was essentially an instrument for imposing social order and discipline." The democrat believed that anyone could make the right moral decisions, provided that society encouraged him to do so. In politics, he hoped that communities would remain sufficiently small to permit citizens to hold one another accountable to proper ethical standards—just as the early Protestant magistrates had hoped. The democrat demanded that the government both reflect and encourage the highest virtues of the people, and he demanded that the people make similar claims on the government.

What applied to politics applied doubly to economics. Indeed, if decentralization was the democrat's third principle of government—after liberty and justice—it was his first principle of economic development. He did not oppose industry. Alexis de Tocqueville pointed out in 1840 that "almost all the farmers of the United States combine some trade with agriculture".[37] Yet de Tocqueville himself was impressed not so much "at the marvelous grandeur of some undertakings as at the innumerable small ones."[38] Industry *had* to remain small, the democrat believed, in order to preserve the "countryside of flocks and herds and cultivated farms, worked in seasonal rhythm."[39]

In short, throughout the nineteenth century, the American democrat attempted to build a society in which the values of the people would come first, their affluence and power second. We can see this clearly in his major campaigns: first, to block ratification of the United States Constitution in 1789; second, to destroy the centralized national bank created between 1789 and 1832 by Whig and Republican financiers to foster economic development; finally, to prevent the destruction of a religious, fraternal, decentralized society even in the face of the Republican triumph following the Civil War. Each deserves consideration.

A. THE ANTI-FEDERALISTS AND THE CONSTITUTION

If many Americans today have come to view the United States Constitution as the last word in political wisdom, to the democrats of 1787, the anti-Federalists, it left much to be desired. The experience of British rule had given the farmers a few notions of their own concerning the appropriate relationship between justice and government in a democracy. In general, they were satisfied with the Articles of Confederation, with its smaller legislative districts, its decentralized distribution of political power, and its mechanisms to permit poor people to exercise their own political muscle against the rich and powerful without difficulty. Whatever else the Constitutional Convention did, they hoped that it would preserve these traditional bulwarks of liberty.

The Convention did nothing of the sort. In place of a Confederation, it proposed a federal system. Instead of granting control over essential public services to the states, it transferred much of this power to Washington, D.C. In place of simple patterns of representation, it suggested a "most complicated" array of "checks and balances." The whole thing smacked of a "conspiracy . . . a continental exertion of the *well-born* in America to obtain that darling domination, which they have not been able to accomplish in their respective states."[40]

Students today read *The Federalist Papers.* Perhaps they should read the anti-Federalist papers as well.[41] They would discover that the arguments that James Madison, Alexander Hamilton, and John Jay presented in support of the Constitution were designed to counter the various arguments against it. Unlike contemporary political scientists, however, the democrats were not persuaded by them.

To achieve justice, the anti-Federalists argued, a government had to remain sensitive to the variety of talents, skills, and resources shared by the people whom it represented. As Melancton Smith[42] observed:

> The knowledge necessary for a representative of a free people not only comprehends extensive political and commercial information, such as is acquired by men of refined education, who have leisure to attain to high degrees of improvement, it should also comprehend that kind of acquaintance with the common concerns and occupations of the people, which men of the middling class of life are, in general, more competent to than those of the superior class.

Richard Henry Lee concurred:

> "A fair representation should be regulated every order of men in the community, according to the common course of elections can have a share in it."[43]

The problem, however, was that if left to themselves some people would use their skills to deprive others of making their best contribution to the community. "The depraved nature of man is well-known," warned Patrick Henry. "He has a natural bias toward his own interest, which will prevail over consideration, unless it be checked."[44] Melancton Smith even evolved a primitive theory of class. "The Author of nature," he noted, "has bestowed on some greater capacities than others: birth, education, talents, and wealth create distinctions among men as visible, and of as much influence, as titles, stars, and garters."[45]

The insurance that such "distinctions" would not create the tyranny of the strong over the weak, then, rested with the strength of the institutions of government itself.

The territory over which a government exercised authority had to be small. The words of the "celebrated" Montesquieu—a French liberal theorist whose *Spirit of the Laws* seems to have influenced both sides of the debate—appeared again and again in anti-Federalist writings. Montesquieu[46] says:

> It is natural to a republic to have only a small territory, otherwise it cannot long subsist; in a large one there are too great deposits to trust in the hands of a single subject; an ambitious person soon becomes sensible that he may be happy, great and glorious by oppressing his fellow citizens, and that he might raise himself to grandeur, over the ruins of his country. In small republics the interest of the public is easily perceived, better understood, and within the reach of every citizen; abuses have a less extent and of course are less protected. . . .

There had to be close ties between the representatives and the people, enforced by frequent elections and relatively small legislative districts. The two-year terms proposed for Congressmen by the Constitution, for example, were too long. One year was sufficient. The Congressional Districts—one for every 30,000—were too large. Locating the capital in far-away Washington, D.C., was, itself, a source of concern. The anti-Federalists feared that Congressmen and Senators would come to form a cabal, an establishment, operating in its own behalf, ill-attuned to the sentiments of the countryside. "You have the peculiar felicity of living under the most perfect system of local government in the world," Samuel Bryan warned, "suffer it not to be wrested from you, and the scourge of despotic power substituted in its place."[47]

The people themselves, finally, had to be willing to fight for equality.

> The few generally prevail over the many by uniformity of council, unremitted and perservering exertion and superior information and address, but in Pennsylvania the reverse has happened. Here the well-born have been baffled in all their efforts to prostrate the altar of liberty for the purpose of substituting their own insolent sway that would degrade the freemen of this State into servile dependence upon the lordly and great.[48]

Everywhere, farmers were demanding reform of anti-democratic procedures in the state legislatures and an end to the concentration of capital in the hands of the rich.

Yet if these steps were taken, the anti-Federalists claimed, a government could guarantee the well-being and self-respect of all.

The Federalists could not accept this prognosis. People were depraved, they agreed, but there was little that government could do about it. The Federalists had no faith that a search for public justice—a collective effort to "build a good society," in modern terms—could provide a positive alternative to the "war of all against all" within a community. Madison argued that each of the small states of the Confederation would become a miniature tyranny.

> The smaller the society, the fewer probably will be distinct parties and interests, the more frequently will a majority be found of the same party; the smaller the number of individuals composing a majority; and the smaller the compass within which they are placed, the most easily will they concert and execute their plans of oppression.[49]

Hamilton predicted disaster for the Confederation as a whole. "A man must be far gone in utopian speculations," he opined, "who can seriously doubt that if these states should either be wholly disunited, or only united in partial confederacies, the subdivision into which they might be thrown would have frequent and violent contests with each other."[50] One could prevent the worst effects of "faction," perhaps, but never its causes.

For this reason, then, the Federalists established, as one recent critic has put it, "a system of rules under which we evil men could struggle with each other over rights, while none of us could gain ascendency."[51] First, they fragmented structures of local representation in such a way as to paralyze any "faction" that sought to effect its will upon the system as a whole. Then, they designed the more powerful branches of government—the Presidency, the Senate—in such a way as to ensure that only the "best" people of the community might participate in them. In *The Federalist Papers*, they tried to clarify what they were doing.

The purpose of creating a three-branched government—each with its own distinct pattern of election or appointment—was, according to Madison, "to break society into so many parts, interests, and classes of citizens, that the rights of individuals, or of the minority, will be in little danger from interested combinations."[52] Moreover, while Madison was worried about "combinations" of all sorts—religious, cultural, ideological—he seems to have been most concerned about the "combinations" that poor people were putting together tc win victories over the rich. "The most common and durable source of faction has been the various and unequal distribution of property. Those who hold and those who are without property have formed distinct interests in society,"[53] he noted. Yet he assured the democrats that they did not have to control Congress to protect themselves. No group would control the Congress, regardless of the public values that it was trying to foster. No one would ever really win; no one would ever really lose. Or so Madison thought.

Nonetheless, a government had to govern; with such fragmentation, the system needed a mechanism to prevent anarchy. It was for this reason that the Federalists gave six-year terms to Senators and a four-year term to the President—in order to attract "some temperate and respectable body of citizens to public service."[54] On the surface, the plan seemed similar to that of the Puritans: Allow the best men of the community to rule. The standards of "goodness" had changed, however. Now it was not the moral leaders of the community whom the Federalists had in mind for the government, but the knowledgeable ones, and, in Hamilton's case, the men of property. Moreover, if the Magistrates had been mandated to inspire their followers with the Divine Word, filling them with a sense of public mission, the "temperate" men of the federal establishment were asked merely to restrain the "passions" of private groups, to "check the misguided career, and to suspend the blow mediated by the people against themselves until reason, justice, and truth regain their authority over the public."[55]

And who would keep this elite under control? First, the checks and balances; second, the people themselves; but third, "a sensibility to marks of honor, of favor, of esteem, and of confidence which, apart from all considerations of interest, is some pledge for grateful and benevolent returns . . . Duty, gratitude, interest, ambition itself, are the chords by which [The House of Representatives] will be bound to fidelity and sympathy with the mass of the people."[56]

In short, the Federalists had formulated an entirely new theory of political virtue for America. Men were evil, they said, but it was neither strong institutions nor accepted common values that would restrain them. It was, rather, power itself that would transform a cheap politician into an elevated statesman. Power no longer corrupted, it enhanced, and those who aspired to position for its own sake, ultimately, would aspire to justice as well.

Needless to say, the democrats were not optimistic as to what might happen under this new scheme. The national government was assuming a number of powers under the Constitution. Without checks imposed directly by the people, they foresaw disaster. They charged that federal taxation would "require a huge national bureaucracy," and a "great number of Congressional ordinances, immediately operating on the main body of the people, which would continually interfere with state laws" until one or the other system of laws would be destroyed.[57] National control of commerce, another innovation, "threatened to give some states—the southern states or the northern states or the large states or the particular states depending on who was making the argument at the moment—the power to throttle and destroy the commerce of other sections of the country."[58] A standing army brought back ugly memories of the British. A national judiciary promised to impose even greater burdens against defendants than the state systems, which were already too dispersed to permit poor people easy access to them.

In general, however, the democrats questioned the Federalists' basic assumption itself—the Enlightenment assumption that knowledge and property alone would impart to their possessors a sensitivity to the problems of an entire society. Justice could not be obtained so easily, they felt. The entire community—*all* the institutions—had to foster it. Justice demanded leaders with an appreciation of the multiple talents, multiple resources, and multiple needs of a country. It demanded a genuine sense of social balance.

From their perspective, the new government was imbalanced: favoring the rich at the expense of the poor; the "well-born" at the expense of the settler on the frontier; the rule of the dollar at the expense of the Golden Rule of the Almighty God. America, they feared, would develop itself accordingly.

B. THE BANK

The implications of this structural conflict became clear after the Constitution's adoption, when democrats and Federalists resumed debate on the appropriate economic policy for the new nation. The specific question was whether the national government should create a national bank designed to accumulate enough capital to control and stimulate economic development throughout the country. For over forty years, between 1790 and 1832, this issue became a *cause célèbre* no less volatile than is the Indochina War today—dividing rich from poor, agrarian from industrialist, Northerner from Southerner and Westerner.

Here, too, moreover, the questions of virtue and power, centralization and decentralization, played a critical role in defining the form the conflict took. The Federalists and later the Whigs viewed the Bank as the key to their entire financial program. "I invest, I acquire, I conquer"—these were their slogans.

The democrats would hear none of this. They understood that the Bank spelled concentrations of power, uncontrolled economic expansion, the rule of the rich. Let the workers in Europe entrust their fate to the factory system; the farmers in America were content with their land. It was "progress" against justice all over again, and this time the democrats were better prepared to fight.

They had a leader—Andrew Jackson. Before Jackson's time as President (1828–36), the fate of the Bank had shifted back and forth, its existence depending on whoever was in power. Under Washington, it had flourished, thanks to Alexander Hamilton. ("The expediency of encouraging manufactures in the United States . . . appears at this time to be pretty generally admitted,"[59] he contended.) Jefferson had allowed the first Bank to go out of business in 1806, only to watch Madison recharter it in 1816 in response to an economic crisis. John Quincy Adams had turned the Federalist program of economic development into a Whig program of "Improvements." "The great object of the institution of civil government is the improvement of the condition of those who are parties to the social compact," he had said in his first annual message in 1825. "Among the first, perhaps the very first, instrument of the improvement of the condition of men is knowledge . . . and . . . the acquisition of . . . the knowledge adapted to the wants, the comforts, and the enjoyments of human life."[60]

Yet to Jackson "knowledge" was hardly the issue at all. In his Message of Veto of the Bank in 1832, he argued:

It is to be regretted that the rich and powerful too often bend the acts of government to their selfish purposes. Distinctions in society will always exist under every just government. Equality of talents, of education, or of wealth can not be produced by human institutions. . . . but when the laws undertake to add to these natural and just advantages artificial distinctions, to grant titles, gratuities, and exclusive privileges, to make the rich richer and the potent more powerful, the humble members of society—the farmers, mechanics, and laborers—who have neither time nor the means of securing like favors to themselves, have a right to complain of injustice in their Government. There are no necessary evils in government. Its evils exist only in its abuses.[61]

The Bank threatened to destroy the institutions that made it possible for the poor people to demand justice from their government. Jackson asked[62]:

Is there no danger to our liberty and independence in a bank that in its nature has so little to bind it to our country? The president of the bank has told us that most of the State banks exist by its forbearance. Should its influence become concentered, as it may under the operation of an act such as this, in the hands of a self-elected directory whose interests are identified with those of the foreign stockholders, will there not be cause to tremble for the purity of our elections in peace and for the independence of our country in war? Their power would be great whenever they might choose to exert it. . . .

Finally, the Bank violated the basic principles of American democracy itself. Jackson concluded[63]:

It is time to pause in our career to review our principles, and if possible revive that devoted patriotism and spirit of compromise which distinguished the sages of the Revolution and the fathers of our Union. If we can not at once, in justice to interests vested under improvident legislation, make our Government what it ought to be, we can at least take a stand against all new grants of monopolies and exclusive privileges, against any prostitution of our Government to the advancement of the few at the expense of the many, and in favor of compromise and gradual reform in our code of laws and system of political economy.

Louis Hartz, a Harvard political scientist, has tried to explain Andrew Jackson's veto of the bank in 1832 solely in terms of the difficult situation in which the commercial classes found themselves. In England, he notes, the merchants, the Whigs, had succeeded by rallying the poor and working people behind them against the kings and landowners, usually on a program of free trade and economic development. Then, they would reject the demands of their allies for a share in the wealth. In the United States there was no king, no real aristocracy. Hence, there was no one against whom the local industrialists could rally the proletariate, no one in comparison to whom they would appear the good guys. Nor, however, could the American capitalists before the Civil War bring themselves to say, as did the Robber Barons somewhat later, "You want to be rich? We want you to be rich, too! There are acres of diamonds in this country if you would just let capitalism find them!" They were too "sophisticated" to make such a vulgar appeal.[64] Therefore, Hartz concludes, "The eighteen thirties, which witness the Reform Act in England and the July Revolution in France, witness also the Jacksonian Revolution in America. Just as the cry *'enrichissez-vous'* goes up in Paris and London, the grim cry of 'monopoly' goes up in Boston."[65]

Jackson's message went beyond a mere assertion of private economic interests, however. It was a statement of fundamental moral beliefs. The elements of religious justice were all there: the notion of a balanced society; the importance of decentralized institutions; the role of a government in holding a country accountable to its highest principles. From this perspective, as Marvin Meyers has suggested, the Bank assumed "the shape of the Monster, the unnatural creature of the lust for wealth . . . To knock down this institution, then, and with it a false, insubstantial world, becomes the compelling object."[66]

Perhaps Hartz is correct. Perhaps under different circumstances, the Whigs might have sold the Bank to the people. After all, the Devil corrupted Faust. Yet that is the way the farmers would have looked at it.

C. "WHEN THE HUMAN SOUL BECOMES IMBUED WITH A GREAT PRINCIPLE"

That the contests over the Constitution and the Bank were merely symbols of a broader demand for a diversified, decentralized society became clear after the Civil War when the industrialists did gain control of the political and economic system. In Europe, Karl Marx was defining the terms of the workers' response, arguing that for all the hardships of industrialism, its growth was inevitable and that after a class struggle, it would redeem the world. Not so in the United States. Here, the Marxists had to wait their turn.

Take, for example, the programs of the National Labor Union and the Knights of Labor, which dominated the labor movement in the 1860s and 1870s. Gerald N. Grob writes[67]:

> The close ideological bond linking the Jacksonian labor movement with the National Labor Union and the Knights of Labor can be found first in the similarity of aims and objectives of each. All three were professed enemies, though in varying intensity, of the financial structure of the United States, and each espoused the destruction of monopoly, to be achieved in part through currency and banking reform. . . . The humanitarian crusades of the 1840s and 1850s had laid the foundation for an irrevocable hostility toward industrial society and the wage

system. Belonging to an America in which the development of an industrial economy had not overwhelmed a predominantly rural nation, these leaders did not think in terms of a permanent wage-earning class and its needs. Regarding the workers as the only legitimate members of the community, they sought to establish a cooperative society based upon a large number of small producers, for only under such conditions could the American democratic ideal be realized.

In 1871, Grob notes, "The Central Committee of the Marxist First International refused to send a delegate" to a session of the National Labor Union "because it had become a bourgeois and agrarian reform body."[68]

Indeed, we cannot divorce the early labor movements from the parallel movements that immigrants initiated to gain control of the cities through political means. "To pull one's self up by one's bootstraps" was hardly an act of individual enterprise when three aunts, two uncles, a next-door neighbor, and a cousin across the Atlantic were hanging onto the boots. The Irish battled for control of Tammany Hall with the Italians. The Jews battled for control of the civil service jobs with the WASPS. Only the English and German immigrants adapted themselves easily to industrialism, many of them becoming staunch Republicans. The other ethnic groups sought "upward-mobility" in other sorts of work—in the professions, as seamstresses, in shopkeeping, in politics—and in neighborhoods that they tried, somehow, to hold together. For years, the spirit of fraternity remained strong, even after the original dreams had been forgotten.

Yet by far the broadest and most effective response to the industrial challenge of the late nineteenth century was made by the poor farmers, black and white, in the Midwest and South, through the formation of the Populist Party in the 1880s and early 1890s. No group has been handled with greater confusion by modern historiography than this one. Michael Rogin, whose *Intellectuals and McCarthy* has tried to undo much of the damage, observes that before such "Prominent and thoughtful writers" as Richard Hofstadter, Seymour Martin Lipset, Nathan Glazer, and Daniel Bell—among others—wrote,[69]

Populist was the name of a particular historical movement for social reform at the end of the 19th Century. Through their influence, Populism has become an example of and a general term for anomic movements of mass protest against existing institutions—the type of movement typified by McCarthyism.

To modern socialists, the farmers' failure to develop an adequate "historical" perspective had disqualified them as a useful movement. Either way, the Populists have emerged as an interesting, but irrelevant footnote to the broad flow of American history.

No set of conclusions could be sillier. In fact, the Populist Party represented the most significant effort to reconcile centralized industry with the American democratic philosophy that the country has seen before or since. In 1892, it won a series of stunning victories, receiving twenty-two electoral votes in the Presidential election; capturing eight to ten seats in the House of Representatives; winning the governorships of Kansas, North Dakota, and Colorado; and making inroads in state and governments throughout the Midwest and South.[70] To get the flavor of this upheaval, imagine if a "People's Ticket" of Ralph Nader and Richard Hatcher were to carry California, Oregon, Minnesota, Ohio, and Georgia in 1972, bringing with them gubernatorial candidates in the last two states. Kansas was so shaken by the Populists that an attempt to organize its House of Representatives, where Republicans held a slight majority, turned into a siege. Populist representatives literally barricaded their opponents in the statehouse in an effort to force their capitulation.

The Populists realized, moreover, that the growth of private monopoly power required more than merely an end to national banks, an easing of credit, and a reform of the currency, although these were all part of their program. The Populist Platform of 1892 brought Andrew Jackson up to date. "The time has come" it proclaimed, "when the railroad corporations will either own the people or the people must own the railroads." It demanded that the "telegraph, the telephone, like the post-office system, being a necessity for the transmission of news, should be owned and operated by the government in the interest of the people."[71]

In 1896, Frederick Emory Haynes, a Harvard economist, noted with some alarm that "although there is thought to be some natural opposition between socialism and the American spirit . . . a study of the present situation in this country leads inevitably, it seems to me, to the conclusion that Populism is the American counterpart of socialism in Europe."[72]

Yet Haynes' analysis was only partially correct. Populism was, after all, an American movement; its roots lay in the democratic tradition. Its differences with socialism, then, were as important as its similarities.

First, while the Populists did speak frequently of a "class struggle" between rich and poor, the laws to which they referred were not the "laws of history" but the basic laws of right and wrong that they had learned as children. "I believe that beneath this serene and placid sleep of centuries sits human liberty" exclaimed Lorenzo Dow Lewelling to his followers.[73]

You ask me how? You ask me why? For my reason, if it must be given, I must reply, a just God sits on the throne in Heaven. So relief will come. I believe this inspiration will be found in every heart. . . . When the human soul becomes imbued with a great principle like that, when we are unified and stand together, then we become Godlike, and the might of the people rises like the tiny zephyr, to the temptuous whirlwind, like the murmuring rills of the surging torrent. Our path will be conflict, but it will also be conquest. It must be so! The demands of the people will be heard. They must be heard!

The Populists fought in the name of a national creed, an American dream, unlike the socialists, who saw themselves as an international movement, freeing followers from the "Mystifications" of nationalism. James Baird Weaver's, "A Call to Action," invoked the memory of the pioneers:[74]

If the master builders of our civilization one hundred years ago had been told that at the end of a single century, American society would present such melancholy contrasts of wealth and poverty, of individual happiness and widespread infelicity as are to be found to-day throughout the Republic, the person making the unwelcome prediction would have been looked upon as a misanthropist, and his loyalty to Democratic institutions would have been seriously called in question . . . But there is a vast difference between the generation which made the heroic struggle for Self-Government in colonial days, and the third generation which is now engaged in a mad rush for wealth.

In contrast with the socialists' uncritical faith in nationalization, the Populists distrusted the power of the state as much as they did the power of the monopolies. In the Platform of 1892, they promised to introduce an "amendment to the Constitution by which all persons engaged in the government" following public seizure of the railroads "shall be placed under a civil-service regulation of the most rigid character, so as to prevent the increase of the power of the national administration by the use of additional government employees." They favored a "constitutional provision limiting the office of President and Vice-President to one term, and providing for the election of Senators of the United States by a direct vote of the people." And, of course, they demanded a "free ballot and a fair count in all elections, and pledged to secure it to every legal voter without Federal intervention, through the adoption by the States of the unperverted Australian or secret ballot system."[75]

In short, the farmers, true to their heritage, saw public ownership of the means of production not as a way of using industry to disembowel existing communities in the name of "strawberries and cream" at some point in the future, but as a way of preserving existing communities against the encroachments of private power. Industrialism itself was on trial. As Ignatius Donnelly summed up the matter:[76]

> But ... remember, we have gotten into a way of thinking as if numbers and wealth were everything. ... It is better for a nation to contain thirty million people, prosperous, happy and patriotic, than one hundred millions ignorant, wretched and longing for an opportunity to overthrow the government.

Patrick Henry couldn't have said it better himself!

Thus, in the course of the nineteenth century, the American democrat evolved an ideology unlike any in the Western world. In Europe, the working class largely accepted or had to accept the main argument that science and industry would be to their advantage, that economic centralization was inevitable, that the new world of secular affluence would be preferable to the old one of theocratic feudalism. American farmers—lacking a feudal past, identifying religion with the small settlements of the prerevolutionary period—found in their God and their heritage a positive alternative to the life-style demanded by the machines. In Europe, societies eventually found themselves facing, in Martin Buber's words,[77] a

> yawning chasm ... which can only be bridged by that special form of Marxist utopics, a chasm between, on the one side, the transformation to be consummated sometime in the future—no one knows how long after the final victory of the Revolution—and on the other, the road to Revolution and beyond it, which road is characterized by a far-reaching centralization that permits no individual features and no individual initiative.

In America, pioneers fought to maintain their settlements, struggling always to strike the appropriate balance between indulgence and virtue to which their own spirit of fraternity seemed best suited.

In Europe, the cry was, "Progess!"

In America, justice survived.

III. LIBERAL COMPROMISE: DEMOCRATIC DEFEAT

Why, then, did the democrats lose? One need only examine a brief passage from *The Octopus*, written in 1900 by Frank Norris, to measure the magnitude of their defeat. The novel describes the efforts of Western ranchers to forestall construction of a railroad over their land near Bonneville, California, a movement that failed when police wiped out its leadership in a battle over the settlers' homes. One survivor remained, a poet, who, near the end of the book, found himself face to face with Mr. Shelgrim, President of the Pacific and Southwest Railroad:

". . . and," continued the President of the P. & S. W. with grave intensity, looking at Presley keenly. "I suppose you believe I am a grand old rascal."

"I believe," answered Presley, "I am persuaded—"He hesitated, searching for his words.

"Believe this, young man," exclaimed (Shelgrim,) laying a thick, powerful forefinger on the table to emphasize his words, "try to believe this—to begin with— that railroads build themselves. *Where there is a demand sooner or later there will be a supply. Mr. Derrick, does he grow his wheat? The wheat grows itself. What does he count for? Does he supply the force? What do I count for? Do I build the railroad? You are dealing with forces, young man, when you speak of wheat and the railroads, not with men. . . ."*

"But—but," faltered Presley, "you are the head, you control the road."

"You are a very young man. Control the road! Can I stop it? I can go into bankruptcy if you like. But, otherwise, if I run my road as a business proposition, I can do nothing. I can not *control it. It is a force born out of certain conditions, and I—no man—can stop it or control it."*[78]

How did this happen? Why did the victors of 1832 become the desperate underdogs of the twentieth Century? By what strange reversal of history and logic did an industrial machine, held accountable to the morality of a people in one period, become a "force borne of certain conditions," uncontrolled and uncontrollable in another?

We must look again at the period which we have just examined.

Thus, far, I have analyzed American history in terms of its conflicts—between farmers and merchants, between democrats and Republicans, between religious justice and the Enlightenment. Yet most of us do not think of America solely in terms of conflict. We think of the "spirit of compromise" that has characterized our society. The "genius" of our system, we tell ourselves, is that it has enabled groups with "conflicting points of view" to work matters out. We may be rich, we may be poor, but we are all supposed to be reasonable. We are all, that is, supposed to be liberal.

To understand America, then, we must understand liberalism—what it says, how it has affected our national debates, where it has led us. Today, we think of liberals as having won the battles against big business that the poor people on their own could never have won; as having persuaded society to accept major programs of social reform; as having transformed itself from a philosophy of *laissez-faire* government to an ideology of state intervention.

Yet the images are deceptive. Liberals have modified the excesses of private power in this century only after their ancestors permitted the defeat of the democrats in the last one. To understand this, we must look briefly at the basic elements of liberal theory; how it influenced the campaigns in which the democrats were engaged; and what happened to the democrats as a result.

A. LIBERALISM

Perhaps it would be easiest to think of liberalism as a religion turned on its head. The religious model of human salvation contains three elements. First, it asks men to take seriously the ideals of justice and truth that set the ultimate standards against which all aspirations can be measured. From there, it argues that without these ideals, human beings will become perverse, they will destroy nature for their own personal aggrandizement, they will war with one another. On this basis, religions try to construct institutions that make it possible for human beings to pursue their ideals and make life difficult when they refuse to do so.

The liberals reverse this equation. They deny that there are any transcendent ideals that should command humanity's attention. Everything is "relative," they say. Even when they do acknowledge the importance of ideals, they claim that to pursue them is not necessary to the achievement of moral goodness. Man, they contend, is reasonably good in his "natural" state. Therefore, they try to discourage people from making "absolute" demands of any kind, while encouraging them to accept the rewards of private existence as they come. Each of these points deserves elaboration.

In its earliest forms, liberalism was an outgrowth of philosophical skepticism. Liberalism emerged in the late seventeenth century in Europe, at a time when scientists, through disciplined and systematic inquiry, were beginning to uncover many of the mysteries of the universe that had baffled people for centuries. Liberals became fascinated with this method, the scientific one, and soon began to debunk any theory that could not be "proved" through its means. Francis Bacon, for example, argued that the "corruption of philosophy by superstition and an admixture of theology . . . does the greatest harm."[79] John Locke speculated that the mind was a *tabula rasa*, a blank slate, upon which the external world merely foisted itself, expecting nothing much in response. As Sheldon Wolin tells us, "Locke had confined man to a middling sort of condition, incapable of omniscience or perfection, 'a state of mediocrity, which is not capable of extremes . . . ' The philosophy best suited to man's limited possibilities was one which concentrated on the 'twilight of probability' between 'sceptical despair' and proud presumption."[80]

Through the discoveries of Newton and Galileo, moreover, liberals became imbued with the notion that the "natural" order that they had found in the universe applied to human beings as well.

In the "state of nature," everyone had been "free, equal, and independent." Government had proved necessary only because of certain "inconveniences" in this condition. Individuals were "uncertain and constantly exposed to the invasion of others."[81] Politics served no positive purpose. The state was, rather, a cumbersome but necessary protection racket designed to conserve, in John Schaar's formulation, "liberty . . . defined as private liberty, namely as the liberty to enhance one's private estate and possibilities to the limits of his power."[82] Each person could do as he pleased as long as he did not interfere with the rights of others. Man's only responsibility was to cultivate those virtues that conformed to the laws of the universe as a whole—prudence, foresight, and industry.

The words "liberalism" and "prudence" were virtually synonymous. It was not a reactionary, but a liberal, Benjamin Franklin, who outlined a list of thirteen virtues, of which eight were temperance, silence, order, frugality, moderation, tranquility, chastity, and humility.[83] As Max Weber[84] noted much later:

> The ideal type of the capitalistic entrepreneur, as it has been represented even in Germany by occasional outstanding examples, has no relation to much more or less refined climbers. He avoids ostentation and unncessary expenditure as well as conscious enjoyment of his power, and is embarrassed by the outward signs of the social recognition which he receives. His manner of life is, in other words, often . . . distinguished by a certain ascetic tendency. . . .

Thus, even though the liberal generally encouraged capitalism, he compensated by counseling caution in speculative dealings, restraint in the amassing of profits, and modesty in patterns of consumption.

Foresight was the second quality that liberals demanded. Foresight entailed the application of the intellect to the task of determining what the effects of personal and institutional behavior would be. Prudence depended on it. A person could not set limits on himself if he did not understand all the consequences of his decisions. This was the sort of calculation demanded in the liberal's plea for "reason" He asked that a person assess what would happen to "Y" and "Z" if he did "X." Since there was nothing to bind "Y" and "Z" to "X" in society, save "natural goodness," or, more precisely, a fear of what would befall man without society, such calculations became the liberal's substitute for a commitment to religious justice.

"Industry" was the final virtue that liberals encouraged. It was Number 6 on Franklin's list of 13. "Lose no time," he urged. "Be always employed in something useful; cut off all unnecessary actions."[85] Unlike the Federalists, however, the early liberal did not view the pursuit of wealth, the conquest of nature, as a means of asserting man's powers. It was, rather, another way of establishing man's limitations. As Sheldon Wolin tells us, Anglo-Saxon liberalism and the French Enlightenment differed substantially in their "contrasting faiths concerning the ability of the human mind to fathom reality and to translate the results into actions,"[86] the liberal being the more cautious of the two. He simply assumed that once released from the false theological "opinions" of the past, he would be unlikely to engage in grandiose experiments in the present and future. Work, then, became a way of avoiding indulgence, waste—the idleness from which romantic dreams of grandeur might arise.

Yet these were the only virtues of liberal men, men locked inescapably in their private selves, without common hopes to bind them, without shared traditions to guide them, without communities to help them discover what they might be. The Puritans and democrats had challenged human passions with a vision of the sacred; the Federalists had goaded them to the destruction of the land. The liberal lived in desperate fear that passions would demand anything at all, for to him only the intellect could contribute to the cause of "harmony" in a volatile and unstable world. Remain calm, he cautioned, imitate the tranquility of nature, and the natural laws would take care of themselves.

B. THE COMPROMISES

The impact of liberalism on America was enormous. First, it effected a shift in the way in which people viewed their relationship to the community as a whole. No longer did they see themselves as participants in an enterprise broader than themselves, obligated to ask, "How can *we* make this place better for *everyone?*" True to the spirit of a liberal Constitution, each person did come to view himself first as an individual, then as a member of an "interest group" or "faction." It was not his responsibility to work toward a "common good." That was the government's problem. He merely had to protect himself against common evils that might be perpetrated against him by the majority, by the minority, or by one man, depending on who was making the argument.[87]

Besides, people came to believe—rather, they were expected to believe—that compromise was possible in *all* human affairs, even those involving the basic principles of the country. This is the spirit with which we identify liberalism today, isn't it? We think of the liberal as the serene optimist, confident that any conflict can be avoided, that any fundamental clash of ideologies can be resolved. Such qualities were characteristic of eighteenth-century liberals as well. "The baneful spirit of party generally . . . serves always to

distract the public councils and enfeebles the public administration, warned George Washington in his farewell address. It agi-
tates the community with ill-founded jealousies and false alarms;
kindles the animosity of one part against another; foments occasionally riot and insurrection . . . "In a government "of the popular
character" it was "a spirit not to be encouraged."[88]

Thus, between justice and progress people were not asked to
choose so much as to equivocate—to see which side would offer
the best deal if forced to bend. Ultimately, the Federalists offered
broad economic improvements throughout the country. The
democrats offered land. In so doing, the real issues between them
began to get lost.

Under the influence of liberalism, the Federalists and Whigs
tried to win over the democrats by pointing to the various opportunities that economic growth opened to them.

Even before Jackson's victory, the Whigs tried to appeal to the
self-interest of the farmers. In his *Report on Manufactures*, Hamilton argued that commerce would provide "extensive domestic
markets" of the "surplus produce of the soil."[89] Henry Clay, director of the Second National Bank under Madison in 1816, agreed.
The "American Plan" of development, as he called it, would[90]

> benefit all classes: the farmer, the professional man, the merchant, the
> manufacturer, the mechanic, and the cotton planter more than all.
> . . . the products of our agriculture command a higher price than they
> would do without it, by the creation of a home market, and by the
> augmentation of wealth produced by manufacturing industry, which
> enlarges our powers of consumption, both of domestic and foreign
> articles.

John Quincy Adams, in 1825, promised the construction of roads
and canals, the exploration of the globe for purposes of scientific
research and inquiry, "and the establishment of a national university"—all as part of his plan for economic development.[91]

After the Jacksonian triumph over the Bank in 1832, however,
the Whigs hit upon the rationale for industrialism that would last
for over a century. They contended that there would be *no* conflict between values and profits, between labor and capital, in the
new scheme of things. "Ours is a country," Calvin Colton[92] proclaimed in the *Junius Tracts,*

> where men start from an humble origin, and from small beginnings
> rise gradually in the world, as the reward of merit and industry, and
> where they can attain to the most elevated positions, or acquire a large
> amount of wealth, according to the pursuits they elect for themselves.
> No exclusive privileges of birth, no entailment of estates, no civil or

political disqualifications, stand in their path; but one has as good chance as another, according to his talents, prudence, and personal exertions. This is a country of self-made men, than which nothing better could be said of any state of society.

Meanwhile, on their own side the democrats had to contend with Thomas Jefferson. In 1791, Jefferson assumed leadership of the forces opposed to Hamilton's financial program. Indeed, anyone who thinks that 1968 marked the first attempt to depose an entrenched establishment by organizing the unorganized into a new political force would do well to read Claude Bowers' account of Jefferson's fight against the Federalists:[93]

When Jefferson assumed the task of organizing the opposition to the policies of the Federalists all the forces most susceptible to organization and intelligent direction were arrayed on the other side. The commercial interests, constituting Hamilton's shock troops, had their organizations in all the large towns and in a crisis could be speedily mobilized in the smaller ones. The various Chambers of Commerce were Federalist clubs that could be summoned to action on a day's notice.

But Jefferson had his eye on other forces, numerically stronger, if less imposing. The farmers comprising ninety percent of the Nation, were resentful of policies that pampered the merchant and left them out in the cold. The private soldiers of the Revolution . . . were embittered because their securities had gone for a song while speculators had waxed wealthy on the sacrifice. . . . There was an undercurrent of feeling, which Jefferson, with an ear marvelously keen for rumblings, caught . . . that laws were passed for the few at the expense of the many. . . .

Including all, and more important than any single one, there was a fervent spirit of democracy running through the land, while the Federalist leaders were openly denouncing the democrats. . . . But how to reach, galvanize, vitalize, organize this great widely scattered mass of unimportant, inarticulate individuals—that was the problem that confronted Jefferson. . . .

As Jefferson's mild eye surveyed the field, he found in almost every state local parties, some long in existence, fighting for popular rights as they understood them; but their fights had been waged on local issues. The party he was to create was to fight in precisely the same cause—on the national field. Here, then, was something already at hand. Why not consolidate these local parties into one great national organization and broaden the issue to include the problems of both State and Nation?

"Soon," Bowers concludes, "very soon, strange disturbing things would be seen even in New England—cabinet makers, shoemakers, mechanics perking up on politics, with evidence of organization here and there. Federalist leaders would be soon complaining that organization was conspiracy against the 'government.' "

Yet if Jefferson was, in effect, the nation's first upper-class reformer, he anticipated the weaknesses of the reform tradition as well. The democrats had argued that unless society made justice its first priority, unless government took positive steps to secure it, justice would be forgotten. They had opposed the effort to create a national government—an effort that Jefferson, with only a few reservations, had supported. Upon the Constitution's adoption, the democrats still insisted that the government take action to control the "interests" on their behalf. They were even afraid that their own representatives might become an entrenched establishment under the Federal plan. A trip to France had won Jefferson to the Enlightenment, however, and while he was not enthusiastic about industrial development, the European liberals had influenced his views on man, society, and government to a considerable degree. As soon as he became President in 1801, he was prepared to bend.

He grew tolerant of the commercial interests. In his *Notes on Virginia,* he had spoken fervently of the agrarian dream, but his "own administration," notes Arthur Schlesinger, Jr.,[94] "became a series of notations on the doom of his Utopia. Jefferson himself helped nourish the serpent in his Eden with one of his favorite measures, the Embargo of 1807, which set on firm footing manufacturing establishments started experimentally along the Atlantic Coast during the twenty years preceding." Later, "in 1816, at the first serious attempt to enact Hamilton's *Report on Manufactures,* Jefferson remarked contritely, 'Experience has taught me that manufactures are now as necessary to our independence as to our comfort.' Eight years of responsibility had made certain the triumph of the statesman over the philosopher."[95]

To compensate for his failure to control the "interests", Jefferson tried to purchase enough land to permit, presumably, both planters and merchants to ease the friction between them. The Louisiana Territory, obtained from the French almost by accident in 1803, would become an "escape valve" for resolving conflicts. It would allow one or both of the warring parties in any dispute to move to a new place. If given enough space in which to wander, if encouraged to leave rather than to fight, Americans would restrain their desires for power over others and learn to accept the natural goodness that the life of the countryside offered.

The Puritans and democrats had insisted on small settlements out of a conviction that intimacy was critical to the search for religious justice. Jefferson gradually began to imply that small communities would produce justice automatically. Isaiah Berlin,[95] a modern liberal, provides a succinct formulation of the view that Jefferson came to see as valid:

> The wish to assert the "personality" of my class, or group or nation, is connected both with the answer to the question, "What is to be the area of authority?" (for the group must not be interfered with by outside masters,) and even more closely, with the answer to the question, "Who is to govern us?"—govern well, or badly, liberally or oppressively—but above all, "who?"... Provided the answer to "Who shall govern me?" is somebody or something which I can represent as "my own" as something which belongs to me, or to whom I belong, I can by using strong words which convey fraternity and solidarity, as well as some part of the connotation of the "positive" sense of the word freedom describe it as a hybrid form of freedom, at any rate as an ideal.

No longer was the preservation of the homestead the means to a good end; it had become an end in itself.

In short, to Jefferson the President, compromise gradually became a matter of high principle as well. In his inaugural address in 1801, he urged:[96]

> Let us, then, fellow citizens, united with one heart and mind, Let us restore to social intercourse that harmony and affection without which liberty and even life itself are but dreary things. And let us reflect that, having banished from our land that religious intolerance under which mankind has so long bled and suffered, we have yet gained little if we countenance a political intolerance as despotic, as wicked, and capable of as bitter and bloody persecutions.... We are all Republicans, we are all Federalists.[96]

The crusader slowly evolved into the conciliator—a road that would be traveled many times by reformers after him.

Yet that was the way with liberalism. It turned a straightforward contest between two strategies for justice into a contest between two strategies for avoiding conflict at all costs. No longer would it be morality vs. the dollar, but "improvements" vs. the land in the interests of "harmony and affection" for all. Other "absolutes" presumably had no place in a democratic society.

C. THE DEFEAT OF THE DEMOCRATS

Whatever advantage these compromises brought to the democrats turned out to be short-lived. Without restraints, the growth of manufacturing was bound to eclipse the purchase of new territories for settlement. Without a public concern for justice, there was no reason to assume that any community, large or small, would take justice seriously. By the Civil War, the democrat was trapped. Vested interests dominated both the North and South, and he had to choose between them. After the Civil War, even his most powerful movements were unable to restore his original position of strength. The story is not a pleasant one.

For a brief period after Jefferson's term, and for a much longer one after Jackson's in the 1850s, territorial expansion did prove to be an attractive program for the democrats. Notes Richard Hofstadter:[97]

> *The failure of Henry Clay's Presidential aspirations became a warning to politicians not to stand in the way of the expansionist drive . . . he had warned that annexation of Texas would bring war with Mexico . . . Clay's remarks were prophetic, but they were also unpopular . . . Neither the ardent expansionists nor their anti-slavery opponents were appeased by his moderate stand; and the expansion issue may have contributed to Clay's defeat in 1844. He lost to the warm expansionist James K. Polk; and the incorporation of Texas into the Union, rejected in 1837, was accomplished under Polk's predecessor, John Tyler, three days before Polk took office.*

Yet the manufacturers were pursing the *daimon* of acquisition as well. Now they *were* demanding the freedom to pursue their talents for exploitation, unfettered by any laws, by any standards save progress, advancement, and gain. They did not need a Bank any longer, they said. They could achieve Hamilton's ends without Hamilton's means. In the long run the poor were bound to lose. For capital, the land provided endless possibilities. It would be easier to conquer nature than to escape to new, greener pastures in an effort to outrun the industrial machine. Industrial dominance would be just a matter of time.

Even the staunch Jacksonian found such temptations hard to resist. As Louis Hartz suggests, "A new social outlook took shape, dynamic, restless, competitive . . . The American democrat was unprepared to meet it . . . he had missed the aristocratic impulse that burned in his own breast."[98] As early as 1840, William Henry Harrison—a Whig—was able to win democratic support by touting his record as a general, a product of the frontier, and a self-made man. The image would not soon be forgotten.

Expansion soon became linked with another issue, moreover—slavery. Indeed, it was not long before *every* issue between North and South, between industry and agriculture, between nationalism and localism, between centralization and decentralization, had converged upon the question of the slaves—the Achilles' heel of the agrarian dream. Would slavery be permitted in the new territories, would it be forbidden, or would each state be entitled to decide for itself? Was the enslavement of a black to his master in the South any worse than the enslavement of a worker to his boss in the North?

In an earlier day, the democrats would have had ready-made arguments to support abolition. Slavery was an unjust, tyrannical institution that violated the laws of God, the spirit of equality, and the fundamental principles of the Declaration of Independence. Indeed, Jackson's successor, Martin Van Buren, did use such arguments in the Democratic Convention of 1848, eight years after his own term had expired. As Arthur Schlesinger, Jr.,[99] describes it:

"From the first institution of government to the present time," Van Buren declared, "there has been a struggle going on between capital and labor for a fair distribution of the profits resulting from their joint capacities. At the beginning, the advantage was always on the side of capital, but lately men of good will have become increasingly concerned with securing to him who labors a consideration in society and a reward in the distribution of the proceeds of industry more adequate than his class have heretofore received. . . . Shall we," Van Buren asked, "whose government was instituted to elevate and ennoble the laboring man, pursue a policy in regard to slavery which tends toward his degradation?"

Yet the Democratic Party of the 1850s was hardly controlled by the radicals. The Jacksonian had been forced to give way to the Secessionist, the poor farmer had been eclipsed by the feudal baron. The agrarian had generated his own aristocracy, every bit as evil as the old landed aristocracies that had coerced small farmers in England. Even when a group of independent democrats did issue a manifesto opposing the slaves, all it did was to "marshall sentiment for the organization of the Republican Party."[100]

Moreover, the Southern plantation owners had found in Jefferson's rationale for "local control" a built-in argument for their own brand of "liberty." "We of the South will not, cannot surrender our institutions," proclaimed John C. Calhoun, the Confederacy's foremost theorist of states' rights.[101]

To maintain the existing relations between the two races inhabiting that section of the Union, is indispensable to the peace and happiness of both. It cannot be subverted without drenching the country in blood, and extirpating one or the other of the races. Be it good or bad, it has grown up with our society and institutions, and is so interwoven with them, that to destroy it would be to destroy us as a people.

Thus, by the Civil War, the American democrat was caught in a vice no less insidious than the one that had destroyed his counterpart in Europe. Now it was the Northern union member forced into an alliance with his employer in a battle against Southern feudal barons to liberate the slaves. Now it was the Southern tenant farmer, joined with the large plantation owner against the interests of the North to protect his land. Yet with the North's victory, it was neither the working people, nor the poor farmers, not even the slaves who ultimately won. The victor was a new Republican wrapped in the banners of liberty and individual initiative, triumphant over the last vestiges of opposition in both political parties, in the driver's seat materially and ideologically, prepared to push through a program of economic development at any price with all the fervor that capitalism could muster.

We have seen that despite the Republican triumph, most major democratic movements after the Civil War still tried to foster the values and institutions of the early nineteenth century rather than accommodate themselves to the demands of corporate life. None of them, however, could withstand the onslaught of the accelerating industrial machine. It had, indeed—as the *Octopus* described it—become a "force born out of certain conditions, and I—no man —can stop it or control it."

How could a Terence Powderly of the Knights of Labor rely upon the "good will" of a Congress to restore the dignity of the working man at a time when all three branches of government had come to accept capitalism as a way of life? Yet Powderly refused to admit defeat. Legislation forcing the decentralization of industry would come, he assured his followers. Once again, the independent producer would triumph. The Executive Committee of the Knights even opposed strikes, in part because it feared that without enabling legislation most of them would fail—a position that subsequent events proved to be correct—but also out of a principled aversion to class warfare as a means of building a communitarian society.

To workers already uprooted from the land—native and foreign-born—such a strategy was bound to seem naïve, unworkable, when measured against their desperate need for relief from the immediate horrors of the factories. The American Federation of Labor, under the leadership of Samuel Gompers, soon began to provide a powerful alternative. As Philip S. Foner notes, "Gompers had only scorn for the doctrines spread by Powderly and other leaders of the Knights which proclaimed that the interests of labor and capital were identical and harmonious."[102] Gompers scorned anyone who urged that the labor movement seek the broad "reform" of society in such a way as to undermine efforts to gain immediate benefits—wages, hours, and working-conditions—for the workingman within the factory. Protest was out. Politics was out. Only strikes were in. By 1895, the Knights of Labor was, for all intents and purposes, dead.

The writings of Randolphe Bourne tell us much about the plight of the urban immigrant in the face of the Hamiltonian triumph.[103]

If freedom means the right to do pretty much as one pleases, so long as one does not interfere with others, the immigrant has found freedom, and the ruling element has been singularly liberal in its treatment of the invading hordes. But if freedom means a democratic cooperation in determining the ideals and purposes in industrial and social institutions of a country, then the immigrant has not been free, and the Anglo-Saxon element is guilty of just what every dominant race is guilty of in every European country: the imposition of its own culture upon the minority peoples.

Bourne's description of the effect of "Americanization" on the ethnics has not been equaled:[104]

Our cities are filled with these half-breeds who retain their foreign names but have lost the foreign savor. This does not mean that they have actually changed into New Englanders or Middle Westerners. It does not mean that they have been really Americanized. It means that, letting slip from them whatever culture they had, they have substituted for it only the most rudimentary American—the American culture of the cheap newspaper, the 'movies', the popular song, the ubiquitous automobile. The unthinking who survey this class call them assimilated, Americanized. The American public school has done its work. With these people our institutions are safe.

What were the immigrants to do? They had to eat. By 1900, any hope that they might have had to gain a foothold in this country on their terms had vanished. Now they had to accept the Enlightenment on its terms and make the best of a bad situation.

The Populist Party fared little better. By 1896, they already had lost so much ground that they had no choice but to work within the Democratic Party. William Jennings Bryan put up a spirited defense in their behalf, but even he was unable to represent the full range of grievances that the farmers were expressing. The critical points in the Populist Platform—public ownership of the railroads, telephone, and telegraph—receded into the background. It was only the "free and unlimited coinage of silver" that survived as a major issue—the focus most consistent with the specific demands of democratic battles of the past. After Bryan lost in 1896, Populism was in no position to revitalize itself. Its yearly conferences dwindled in size and importance, until by 1904 even its most devoted followers had to admit that the farmers' movement was dead.

Thus, liberalism had presided over a compromise between Whigs and democrats that, ultimately, had undermined everything that the democrats were seeking. Henry Clay and John Quincy Adams had promised "improvements." As of 1900, the poor were still waiting. Jefferson had offered land—the land was vanishing. The society that the democrats had tried to preserve—religious, fraternal, distinctive—was dying. Religious justice had lost, and with its defeat the character of American politics would never be the same.

IV REBIRTH OF THE RADICAL DEMOCRAT

Today, Keynesian liberals take credit for having restored the democratic program to American politics. They point to the structural reforms that have taken place in the twentieth century: popular election of Senators, woman's suffrage, reforms in the electoral college, the enfranchisement of blacks, and, most recently, the "one-man, one vote" principle applied to apportionment of Congressional Districts. They boast of the economic revolution of the past seventy years, the abundance that industrialism has created and the services that the welfare state has provided to a large number of individuals and groups. They take credit for the social revolution of the modern age, for urbanization, then suburbanization; for the eight-hour work day, for mass education; for public acceptance of labor's right to organize; for a "new spirit of equality." They say that the important parts of the Populist Platform—the suffrage, the income tax, the secret ballot, controls over monopoly, a regulated program of international trade—have been adopted.

The liberals cite the transformation of their own ideology in the past three centuries as additional evidence of the progress that society has made. In the 18th century, the argument goes, liberals underestimated the need for government intervention; today, they insist upon public regulation of the private sector. "Classical" liberalism believed that an "individual hand" would produce an equitable distribution of scarce resources; Keynesian liberals understand that government manipulation of fiscal and monetary policy is critical to the success of the economic system. Traditional liberals were, perhaps, too optimistic about human nature. They sought only the "freedom" to develop themselves in their own way. Today, liberalism realizes that without society there can be no freedom; that without some measure of regulation, there can be no society.

Therefore, the Keynesians conclude, the democrats should not complain. The critical elements of the Populist Platform have been written into law. Their theories have been incorporated into liberalism itself. Their social objectives have been taken seriously and fulfilled. All that remains is to ensure that the system maintain its high level of performance and its resiliency in the face of the new challenges of a "postindustrial" society.

If the written words of a platform are to be understood as the extent of a political program, then the liberals are correct. Many of the democrats' formal demands have been met. Yet if the essence of a movement lies not simply in its list of proposals but in its vision of what life should be, then shouldn't we look beyond specific "reforms" to judge whether liberalism has remained true to the democratic heritage of this country? The first premise of the democrats was that religious justice should govern technological progress; the first premise of modern society is the opposite. The democrats contended that a country needed strong communities, bound by customs and traditions, both to permit popular participation in decision-making and to foster a higher quality of life than would be possible in an urban environment. Modern society has destroyed communities as a matter of principle, arguing that mobility is a more important goal. The democratic philosophy sought to challenge man to pursue moral excellence, the search for which would make an equitable distribution of private wealth seem logical, necessary, even enjoyable. Liberalism has acquiesced to the doctrine that says that if man's aggressions are harnessed to the conquest of nature, material abundance will render disparities of wealth and power between rich and poor irrelevant.

Nor is the claim that Keynesianism represents an "advanced" form of liberalism particularly accurate. Here again, if program is the guide, then the proposition is correct. The techniques of liberalism have changed substantially. Yet the basic premises of liberals have remained constant. From 1690, when John Locke contended that the only purpose of civil government was to help human beings resolve the "inconveniences" that arose in the "state of nature," to the 1970s, when liberals in the United States argue that the only purpose of government programs for the poor is to "bring them into the mainstream of American life," liberals have placed all hope for man's redemption in the presumed perfectability of the "natural workings" of society itself. Modern government does not attempt to build a political community of citizens committed to do what they ought to do. Instead, it attempts to "temper" the excesses of private institutions—an art that has come to be called "social planning" or social "engineering;" or it "rehabilitates individuals to "perform" more effectively within the industrial system. Behaviorialism, psychiatry, casework—these are the modern liberal's substitute for positive politics—the outcome of the alliance between his concept of freedom and the Enlightenment's belief that through knowledge man can "handle" every private problem, meet every private need.

Indeed, it is possible to argue that modern liberalism is not even as humane as the classical ideologies that it replaced. Early liberals, particularly in the United States, at least sought to preserve the elements of a society that was trying to be virtuous, at least at its lower levels. Modern liberalism is trying to modify an industrial system so far removed from virtue that it has had to revise the meaning of the term.

How would Jefferson respond to the corporate megalopolis that we have created today? Would the man who attempted to build a popular movement to challenge the business interests, who insisted that a decentralized government and economy was critical to the success of a democratic society, tolerate the technologism that now masquerades as liberal theory? The modern political figure closest to Jefferson's thought, perhaps, is Eugene McCarthy, with his deep suspicion of centralized power, his aversion to the military-industrial complex, his sympathy with grass-roots political organization balanced by his affinity with the "natural aristocracy" or cultivated citizens and his concern that people "work within the system." If a latter-day Jeffersonian finds himself on the far left of the liberal spectrum, where does that put the liberal establishment?

And what has happened to the old liberal virtues—prudence, foresight, and industry?

The modern program for prudence seems to have spawned three branches. Through the enactment of federal legislation against trusts and monopolies, the liberals demand that large corporations limit some of the wealth and power that they appropriate to themselves. This is the economic branch, which obeys number 9 of Benjamin Franklin's Rules—"Moderation" ("Avoid extremes; forbear resenting injuries so much as you think they deserve.") Next, the liberals make speeches urging political activists to restrain themselves, to modulate their voices. This is the social branch, and though it, too, lives by Rule number 9, it also owes a great deal to rules number 2—"Silence" ("Speak not but what may benefit others or yourself; avoid trifling conversation.") and 13—"Humility." ("Imitate Jesus and Socrates.") Finally, there is the personal branch of the program, perhaps the most important of all; it demands a cool, detached, almost clinical approach to the world. This, surely, obeys Rule number 3—"order" ("Let all your things have their places."), but also number 10,—"Cleanliness" ("Tolerate no uncleanliness in body, clothes, or habitation.") and number 11,—"Tranquillity." ("Be not disturbed at trifles or at accidents commonly unavoidable.")[105] It is quite a program, this effort to restore "prudence" to a world with nuclear weapons, but it has one problem. It isn't working.

The welfare state includes many programs that either reflect or are designed to foster foresight: mass public education; social security; child welfare bureaus; summer jobs for ghetto youngsters who might otherwise riot in the streets. Have these programs forestalled or shortened the list of problems that reflect a lack of foresight: the War in Vietnam; urban blight; rural poverty; university revolts; pollution; racial tensions; male chauvinism; and, for that matter, riots in the streets? Liberals tell us that their planners are working to solve these things if only we would just give them a little more time, but time seems to be running out.

In fostering "industry," the liberals have been experiencing difficulty as well. People don't enjoy their jobs any longer. Work in a factory or even in a corporation, it seems, is not as satisfying as work over which the individual has control, or work to which he feels some ideological commitment. The liberal has a whole range of solutions: higher pay; shorter hours; longer lunch breaks; Muzak in the halls; new coffee machines in the waiting rooms; an added four days to vacation time. And, of course, if the production gets dull, there is always that after-hours compensation, conspicuous consumption, to keep the citizenry at its desks. Yet have these solutions worked? Are the young graduates of today's universities, for example—the very symbol of the success that liberalism claims for itself—now flocking eagerly to all the exciting programs that our society offers them?

No, the answer is clear. Modern liberalism has squeezed the entire spectrum of American politics into the framework of the old Federalist Party and told everyone in the country—indeed, in the world—to love it or leave it. In 1972, at a time when we should be exploring a wide range of social alternatives to combat the problems of our nation, we find ourselves entangled in a debate between Alexander Hamilton and Henry Clay over whether technology without much interference will yield the good life, or whether society needs "improvements" from the government as well. We have become prisoners of the very system that even early liberals were hesitant to permit in this country—the system of industrial enlightenment.

And if modern liberalism has failed to restore even its own original vision, what must be the plight of an American democrat in our society? What would a Patrick Henry, a Samuel Bryan, or an Andrew Jackson say were one of them to materialize in our era? Chances are he would look around in amazement and ask, "What happened? How did it all get so out of hand?" Then he would ask, "On what basis does our program survive?" How would an "enlightened" American respond?

He would have to explain to the democrat why the old religious virtues have vanished. "Well, you see," he might say, "there was neither time nor energy for them in our society, nor were they particularly practical. We discovered that you could achieve quite a bit just by working eight hours a day, spending time at home with your wife and family, and trying to ensure that your kids get a good education. Oh, we send our kids to church, mind you, but beyond that, there doesn't seem to be much need for religion anymore. The kids are losing interest in it altogether."

The democrat would want to know what happened to the old

communities. He would not expect to find them in the cities; in fact, he would wonder why the country permitted cities to grow to such size in the first place. Nor would the suburbs satisfy him, however. He would look for assembly halls, for fraternal societies, for political clubhouses. He would ask when the town meetings took place, then why the community had done so little to encourage them. His guide would answer that we don't need those things anymore; we have television.

As the democrat traveled along the New Jersey Turnpike, his nostrils would inhale the stench of sulphur from industrial plants. As he moved westward, repeating the trips that his own countrymen had made, he would discover not the open frontier, but lakes filled with the sludge of municipal sewage systems. He would eat at truck stops that served him hamburgers filled with cereal and dyed carrots.

From there, he might visit the office building of one of the nation's large corporations. He would stand in awe at its size, at the number of people who poured in and out, and then he would wonder: How many people really know each other in there? Upon entering, he would be struck with the sameness that he would encounter. Everyone would be dressed alike. They would remain at their desks, saying little to one another beyond what was important to the completion of their particular tasks. They would leave their desks at regular intervals and return to them at equally regular intervals. Someone would explain to the democrat that this procedure guaranteed both equality in competition and regularity in administration. What would the democrat say—he, whose whole effort had been to construct a society in which the goal of political and economic equality could be pursued without sacrificing human individuality?

Doubtless, he would wonder about equality—whether a few people controlled more wealth than the great majority. His guide would have to admit that this was the case, but that, again, it didn't really matter, because everyone, basically, had enough to eat. Then, when the democrat saw the slums of the cities, when he passed the wooden huts in which the rural poor of Appalachia must live, he would ask again, "Why does the country not share its enormous wealth to create equality? Has it forgotten the principles for which its pioneers risked their lives?" Again, the guide would have to admit that this was the case, but that it didn't really matter, because eventually, there would be enough wealth for everyone, even those at the bottom, and besides, the politicians were trying to guarantee full employment. What else could they do?

At this point, the democrat would be growing angry. "How could an American tolerate this kind of system?" he would ask. A system dominated by the same sort of technocrats whom he had spent years trying to control? "Why don't the people rebel? Have they become so deadened to the meaning of life that they seek no goals beyond the satisfaction of their immediate needs? Have they lost so much appreciation for one another that they no longer care about the character of their communities? Have they lost so much touch with the land that they are willing to allow industry to do anything it damn well pleases? Have they become so callous as to turn their backs on the sick, the hungry, and the starving? Will they even force women whose husbands have left them to work rather than to care for their children, when most Americans seem to be able to afford cars, television sets, and expensive clothes?"

The guide would be puzzled, wondering what sort of dangerous radical he had expropriated from the past. He would find himself explaining that the black people of the country, at least, were raising the sort of questions that he asked and that some of the young people were equally troubled by the direction in which the country was going.

The democrat would continue. "What success have they had? Have they been able to talk about the things that we fought for? Have they tried to make people understand that modern America has done little of what the early settlers hoped that their country would accomplish?"

Again, the guide would have to admit that he had never heard the young refer to early democratic programs particularly, although, he would say, they do talk about the "ideals" of the country on occasion. The black people have moved more in this direction, the guide would recall. Dr. Martin Luther King used to talk about justice frequently, even citing the Declaration of Independence and the Constitution to support what he was saying. But then, the guide would have to add, the country didn't listen. It seemed that only violence would attract the media's attention, and that just turned the people off.

Surely, the democrat would persist, there must be something that could be done? Has everyone just given up?

"Your guess is as good as mine, mister," the guide would conclude, "but let me tell you something. The things you're talking about have become very hard to fight for. There are people, plenty of them, who might want to achieve the Kingdom of God here on earth, but they'll be damned if they're going to risk their lives in a fruitless effort to do it. People have to work; they have to live; they have to eat. If somebody makes it possible for them to live, work, and eat a little better, they'll take it; but the other guy has to make the move. They don't know what to do any more than I do. They just know that the system seems to produce more than it used to produce; and that everyone is supposed to have an equal chance to succeed. What more can we expect? What more is worth having?"

The democrat would wonder whether he had landed in the right country.

Indeed, we are back where we started, wondering whether the society in which we live is the right country in which an American ought to be living. We have touched briefly on the transformation of ideologies and institutions from the world of traditional America to the one in which we now attempt to survive. We have relived for a few minutes the dream that our grandparents and their grandparents shared that this country might become a "city on a hill" in a new world. We have come to understand that the various "problems" of our age did not just "happen," nor were they even unexpected. They have multiplied because the twentieth century has refused to listen to the best lessons of the previous nineteen: that power and virtue are at odds with one another; to pursue one for its own sake is to deny the other.

We should also now be clear about something else, something about the character of today's "dissenters," white and black. They are not "new liberals," at least not in any conventional meaning of the term. Unlike descendants of John Locke, they are not so naïve as to assume that man is simply what happens when you add his "emotions" to his "reason." They understand that the third human faculty—the capacity to imagine—is what really differentiates us from lower animals. A dog has feelings; a monkey can learn to solve simple problems. Neither of these animals can imagine themselves as anything other than dogs or monkeys. A man can. That is what makes him a human being. "A favorite commonplace of the Puritan preacher," writes Perry Miller, "was that the mind is great if the object of its desire is great; 'as the things and objects are great or mean, that men converse withall; so they are high or low spirited.' "[106] To the movements, if modern society itself has become low-spirited, it reflects the character of its goals.

Nor can we describe the uprisings as being "socialist." Oh, if we mean by "socialism" any political system that encourages its people to share with one another, then the young radicals, of course, are socialists, as are all those who ever have rebelled in the name of justice. Yet socialism in the past two centuries has meant both more and less than its vision of brotherhood. In its Marxist formulation, it has replaced morality with technological progress, communities with corporations, no less enthusiastically than has liberalism. It, too, has believed that to be "local" is to be "primitive," to be "idealistic" is to be "naïve." Utopian socialists, by contrast, have tried to realize their ambitions by isolating themselves from society rather than confronting it. Both schools of socialism have been conspicuously silent on the problems of developing popular participation in decision-making—a critical goal of the New Left. So to describe the rebellions as "socialist" is to miss a great deal, just as socialism itself misses a great deal in its prescriptions for human improvement.

What we are witnessing, in fact, is a last, desperate attempt to revive the American democratic tradition. It is within the tradition that a young person becomes impatient with inequities, that he insists upon results "now," that he refuses to wait for "time" or "progress" to bail his country out of its difficulties. It is within this tradition that he demands public control of private corporations, even "public ownership of the means of production," not as an end in itself but as a means to prevent the destruction of local communities by the machines. It is within the democratic tradition that a young person demands that the Federal Government use its power to redistribute the wealth, even as he organizes the people to control the enormous power of the Federal Government. Liberals may cry, "Work!" in accordance with the technological imperatives of the day. The young demand religious justice, a justice that might govern us all, rich and poor, in a country that would be dedicated to the fulfillment of what it means.

Why, then, do the campaigns become so confused? Why do the movements themselves seem so unable to identify their real objectives?

The answer, sadly enough, is that contemporary radicalism has unwittingly borrowed so much of the Enlightenment's ethic itself that even its own attempts to restore the hopes of America have foundered on the shores of "reason." After 1965, when the public showed signs that its commitment to Dr. Martin Luther King's "dream" was limited, one would have expected the new democrats to explore the roots of idealism in men—what conditions encouraged it, what conditions discouraged it, how our system affected it one way or another. Instead, they jumped into the various pits dug for them by the Old Left of the thirties—the pits that promised that a "dialectical" understanding of history would yield some inner insight into morality as well. Ever since, the radicals have tried to raise "consciousness", to put forth the "correct" analysis of reality, rather than to raise expectations and a sense of vision. Their capacity to project an image of a higher morality has vanished.

Democrats in early America could claim that their goals and ideals were legitimate; the movements today have been denied this right. To use the language of "justice" is to accept implicitly the best elements of the traditions that have given us ideas of justice in the first place: the religious traditions; the Western political tradition, the Jacksonian tradition. Yet liberalism has permitted religion to become a slave to technology, the Western political tradition to become the handmaiden of "Progress," the Jacksonian tradition to become little more than a primitive forerunner of the welfare state. Where, then, can the new radical democrats turn to legitimize their quest for moral purpose in the world? Prior to 1965, when the New Left did pursue a vision, they were accused of the worst crime that a modern man can commit—"utopianism."

Finally, unlike their ancestors, the new democrats despair of finding ways to assert that life in the pursuit of an ideal is even possible in our society. How can they do otherwise? Their parents assure them that they will sell out. Their professors tell them that they are too impatient. Their political leaders ask them to work within a system whose premises are circumscribed entirely within the framework of the Enlightenment. The newscasters, the commentators, the columnists, make wry jokes about the problems that these "young rebels" will face when they have to "find jobs within the Establishment." The choice is placed before young people in terms no less stark than it was presented to their immigrant parents one generation ago and to the agrarian democrats one generation before that. If you want justice, you will never "make it;" if you want to make it, you have to "sacrifice your dreams" for those which technology can handle. Without an understanding of their own roots, without a feeling that somebody else has taken their country away from them, the young have had to look elsewhere for their hopes—to countercultural experiments in the farmlands of Vermont and to the revolutionary collectives of Cuba and North Vietnam. The virtues of the American past seem to find support only in the underdeveloped worlds of the international present.

Yet escape is no more possible for the radicals of today than it was for the democrats of one hundred years ago. If the nation's crisis does have to do with its moral purposes; if its agony does reflect the feeling that society no longer cares about aspirations that at one time gave meaning to human life; if so-called "leaders" and "experts" have betrayed justice in the name of Progress, even as they have urged activists to "change things peacefully" in the name of "prudence," then merely to reconstruct the physical environments of early America will not restore the sense of dignity that those environments were attempting to foster.

The task of the new democrats must be to reawaken ideals, to revive the traditions that gave them meaning, to rebuild the institutions through which people can pursue them, and to restore, as much as they can, the sense that life will be worthless unless we follow a course other than the one that a liberal system urges upon us. That is the mandate of our heritage, that is what the search for justice entails, that is the only revolution that has a chance to succeed. It is not a revolution of men's minds, nor even a revolution of their hearts, but a revolution of men's dreams and of what they are willing to do to achieve them.

REFERENCES

1. Karl Marx, *The German Ideology* (New York, International Publishers, 1947), p. 22.
2. John Schaar, conference sponsored by International Association for Cultural Freedom, May 11, 1970.
3. Jean Jacques Rousseau, "A Discourse on Political Economy," in G.D.H. Cole ed., *The Social Contract and Discourses,* (New York, Everyman's Library, 1950), p. 307.
4. Martin Buber, *Paths in Utopia* (Boston, Beacon, 1949), p. 13.
5. Rousseau, *op. cit.,* p. 301.
6. Rousseau, *Social Contract,* Book II, Chapter 9, *op. cit.,* p. 44.
7. Buber, *op. cit.,* p. 140.
8. Rousseau, "A Discourse on Arts and Letters," *op. cit.,* pp. 150, 163, 164.
9. Frank E. Manuel, *The New World of Henri St. Simon* (Notre Dame, Ind., University of Notre Dame Press, 1963), p. 68–69.
10. Perry Miller, *The New England Mind: The Seventeenth Century* (Boston, Beacon Press, 1954), pp. 8–9.
11. *Ibid.,* pp. 416, 409, 429, 421.
12. *Ibid.,* p. 44.
13. *Ibid.,* p. 416.
14. Miller, *Ibid.,* p. 473.
15. Perry Miller, *The Puritans* (New York, Harper, 1963), p. 5.
16. Perry Miller, in *From Colony to Province* (Boston, Beacon, 1961), p. 308.
17. Miller, *Mind,* p. 475.
18. Miller, *Colony,* p. 319.
19. *Ibid.,* p. 313.
20. *Ibid.,* p. 311.
21. Quoted in Edward S. Morgan, *The American Revolution: Two Centuries of Interpretation* (Engelwood Cliffs, N.J., Prentice-Hall, 1965.), p. 18.
22. James Madison, *The Federalist Papers: No. 10,* Clinton Ros-

siter, ed., (New York, New American Library), pp. 79–80.
23. Timothy Dwight, "Duty of Americans At the Present: 1798," in Albert Fried, *The Jeffersonian and Hamiltonian Traditions in American Politics* (New York, Doubleday, 1968), p. 44.
24. Quoted in Arthur Schlesinger, Jr., *The Age of Jackson* (Boston, Little Brown & Son, 1945), p. 266.
25. Cecilia M. Kenyon, "Men of Little Faith: The Anti-Federalists on the Nature of Representative," *William and Mary Quarterly XII* (1955), pp. 3–43.
26. Quoted in John D. Lewis, *Anti-Federalist versus Federalist: Selected Documents,* (San Francisco, Chandler, 1967), p. 25.
27. Claude G. Bowers, *Jefferson and Hamilton* (Boston, Houghton mifflin, 1966), p. 70.
28. Andrew Jackson, quoted in Marvin Meyers, *The Jacksonian Persuasion: Politics and Belief* (New York, Vintage, 1957), p. 20.
29. John Jay, *Federalist No. 2, op. cit.,* p. 38.
30. Tom Paine, "To the Citizens," in John Dos Passos, *Living Thoughts of Tom Paine,* p. 153.
31. Tom Paine, "Agrarian Justice," *Ibid.* p. 143.
32. Alexis De Tocqueville, *Democracy in America, Vol. 1* (New York, Vintage, 1954), p. 316.
33. Albert Fried, *The Jeffersonian and Hamiltonian Tradition in American Politics* (New York, Doubleday Anchor Books, 1968), p. 14.
34. Schlesinger, *op. cit.,* p. 16.
35. Miller, *Colony,* p. 50.
36. Henry Mumford Parkes, *The American Experience* (New York, Vintage, 1959), p. 179.
37. De Tocqueville, *op. cit., Vol. 2,* p. 166.
38. *Ibid.,* p. 167.
39. Marvin Meyers, *The Jacksonian Persuasion: Politics and Belief* (New York, Vintage, 1957), p. 26.
40. Samuel Bryan, *Centinel IX,* Lewis, *op. cit.,* p. 148.
41. The Lewis collection from which I have taken a number of these citations includes many of them. See No. 26.
42. Melancton Smith, "In the Ratifying Convention of New York," *Ibid.,* p. 234.
43. Richard Henry Lee, "Letters of the Federal Farmer, Letter II," *Ibid.,* p. 202.
44. Patrick Henry, "In Ratifying Convention of Virginia," *Ibid.,* p. 223.
45. Melancton Smith, "In the Ratifying Convention of New York," *Ibid.,* p. 235.

46. George Clinton, "Cato III," *Ibid.*, p. 190.
47. Samuel Bryan, "Centinel IX," *Ibid.*, p. 147.
48. *Ibid.*, p. 148.
49. Madison, *The Federalist Papers*, No. 10, *Ibid.*, p. 273.
50. Hamilton, *Ibid.*, No. 6, p. 248.
51. Christopher Reinier, "Politics as Art: The Civic Vision," in Dennis Hale & Mitchell Cohen, *The New Student Left* (Boston, Beacon, 1967), p. 29.
52. Madison, *Ibid.*, No. 51. p. 352.
53. Madison, *Ibid.*, No. 10, p. 268.
54. Madison, *Ibid.*, No. 63, p. 371.
55. *Ibid.*, p. 371.
56. Madison, *Ibid.*, No. 57. pp. 357. 360.
57. Lewis, (The citation within the Lewis summary—see No. 26 —is Richard Henry Lee, "The Federal Farmer, Letter III" (10 Oct. 1787), Ford, *Pamphlets*, p. 302.), *Ibid.*, p. 5.
58. *Ibid.*, p. 6.
59. Alexander Hamilton, "A Report on Manufactures," in Richard Hofstadter, *Great Issues in American History From the Revolution to the Civil War: 1765–1865* (New York, Vintage, 1958), p. 216.
60. John Quincy Adams, "First Annual Message, Dec. 6, 1825," in Fried, *op. cit.*, p. 130.
61. Andrew Jackson, "Bank Veto Message," in Hofstadter, *op. cit.*, p. 294.
62. *Ibid.*, p. 293.
63. *Ibid.*, p. 295.
64. Louis Hartz, *The Liberal Tradition in America* (New York, Harvest, 1954), Chap. 4, *passim*.
65. *Ibid.*, p. 91.
66. Marvin Meyers, *op. cit.*, p. 26.
67. Gerald N. Grob, *Workers and Utopia* (Chicago, Quadrangle, 1961), p. 39.
68. *Ibid.*, p. 29.
69. Michael Paul Rogin, *McCarthy and the Intellectuals* (Cambridge, MIT Press, 1967), pp. 5–6.
70. John D. Hicks, *The Populist Revolt* (Lincoln, Nebraska, University of Nebraska Press, 1959), p. 267.
71. *Ibid.*, pp. 275–281.
72. Frederick Emory Haynes, "The New Sectionalism," in George B. Tindall, *A Populist Reader*, (New York, Harper, 1966), p. 180.
73. Lorenzo Dow Lewelling, "Speech at Huron Place," July 24, 1896, *Ibid.*, p. 157.
74. James Baird Weaver, "A Call To Action," *Ibid.*, p. 61.
75. Populist Party Platform of 1892, *Ibid.*, p. 90.

76. Ignatius Donnelly, "Gabriel's Utopia," *Ibid.*, p. 115.
77. Martin Buber, *op. cit.*, p. 13.
78. Frank Norris, *The Octopus* (New York, New American Library, 1964), p. 405.
79. Francis Bacon, *"Novum Organum,"* in Walter Kaufman, *Philosophic Classics: Bacon to Kant* (Engelwood Cliffs, N.J., Prentice-Hall, 1961), p. 20.
80. Sheldon Wolin, *Politics and Vision* (London, George Allen & Unwin, Ltd., 1961), p. 298.
81. John Locke, "True End of Civil Government," in *Social Contract* (New York, Oxford, 1962), p. 73.
82. John Schaar, "On Community," from a transcript of lecture delivered at session of International Association for Cultural Freedom, Cambridge, Mass., May 11, 1970.
83. Benjamin Franklin, *Autobiography* (New York, Lancer, 1968), pp. 123–124.
84. Max Weber, *The Protestant Ethic and the Spirit of Capitalism* (New York, Charles Scribner & Sons, 1968), p. 71.
85. Franklin, *op. cit.*, pp. 123–124.
86. Sheldon Wolin, *op. cit.*, p. 298.
87. See Wilson Carey McWilliams, "Political Illegitimacy," unpubl. ms., p. 7. See also, Ewart Lewis, "The Contributions of Medieval Theory to American Political Thought," *American Political Science Review*, Vol. L, 462–474.
88. George Washington, "Farewell Address," in Richard Hofstadter, *Great Issues in American History From the Revolution to the Civil War: 1765–1865* (New York, Vintage, 1958), pp. 216.
89. Alexander Hamilton, "A Report on Manufactures," *op. cit.*, p. 175.
90. Henry Clay, "Speeches on the 'American System,' Feb. 2, 3, 6, 1832, *Ibid.*, p. 125.
91. John Quincy Adams, "Inaugural Address," *Ibid.*, pp. 105–106.
92. Calvin Colton, From *Junius Tract No. 7*, Quoted in Edwin C. Rozwenc, *Ideology and Power in the Age of Jackson* (Anchor, New York, 1964).
93. Claude G. Bowers, *op. cit.*, pp. 140, 141, 142, 143, 151.
94. Arthur Schlesinger, Jr., *op. cit.*, pp. 9, 18.
95. Isaiah Berlin, *Four Essays on Liberty* (New York, Oxford University Press, 1969), p. 267.
96. Thomas Jefferson, "First Inaugural Address," March 4, 1801, in Hofstadter, *op. cit.*, pp. 187–188.
97. Richard Hofstadter, *op. cit.*, p. 311.
98. Louis Hartz, *op. cit.*, p. 111.
99. Arthur Schlesinger, Jr., *op. cit.*, p. 462.

100. Richard Hofstadter, *op. cit.* p. 354.
101. John C. Calhoun, "Senate Speech on Slavery," Feb. 6, 1837, in Fried, *op. cit.*, p. 159.
102. Philip S. Foner, "Class Collaborator," in Emanuel Stern, *Gompers* (Engelwood-Cliffs, N.J., Prentice-Hall, 1971), p. 147.
103. Randolphe Bourne, "Trans-National America," In *War and the Intellectuals: Collected Essays: 1915–1919* (New York, Harper & Row, 1964), p. 112.
104. *Ibid.*, p. 113.
105. Benjamin Franklin, *op. cit.*, pp. 123–24.
106. Perry Miller, *The New England Mind: The 17th Century, op. cit.*, pp. 46–47.

Making Change—
Where We Are

5 Yes, but how?

To say, "reawaken ideals, rebuild institutions, revive the traditions that gave them meaning" is to raise questions, not to answer them. How do we go about this grandiose undertaking of restoring a democratic vision to modern America? What institutions do we change? From what, to what? How does an effort to change any one institution influence the directions of society as a whole? Psychology, history, philosophy—these subjects are all very interesting, but how do we make things work?

To answer such questions in any period would be hard. "Justice" itself is an elusive image, almost as hard to understand as it is to achieve. Truth is difficult to define and determine as well. There is always a slightly different perspective that shows us that the "truth" may not be quite as we imagine it to be. If we are never fully certain as to the nature of justice; if we are never fully certain as to the nature of truth, then how can we make the truths of reality correspond to the justice of our noblest dreams? For this reason, in any period, the task of creating change becomes one of our most taxing occupations.

Moreover, in this period, the task becomes doubly difficult. Liberals have not merely perverted our highest values, they have destroyed the institutions through which the people might pursue them. In the nineteenth century, farmers and urban immigrants looked to the national parties, particularly the Democratic Party, for help in organizing their communities and in articulating their goals for the country as a whole. Modern historians have not shown us the records of the nineteenth century democratic clubhouses, nor have they paid much attention to the meetings that the Populists sponsored in the churches of the Midwest and the South, but one suspects that they must have sounded much like the conventions of poor peoples' movements for tenants' rights and "adequate income" today. The pre-industrial clubhouse could organize a march as well as a canvass; it might storm the headquarters of the opposition until its demands were met as easily as it might run a candidate for an elective office. Moreover, the pyramid of power was clear. Party leadership rewarded followers with patronage jobs in exchange for votes, just as their constituents rewarded leaders with continued support for delivering favors to their districts. Local clubhouses would hold urban and state representatives accountable to the party; these, in turn, would bargain at a National Convention for a Presidential nominee. Fraternity, solidarity, mutual support—these were the primary values. The entire system was designed to reinforce them.

With the Populist defeat, however, not only did the prospect of national influence slip away from the Democrats, but also their ability to exercise local power effectively. By the early twentieth century, an urban political leader was placed in direct competition for resources with a local business leader. If the politician hoped to preserve what Robert Merton[1] has called the "latent" functions of the machine—its role in preserving ethnic ties, fraternal solidarity, and community values—he had to compete effectively with the business interests on their own terms. "I seen my opportunities and I took 'em," boasted George Washington Plunkitt of Tammany Hall around 1900:[2]

> Just let me explain by examples. My party's in power in the city, and it's goin' to undertake a lot of public improvements. Well, I'm tipped off, say, that they're going to lay out a new park at a certain place.
>
> I see my opportunity and I take it. I go to that place and I buy up all the land I can in the neighborhood. Then the board of this or that makes its plan public, and there is a rush to get my land, which nobody cared particular for before.

Plunkitt had to deal in this way. Not to do so meant to lose to the downtown establishment—to the merchants and bankers who were taking everything else away.

The machines had to protect the immigrant's culture as well. Already, the public school—compulsory now, at the behest of liberal reformers—was forcing the children of the foreign-born to comb their hair, don respectable clothes, and sit in straightback chairs while an English schoolmarm and *McGuffey's Readers* impressed upon them the merits of Horatio Alger. A social worker from the local settlement house would visit the neighborhoods periodically, encouraging them to clean their houses, get jobs, and appease the bureaucracies around them—all in the interests of "saving" themselves from poverty. The "rayformers"—as satirist Peter Finley Dunne described the political spokesmen of a growing middle class—were seeking out a different kind of candidate for local office—the urbane lawyer, the educated businessman, the college professor.

> "I don't like a rayformer," said Mr. Hennesy.
> "Or any other Raypublican," said Mr. Dooley. [3]

To all of this, the machines had to make a strong response. They centralized their structure. If in principle, the people in the party were supposed to control its representatives and leaders, encouraging all to adhere to a spirit of democracy, in practice the "boss" assumed absolute power over the political structure in order to keep it together. To be sure, many of the old democratic virtues survived, at least long enough for Plunkitt to sing their praises:[4]

> You hear a lot of talk about the Tammany district leaders bein' illiterate men. If illiterate means havin' common sense, we plead guilty. . . .
>
> To learn real human nature, you have to go among the people, see them and be seen. . . .
>
> But I am one sort of man always in one respect: I stick to my friends high and low, do them in good turn whenever I get a chance, and hunt up all the jobs going for my constituents.
>
> Puttin' on style don't pay in politics . . . Live like your neighbors even if you have the means to live better . . .

Yet now even the democrat was paying obeisance to efficiency by any means necessary:[5]

> Then see how beautifuly a Tammany city government runs, with a so-called boss directin' the whole shootin' match! The machinery moves so noiseless that you wouldn't think there was any. If there's any differences of opinion, the Tammany leader settles them quietly, and his orders go every time.

In contrast with its agrarian and urban predecessor, the machine began to narrow its sights considerably. If the nineteenth century democratic movements had spoken in the broad language of the "people," and of "justice" and "equality" for all, the new machine concluded that there could no longer be justice—at least not the kind of justice that the immigrants had attempted to obtain. Therefore, it was enough merely to deliver those services readily available to them. To be sure, the services were administered generously; Plunkitt would have had few problems with today's National Welfare Rights Organization:[6]

> *If a family is burned out I don't ask whether they are Republicans or Democrats, and I don't refer them to the Charity Organization Society, which would investigate their case in a month or two and decide they were worthy of help about the time they are dead from starvation . . . I just get quarters for them, buy clothes for them, if their clothes were burned up, and fix them up till they get things runnin' again.*

Yet the cleaned streets, the new traffiic light, the favor for a grandmother who needed a new rest home, gradually stretched the machine's powers to its limits, while the corporations and professions were gathering strength around them.

By the 1920s, the broad outlines of machine politics had evolved to the condition in which we find them today—a source of rewards and favors, as well as of personal loyalties and ties throughout the community; a structure that might compete with small businesses for economic control of the city: and an army for the "Boss" who managed to bring the system under his personal dominion. Muckrakers charged machines with "corruption," but Plunkitt understood what was happening.[7]

> *I don't believe that the government of our cities is any worse, in proportion to opportunities than it was fifty years ago. I'll explain what I mean by "in proportion to opportunities." A half a century ago, our cities were small and poor. There wasn't many temptations lyin' around for politicians. . . . It makes me tired to hear of old codgers back in the thirties or forties boastin' that they retired from politics without a dollar except what they earned in their profession or business. If they lived today, with all the existin' opportunities, they would be just the same as twentieth-century politicians.*

Patrick Henry himself would have agreed.

The "rayformer," the new Progressive, the Yankee, would hear none of this. To him, industrialism may have created abuses—unhealthy "excesses" on the part of rich and poor alike—but its ethic was basically the correct one. No longer, he felt, did politics have to play a part in the overall process of economic and social development. There was a "right," "scientific" way to accomplish anything, an "answer" that those with the "right" training and the "right" methods and procedures might understand. There was a right way to allocate scarce resources as well as a right way to manage conflict for the good of all. These were, in Eric Goldman's words,[8]

> *men in a hurry, and even at their best legislatures must always seem slow and cumbersome . . . Under the circumstances, progressives relied*

increasingly on the "good man" who would bring to reform the deci-
siveness of a Carnegie and would maneuver, drive, or skirt around a
legislature. The desire to provide efficient by-passes heightened progres-
sive enthusiasm for the administrative commission, the device which
gave long-time, quasi-legislative powers to a few men appointed by the
executive.

Consequently, when the reformer faced a political system that
no longer cared about justice, that had centralized power in the
hands of a few people, he sought not, strangely enough, to reform
it—to fight for a more vigorous, class-conscious program for the
machines and for the participation of the people in the formulation of their decisions—but to destroy it. Nor was the administrative commission the only technique that he used. The urban civil
service transferred power from the poor to the middle-class, from
the "loyal" ones to those judged technically competent to run a
city by the merit system. The bureaucracy itself assumed greater
and greater importance in "managing" things, even in comparison with elected officials. And when the Progressives could not
"depoliticize" a city, they hopelessly fragmented its political structure through the development of their own system of clubhouses
and leaders, again, separate from those of the immigrants, while
equal in their claims to the wealth and power that the metropolis
provided.

The New Deal did nothing to reverse this trend—indeed,
Roosevelt carried it to its logical conclusion. If Progressives had
replaced, or tried to replace, local machines with local bureaucracies, the whole range of Keynesian legislation—bringing with it a
maze of new federal agencies—ensured that the professionals
would control the national bureaucracy as well. The social-welfare
professions date their coming of age with the New Deal. The
"responsible" charity workers of the city became the 'dedicated"
administrators of the Social Security Act of 1935, the Works Progress Administration, and the other programs designed to "help
people who could not help themselves." The lawyer replaced the
party "hack" as a top national adviser. The clash of "ideas,"
"proposals," "programs," acquired the mystique of high science,
even when the ideas were not terribly good; the proposals, not
terribly far-reaching; the programs, not terribly substantial. Perhaps the Federal Government did impose some measure of regulation upon the "interests" during the thirties—even in the name
of equality—but it was not a government of the people that did
so but a government of the "experts," committed to making the
industrial system work without rebuilding local party organization
in the process.

The result was not simply to narrow the range of establishment politics in this country but to impose serious limits on the practice of politics altogether. Wilson Carey McWilliams writes:[9]

The only general ideology of American politics has been the doctrine of "reform," which aims at institutional and legal changes to guarantee that government is established on a basis which permits the individual to abstain from active political concern. "Reform" postulates an obligation limited in time, not a continuing public activity. It is based on the aim of reestablishing the "system" in such a manner that individuals may pursue their private, unregulated claims "within" its rules.

This philosophy has held true to this day. Not only are radical democrats asked to compromise, they are asked to forget any system of values that does not *invite* compromise—even a system of values central to the American tradition. Moreover, those who accept established institutions know what they are doing. They realize that our society is no longer structured to "handle" fundamental questions of justice between people, groups, and within the nation as a whole. Such questions are no longer "productive." They take us away from the more "useful" task of promoting economic growth and of ensuring that everyone can get a chance to "pitch into the effort."

The result is that all movements for change come to accept the liberal values of privatism, stability, and growth almost before they begin. Some try to dramatize the inequalities between rich and poor, both here and abroad, generally employing the techniques of conventional electoral politics. A second group fights the conditions of "powerlessness," largely by attempting to organize the unorganized around specific demands for "control over the decisions that affect our lives," or by seeking recognition as a group with legitimate claims to additional rewards from the system as a whole. A third group seeks to combat the "dehumanizing" effects of technology by constructing alternatives to specific institutions within the social structure—institutions that emphasize personal exploration, growth, and self-expression.

Sadly, they all seem to lead downhill. Let's look at a few examples of each.

I. EQUALITY AND THE ELECTORAL SYSTEM

Most champions of social and economic equality between rich and poor argue that electoral politics provides the most effective vehicles to obtain it. The government, they say, is the one institution with the power to redistribute wealth. Therefore, one cannot accomplish this objective without persuading political leaders that it is in their interests to do so.

Indeed, they contend, all the great progressive advances in this century have come about as a result of revolutions within the system whereby a President—most often, a Democratic President —undertook a program of major social reconstruction on the basis of his own personal vision. They cite the New Deal as the primary example, but also the broad programs of the "New Frontier" and the "Great Society"—the Civil Rights Bills of 1964 and 1965, recent expansion of social-welfare programs, and the War on Poverty—as evidence of what electoral politics has done and can do. The "electoralists"—if I may coin a social category—always admit that there is "much to be accomplished. They acknowledge that the imbalances between rich and poor remain enormous. Yet to them, these crises merely reinforce their insistence on direct involvement within the political system. Since the candidates ultimately will make the changes, they say, a radical will gain most mileage by joining a campaign staff, becoming a politician's trusted "adviser," then using personal influence to push him in the right direction.

Besides, they say, electoral politics provides a golden opportunity to engage in political education. The candidate can speak to a large number of groups. He can gain access to newspapers, to television programs, to evening news broadcasts. He addresses rallies, he shakes hands with people at supermarkets, he distributes leaflets, his supporters undertake door-to-door campaigns designed to win popular support for his cause. What better chance does an activist of any persuasion get to present his ideas and programs to the American people? More than one radical has had to answer these arguments in the past, and, I suspect, more than one radical will have to answer them in the future.

The case that the electoral politics and their advocates make is a powerful one. In fact, student radicals themselves have not always spurned electoral politics. One of Rennie Davis's first political undertakings was to engineer the nomination of John Kennedy in a mock convention at Oberlin College in 1960. Tom Hayden speaks of the "optimism" of the Kennedy days in *Rebellion and Repression*.[10] In the *Making of an Un-American*, Paul Cowan[11] now writes: "I had a special, private reason for believing that Kennedy was more sensitive to problems like segregation than the Harvard professors he had named as his advisers. He was a member of a minority group and he had graduated from Choate." Nor did participation in presidential campaigns end in 1960. In 1964, the Students for a Democratic Society printed a button reading, "Part of the Way with LBJ"—a slogan that, perhaps, found more adherents than any that the organization conceived before or after.

A number of local races have attracted the Left as well. In Manhattan in the early sixties there was Assemblyman Mark Lane who threatened to turn the New York Reform Movement into a movement for social change. In Massachusetts, Thomas Boylston Adams undertook a "Peace Campaign" for the Senate in 1966— a dismal failure, but one that involved a number of SDS members. Roberts Scheer's near-successful attempt to unseat Berkeley Congressman Jerry Cohelan in 1966 is well-known, as is—since the publication of *Do It!*—Jerry Rubin's bid for the mayoralty of Berkeley. Even now, radicals will use the system when it seems appropriate—witness the election of Ron Dellums to Congress from the Berkeley District; the election of Bela Abzug from Manhattan; and, more recently, the successful campaign of a radical slate of candidates for the Berkeley City Council—all undertaken with the support of both "New Politics" liberals and of radicals committed to a fundamental transformation of the system from top to bottom.

Nonetheless, for the most part these efforts have served to alienate the Left more than to excite it. A few examples are well-known. In 1960, Kennedy promised to "get the country moving again," only to wait three years before pressuring for a Civil Rights Bill. In 1964, Lyndon Johnson endorsed a peace platform, only to escalate the war in Vietnam. A billy club in the head was the reward given to many supporters of Eugene McCarthy for working at the Democratic Convention in 1968.

Yet even these public disappointments were not the most significant ones. The challenge of the Mississippi Freedom Democratic Party (MFDP) remains the most vivid and bitter memory of radicals surrounding the Democratic Convention of 1964. The movements to attract "moderates" to the anti-war movement before the McCarthy Campaign were as annoying to the New Left as the McCarthy campaign turned out to be. Finally, there was the experience of working within the "system" itself—how it really worked, and why it didn't work in the way that radicals had expected.

A. THE MFDP CHALLENGE

The attempt of the MFDP to unseat the segregationist "regular delegation" at the Democratic Convention of 1964 remains one of the unhappiest stories of the Civil Rights Movement.

Throughout the summer months prior to the Convention, members of the Student Non-Violent Coordinating Committee (SNCC) and volunteers in the Mississippi Summer Project had been trying to build a broadly based, democratically run organization to parallel the Southern Democratic Party. Their aim was to organize a coalition of poor blacks and whites throughout Mississippi, then to bring representatives from the coalition to Atlantic City to challenge the regulars on the floor. The MFDP was both a protest movement and a political party, as close a replica of the early Populist organizations as any that have been created in the past fifteen years.

Unfortunately, like the Populists, the MFDP failed. MFDP delegates arrived in Atlantic City believing that they had won the support of both the Credentials Committee and the Johnson administration, only to learn that they had to work out a compromise. They expected their representatives—Allard Lowenstein and Joe Rauh—to represent *their* interests, only to discover that both were as committed to the Vice-Presidential aspirations of Hubert Humphrey as they were to anything else. Suddenly, in fact, Humphrey's chances hinged on a "peaceful" solution to the Mississippi affair. Wily old LBJ had thrown the process of negotiations between the party and the radicals into the Senator's lap. The liberals caved in. The MFDP was told to "make do" with a bargain—cede Mississippi to the regulars; accept a position as a symbolic, "at large" delegation.

Even from the standpoint of conventional politics, there was reason to question the compromise. The MFDP Slate was committed to the national ticket; the regulars were not. The MFDP was integrated; the regular slate was not. The MFDP slate supported the national party platform; the regulars did not. What good would Humphrey be, the poor people asked, if in seeking the Vice-Presidency, he chose to prostitute his fundamental principles? What good, indeed? The word was out, however, and the MFDP had to accept it. To this day, there exists a large group of former Civil Rights workers whose disenchantment with the system dates from that moment.

B. LOWENSTEIN, LETTERS, AND THE WAR

Perhaps the bitter taste of the MFDP incident might have receded into the background were it not for the electoral effort to end the war in Vietnam. Here, too, the liberals compromised the Left. In fact, much of the damage already had been done prior to the "Dump Johnson" movement and the McCarthy campaign, through an effort in which I, as a National Student Association (NSA) officer, was heavily involved. Was our approach to winning "moderate" support for the peace movement the only one, or even the best one that we might have developed? I wonder.

In 1966, Allard Lowenstein made one of his regular visits to the annual conference of the NSA. Such appearances always generated lots of enthusiasm, and, occasionally, a plan of action on a major issue of the day. In 1965, for example, Lowenstein had persuaded a number of student leaders that the most effective way to challenge our growing involvement in Indochina was to question the basic assumptions of the policy of the United States government toward Asia as a whole, particularly as it related to the recognition of the Peoples' Republic of China and to their admission to the United Nations. Thus, between 1965 and 1966, the acronym "ARFEP"—something like "Americans for a Reappraisal of Our Far Eastern Policy"—became part of the Movement alphabet soup, as local chapters of a new organization popped up at scattered campuses throughout the country.

ARFEP turned out to be a magnificent failure, all the more a failure because the outcry of radicals against the war—expressed in marches, campus demonstrations, disruptions of meetings at which government officials spoke—was becoming a source of national concern at the same time. By 1966, Lowenstein was anxious. Never an admirer of those farther to the Left than he was himself —he referred to the New Left often as the "New Gauche"—he saw in the militancy of the student movement a threat to peace almost as serious as the Indochina War itself. "If the issue is phrased as the radicals argue it," he would say—"that the United States is on the wrong side—then Johnson merely can isolate 'us' [always "us," the grand "us," in a Lowenstein speech] and win a major victory. Somehow, we have to find a new approach."

At the NSA Congress in 1966, then, he persuaded a contingent of student-body presidents to prepare a politely worded letter to President Johnson announcing that even "patriotic young people" questioned whether the President was committed to a diplomatic, rather than a military solution in Vietnam; that these same students were becoming "deeply troubled" by the unresponsiveness of the administration to student questions about the war; that were the war to continue, many young "men and women who would have willingly fought in Germany and Korea" would find it necessary to "go to jail" rather than to fight for a cause in which they could not possibly believe. Ingeniously worded, the letter merely asked the administration to "clarify its position on these matters."

It took four months for Lowenstein and others to persuade one hundred student-body presidents, scattered throughout the country, to sign the document. When they did, however, and when it appeared on the front page of the *New York Times* on December 30, 1966, its impact was enormous. First, it converted students at colleges and universities throughout the country to the "Dove" position—a situation that had not been the case up to that time, recent rhetoric to the contrary. It encouraged opposition to the war elsewhere. In rapid succession, Lowenstein solicited a "Returned Peace Corps Volunteers" letter against the War; then a pained, four-page, single-spaced "Rhodes Scholars Against the War" letter. Independent letters and ads popped up—Businessmen against the War; Professors against the War; Clergy against the War. It got to be a joke, with some of us expecting a "2,000 Former High School Basketball Centers Against the War" advertisement to appear at any moment. Nonetheless, the growing criticism from the "mainstream" had the effect that Lowenstein had anticipated. "Peace" became respectable on Capitol Hill, as the Kennedys, Albert Gore, Mike Mansfield, Mark Hatfield, and others joined the hitherto lonely men on the Senate Foreign Relations Committee as administration critics.

All of this would have been perfect were it not for a second result of our efforts: The case against the war had changed as well. Before, the radicals had been trying to focus on the similarity between bombings of peasant villages in Vietnam and the bombings of Civil Rights headquarters in Mississippi. As Bob Moses of SNCC put it, "When I heard the President, LBJ, tell me that the Vietnamese were being led by Communists, I *knew* that there was something wrong. Hell! That's what they say about us." In effect, the New Left was trying to mold a coalition that has eluded the Peace Movement to this day—between the poor people of the country and the middle-class liberal whites—a coalition designed to fight for social justice and equality both within the United States and between the United States and the Third World.

Lowenstein was a Jeffersonian, however—a mediator, a liberal. He believed in equality, but he had learned to identify it more with a Norman Thomas or an Eleanor Roosevelt than with a John L. Lewis or with a group of anynonymous blacks fighting for the rule of the Golden Rule over the South: To him, egalitarianism somehow meant "conciliation" between men, the "benevolence" of the rich and respectable people toward the poor, the "responsiveness" of the elite to the people—as opposed to an exacting principle of religious justice that a country had to understand and to obey, whether the people's "natural instincts" conformed to the principle or not. Once again, equality between rich and poor in the United States became "Harmony between the classes and between the races"; parity between the Vietnamese and the American people became "peace." Now we opposed the war because it was "too costly"; because it was "dividing the country"; because it was "the wrong way to fight Communism." Now a "negotiated" settlement was possible, and a U.S. withdrawal would result in something other than a victory of the National Liberation Front (NLF).

Apart from the ethical dilemmas inherent in such a position— to this day, the liberals have not provided a direct answer to those who charge that a "premature" pullout of U.S. troops will result in a Communist victory—it posed practical problems as well. To be for "peace" as an end in itself meant to be peaceful as an end in itself, that is, to become as concerned with the tactics employed in social conflict as with the goals that the various groups were trying to achieve. We were at the mercy of changes in behavior on the part of one side or another. Who looked peaceful this week? Was it Johnson, when he dispatched Rusk on a diplomatic mission? Was it ourselves, with our latest letter? Was it Tom Hayden, with his efforts to gain the release of American prisoners of war? Conversely, which was the more warlike—the bombing of the North, or the storming of the Pentagon?

Indeed, by the elections in November, 1968, the public debate on the war had degenerated into a discussion of how the various candidates *felt* about it. At first, McCarthy seemed to feel the worst, tramping around the lonely snows of New Hampshire like that, when no one else was willing to stick his neck out against Johnson. When Kennedy declared, matters became complicated. Even though he had hesitated before risking a challenge, his speeches were far more passionate than McCarthy's. Perhaps his was the most intense emotion. How did Humphrey *really* feel about the war? Did he believe his rhetoric, or was he merely trying to appease Johnson? Among Senatorial candidates, who had been with "us" the longest?

Then the insurgents became enchanted with that peculiar form of double-think that the electoral system imposes on everyone who touches it. McCarthy lost Naw Hampshire, but he had really won it. His was, moreover, a victory for the "anti-war" position, even though subsequent polls showed that many of those who had voted for him thought he was a hawk. The white working-class people who supported Kennedy for President also supported "our boys in Vietnam"—who, after all, tended to be their boys in Vietnam—but the liberals said that Kennedy, too, was winning new forces to "our side." It took no more credible a character than forthright, perservering, "I've-clawed-my-way-up-to-the-top-with-the-worst-of them" Richard Milhouse Nixon to coopt the mild "peace" sentiment that the liberals had generated in 'middle America' by promising a Vietnamization program no different from Lyndon Johnson's stated position—to fight only so long as it took to train the Vietnamese "to carry the ball themselves"—but buttressed with a rhetoric that pledged "to end this dirty war as soon as possible!"

Even then, when the illusion of liberal strength did crumble after the elections, the doves chose not to examine their own failures but to attack the very radicals who had put them into business in the first place. In 1967, the student presidents had gained strength by warning of disruptions, of jail, were the war to continue. As their prophecy proved correct, however, they joined the Right in condemning the protesters. Lowenstein, now a Congressman, led the way. He fulminated against the radicals in speeches throughout the country. He dispatched a staff member to seek the NSA presidency on an anti-Left, pro-"peace" platform. He privately attacked Moratorium organizers for refusing to follow his suggestion that the October extravaganza be billed as a protest against violence of all kinds. Here was the man who before the 1968 Convention had said, "I don't know. After Chicago, we might all be in the streets." Where was he now?

Ultimately, without leadership, the McCarthy kids became the McCarthy clique, floating from one organization to another, undermining each other, jockeying for position. The best of them ceased to think seriously about the direction in which the country was moving under Nixon; the worst, merely indulged themselves in name-dropping, nostalgia, and oblique references to parties at "Gloria's" place in New York. And as final ironies, Sam Brown, Richard Goodwin, *et. al.* had to prevail not upon "one of their own" but Edmund Muskie to deliver the rebuttal to Spiro Agnew during the 1970 campaign; and Allard Lowenstein, gerrymandered into a Republican district, became the *only* incumbent Representative to lose his seat in the elections that followed.

C. MAKING SENSE OUT OF THE ELECTORAL SYSTEM

When such experiences pile up—one on top of another—we must go beyond berating specific tactics employed by each side to explain them, however. Even the "kids" now have gone beyond mourning the failures of the past. They are trying to understand why they occurred. None of them, at this point, is so sanguine as to expect that an effort to put one or two candidates in an office in Washington, D.C., will bring the millenium, as much as Allard Lowenstein and others may want them to believe it. The liberals may say, "Work within the system," but the students are still trying to find out where the system is.

On a local level, the radical today finds no place where he can engage in political activity on a regular basis. The machines will not have him, at least not one on his terms. They are too determined to set their sights on those programs that they can "get." Broad visions might disturb their relationships with local or national elites, with fatigued constituents, or all three. They exercise power, and, to the extent that they do "deliver" goods and services, even some measure of authority, but they define themselves out of the task of building a sense of civic duty that extends beyond the St. Patrick's Day Parade.

Look at Mayor Daley's operation in Chicago. His supporters boast of the "efficiency" with which he administers essential services; his opponents brand him a "tyrant." The mayor's power is not the issue, however, but its use—a use determined by a parochial conception of what people really need. "The Mayor and his fellow Irish politicians," notes Perry L. Weed, "do not judge their actions by ethical standards, but by the test of practicality. To them politics is a source of power to be used for individuals rather than in the public interest. Daley views sin as a personal matter, for which one is answerable to God."[12] In the Old Testament, God judged Israel for the sins of all its citizens; in the New Testament, Christ died for mankind. Were the Mayor to take these Biblical lessons seriously, he might use his authority to challenge the poor whites to reconsider their attitudes toward blacks, in accordance with the Sermon on the Mount. He might challenge the business interests, locally and otherwise, to provide economic resources for blighted neighborhoods. He might demand that the community as a whole participate in a discussion of what it might be and do. Instead, he sanctifies the hatreds of every group with the promise that they need *never* concern themselves with public justice while he's running things. He points with pride to the municipal auditoriums that he can construct—temples to the false god of progress. He glorifies stability as an end in itself—even a stability achieved at the expense of mutual trust and confidence between the people. The streets are clean; the garbage is collected; but each day, the unchanneled, unchallenged anxieties and frustrations of modern life build to the point of explosion. One wonders how long such a solution can last.

The reform clubs are little better. They might permit the radical to participate, but they tend to be ineffective encouraging political action only during a major social crisis, or around election day. In 1900, Plunkitt commented that the reformers were "mornin' glories—looked lively in the mornin' and withered up in a short time, while the regular machines went on flourishin' forever."[13] Nothing has changed. Barbara Jeffers, a leader of recent reform movements in New York City, expresses similar sentiments in *The Airtight Cage*:[14]

> Our club lasted as long as any I've seen, and that's something. But I've concluded that, if you're going to have a good-government organization that means anything, it has to be built out of intelligent, articulate, hard-working, emotionally involved people who completely control, completely run the organization. They sit in the driver's seat and drive the officers; the officers do not drive them. But when you get this driving type of membership you build an organization that in the long run will tend to destroy itself because it is undisciplined. It comes into being to fight an authority and it dies because it cannot trust the new authority it has erected for itself.

The reformer is, in James Q. Wilson's words, an "amateur democrat"—a democrat who has found fame and fortune in some lucrative occupation other than reform. In politics, he sees himself not as part of a group of people trying to encourage a "common good," but as a private man for whom politics has become a medium through which to "express" his private moral beliefs. Often, he appears to be a purist, but it is a flimsy, extracurricular sort of purity that he displays. Neither his material nor his spiritual life depends on the movements in which he participates; his love of justice extends only so far as it doesn't cost him anything. The moment someone offends his sensibilities, he walks out in the name of his "right" not to tolerate "this sort of abuse." Both New York City and Cambridge, Massachusetts, are filled with such people, and for every seven of them, there is a clique no less insular, no less embittered and protective, than the ethnic cliques of Chicago.

Even when a radical does find that rare electoral organization that cares enough about social change to endure the hard work involved in creating it, he comes to understand how unorganized the rest of the population is. Whatever the weaknesses of early forms of party discipline, they at least ensured that an elected official would have to answer to someone on a regular basis. Whatever the strength of the era of "independent voting," it has failed to produce mechanisms of control comparable in their effectiveness. The people communicate through polls, and if these tell a candidate that he has support among three loose groups of voters, he will try to blur his appeal to maximize his chances with all three of them. The "spirit of compromise," the social scientists say, but the radical has to wonder who is compromising whom.

Finally, if the radical transcends these difficulties—if he finds a club; if his candidate wins on a decent enough program—he discovers that an elected official can neither pass the laws that need to be passed nor enforce the laws that need to be enforced. It is common knowledge, yet its significance escapes us. Everyone knows that a President's power to achieve social change is far less than his power to order the military destruction of foreign nations, even when the public-opinion polls are demanding the opposite. Yet is this conditon his fault, the fault of the American, or the fault of the institutions and ideologies that we have inherited?

The answer is fairly clear: The system itself must be blamed. In part, elected officials are afraid of the corporations. They need money, after all, and since political parties no longer can attract contributions from the "little guys," the rich tend to dominate the field. Yet "tolerance" of government by private corporation governments has become a matter of principle as well—an extension of the Enlightenment's faith that with technology society will "naturally" regulate itself in a manner satisfactory to all. As Theodore Lowi,[15] a political scientist from the University of Chicago, puts it:

> *Modern liberals are ambivalent about government. Government is obviously the most efficacious way of achieving good purposes in our age. But alas, it is efficacious because it is involuntary. To live with their ambivalence, modern policy makers have fallen into believing that public policy involves merely the identification of the problems toward which government ought to be aimed. It pretends through "pluralism," "countervailing power," "creative federalism," "partnership," and "participatory democracy" that the unsentimental decisions about how to employ coercion need not really be made at all. . . .*

When such a doctrine impedes the ability to make law, it is bad enough. When it destroys the institutions designed to enforce law, the country verges on despotism. Lon Fuller, Professor of General Jurisprudence at Harvard Law School, lists in *The Morality of Law* [16] eight ways in which a legal system can miscarry—eight distinct "routes to disaster." These, he notes, are (1) "A failure to achieve rules at all, so that every issue must be decided on an *ad hoc* basis; (2) failure to publicize, or at least to make available to the affected party, the rules he is expected to observe; (3) the abuse of retroactive legislation; (4) a failure to make rules understandable; (5) the enactment of contradictory rules; (6) or rules that require conduct beyond the powers of the affected party; (7) introducing such frequent changes in the rules that the subject cannot orient his action by them; and, finally, (8) a failure of congruence between the rules as announced and their actual administration." Radicals have encountered instances of *all* of these malpractices in pursuing their work.

I. "A failure to achieve rules at all . . ."
Example: Hippies in a relatively small community decide that a neighborhood park is a pleasant place to congregate on a Sunday afternoon, only to be attacked by residents of the area, complaining that long-haired, scraggly "types" upset the mores of the community. The police clear the area even though there is no law against long hair or sitting in the park.

Example: For all the wire taps that it has denied, the Federal Bureau of Investigation boasts of its monitoring of hotel rooms in which Dr. Martin Luther King was staying. Former Attorney General Ramsey Clark expresses outrage at the revelations, claiming that Hoover had violated government regulations.

II. "Failure to Publicize the rules"
Example: The Massachusetts Department of Public Welfare for

many years failed to inform welfare recipients of provisions entitling them to "special needs" allocations above their regular budget allotment for use in hardships. Thus, welfare mothers often failed to receive winter clothes for their children; fuel and utility money; extra food orders; and furniture, even though all of these benefits were guaranteed to them.

III. *"The Abuse of Retroactive Legislation"*

Example: Ex post facto legislation so clearly violates the Constitution that even the courts rule against it, but this doesn't prevent a bureaucrat from occasionally trying. In 1967, General Lewis B. Hershey issued a secret memorandum to local draft boards suggesting that participants in "disruptive" protests be reclassified "1-A." The document might have remained in effect were it not that the son of a member of a local draft board forwarded it to the national o ffice of the NSA at the behest of his troubled father. The general was somewhat upset, we learned, when an Associated Press reporter confronted him with a zeroxed copy of his own memo.

In the weeks that followed, local draft boards throughout the country began reclassifying registrants, some even specifying that political activities were the cause. The public outcry that followed was insufficient to arouse the White House, but when the NSA insituted legal action against the Hershey directives, demanding their nullification by the courts, the government acted. In a letter to university presidents, Joseph Califano, special assistant to the President, stated that under no circumstances would the draft become an instrument to "Punish" past dissent. One year later, an appellate court ruled in NSA's favor on the case.

The Hershey directives, admittedly, lost in court, but more than one student, we discovered, subsequently became reluctant to fight the draft for fear of reprisal by his local board.

IV. *"A Failure to Make Rules Understandable"*

Example: Laws governing landlord-tenant relations in most states are so complicated that tenants rarely know when they can or cannot be evicted. Nor do various tenants' rights handbooks help, for they include only the letter of the law, not how the courts will enforce it.

Example: The loopholes of the draft law in the sixties became a boon to middle- and upper-class young people who could afford competent attorneys. Yet working people and the poor often weren't even aware of their basic rights under the law. The composition of the army, particularly before the reform of the Selective Service Act, spoke for itself.

V. *"The Enactment of Contradictory Rules"*

Example: An organizer's remarks on Mississippi, written in 1965, tell the story:[17]

The ironies here are enormous. Consider that just last summer, when hundreds of northern students flooding into Mississippi were threatened with brutality and murder (threats quickly carried out), Robert Kennedy, the Attorney General, plaintively explained to the nation that he had no power or authority to dispatch any Federal presence to Mississippi to protect the young civil rights volunteers. Kennedy's rigidly minimal interpretation of both the situation in Mississippi and the limitations on the exercise of Federal power was disputed by a host of constitutionalists, legal experts, and liberals and radicals more interested in the realities of combatting the violence and illegality of racism in Mississippi than in the political tightrope on which Robert Kennedy was balancing. But what nobody (except SNCC) realized was that already existing Federal machinery in Mississippi could reassert the rule of law and the formal equality most states of the union took for granted, if that Federal machinery followed its own rules and guarantees instead of accommodating to the mores and customs of segregation.

VI. *"Rules that Require Conduct Beyond the Powers of the Affected Party:"*

Example: Housing codes in most states require that buildings maintain adequate standards of health, sanitation, and security. Many tenements, however, are so dilapidated as to be beyond rehabilitation. The result is that attempts to enforce the codes against landlords become self-defeating. They merely result in evictions from the substandard dwellings without alternate housing being available for the tenant's use.

Massive construction of low-income housing might make obedience to the law possible by *both* landlords and tenants, but under the circumstances, the codes exist more as ideals than as statutes.

VII. *"Such Frequent Changes in the Rules that the Subject Cannot Orient His Action by Them."*

Example: First, they were drafting everyone but students, oldest first, with a cut-off at 26. When that didn't work, they tried drafting everyone but students except the students who didn't do well on this test that they started to give. Then they started drafting protesters, but they changed their minds. They changed their minds on the students; instead they decided that a lottery would be better that took the youngest first except for college graduates, who remained eligible for one year after school. Then they said they were going to let the students decide when to put themselves in the pool with the nonstudents, so that the liability of the nonstudents would go up again, but that was all right, because soon, they said, they were not going to draft anyone. Except in cases, that is, when . . .

VIII. "A Failure of Congruence Between the Rules as Announced and Their Actual Administration"
The various Nader reports provide a number of examples, of which these are representative:
Example: "The FDA's (Food and Drug Administration's) concept of law enforcement is not the creation of evil and destructive inspectors; it comes from higher up in the organization. In fact, the enforcement personnel of the FDA have shown consistent sensitivity and dedication. But agency policy has consistently channeled their work into relatively unimportant areas and away from areas in which strong enforcement activity is clearly needed."[18]
Example: "Between 1965 and 1970 only eleven abatement actions were initiated by NAPCA (National Air Pollution Control Administration) . . . High level administrators at NAPCA and in HEW must take full responsibility for the government's shoody inspection and enforcement programs."[19]
Example: "The Federal Trade Commission has found several separate methods for not performing its enforcement duties properly under existing law. First, the FTC has allowed a general decline of formal enforcement activity of any kind. Instead, it has shifted—unwisely—toward "voluntary" enforcement tools. To compound that, it has also permitted compliance by those whose practices have been challenged to become almost entirely voluntary. Finally, the FTC saps all of its enforcement programs by excessive delays."[20]

The abuses here are but a fraction of those that radicals have encountered. Daily, they learn of police harassment, wiretaps and bugs, excessive bail, prisons in which community leaders and organizers rot for months before coming to trial, sadistic punishments administered in the prisons themselves—all in the name of "law and order." Such practices constitute systematic persecution of the poor, the minorities, and the young in the name of local and national property interests and those who would defend them.
No, the situation is clear. Young people have given up on electoral politics because their parents have given up on electoral politics. It is frightening, isn't it, that the search for a national leader to "bring us together again" has now become the only way in which the citizens of a democracy can express their dismay at the state of the world? Yet without resistance, the American people have let the Progressives supplant local party organization with professional bureaucracies. They replaced the morality if justice and loyalty with the ethic of expertise and stability. They have traded the institutions of collective power for civil-service requirements designed to weed out the "best men" who might

then make all the decisions. Now these same people ask that radicals work within a system that is not really designed to work itself. It is, at best, an auxiliary to the real government—the industrial government, charged with glutting us all. Equality is left at the starting gate.

II. INTEREST GROUPS AND THE PROBLEM OF POWER

The breakdown of the electoral system has prompted many of the dissatisfied to organize themselves into voluntary associations to function as pressure groups for benefits of various kinds. The pattern is familiar; a group has been denied public recognition. No one grievance is at stake, the problem reflects its overall relationship to existing institutions—a subordinate relationship that prevents its members from fulfilling goals that they want to achieve. Therefore, they seek power over their own destinies so that they can deal with society on a relatively equal basis. Even if initial campaigns do not yield economic resources—the situation which faces a black candidate who assumes the mayoralty of a city like Newark—in the end, the feeling of control, of determining the direction of one's personal and collective life compensates for the loss.

Yet here again, the premises of the system often render impotent the best efforts of people to change it. Either a movement encounters an elite that is so powerful that it can determine the demands of its opponents as well as its own response. Or, sometimes, an idealistic movement, often functioning at a local level, ends up adopting accepted standards of militancy and acquisitiveness in order to remain within the framework of politics as they understand it. Or, most frequently, the breakdown of lines of access between the people and their representatives makes impossible effective advocacy in their behalf.

In every case, a public demand, appealing to a higher sense of value, gives way to a private one. Three examples come to mind —The NSA-CIA Relationship; the odyssey of the Massachusetts Welfare Rights Organization; and my own efforts to advocate "Student Power" as president of the NSA in 1968.

A. THE NSA AND THE CIA

As the nation's "largest and most representative," according to its brochures, student organization, the National Student Association always faces problems in reconciling the strains between the views of the young people for whom it speaks and the attitudes of the establishment with which it must deal on a day-to-day basis. During my own term of office in 1967–68, the national office faced many such dilemmas. Should we take money from the Office of Education to encourage students to cooperate with faculty members in the evaluation of courses, at a time when students were printing their own "course and teacher evaluations" at many universities? Should the organization continue to administer tutorial programs for young children funded by the Office of Economic Opportunity, programs designed to help children adjust to the schools rather than to fight to change them? Should NSA even talk to the State Department?

Yet no decision in our administration came as close to dramatizing the difficulty of pursuing power for its own sake as the problems that previous NSA presidents had to endure in dealing with a certain covert government agency.

In 1967, *Ramparts Magazine* revealed that for fifteen years the Central Intelligence Agency had been financing the international programs of the NSA and, by consequence, much of the Association itself. The agency had channeled funds—which supported American participation in international student conferences, youth exchange programs, grants to Third World student unions —through *conduit* foundations to which the association would submit ostensibly legitimate proposals. Yet the proposals were a façade. The *real* arrangements had been made in private meetings between representatives of CIA "Covert Action Division 5" and "witty" (agency jargon for "privy") NSA officers. Over three million dollars had come to NSA through this process, undetected by its board, its membership, and the general public. Only since 1964 had the officers attempted to terminate the relationship and seek new means of support.

Subsequent articles about the revelations pursued one of two lines of attack. Liberals generally focused on the problem of accountability. Who within the government had authorized the program? Which committees in Congress maintained jurisdiction over the CIA? Similarly, within NSA—had the officers acted contrary to resolutions passed by delegates to NSA's congresses? Had CIA operatives interfered in NSA elections, in its debates, in the implementation of its program? Needless to say, as the answers to such questions confirmed all the liberals' worst fears, they demanded that *both* the CIA and the NSA be brought under better control—the former, by the government; the latter, by its membership of student government leaders.

Radicals examined the question of organizational autonomy, contending that the relationship had perverted NSA's independence from an establishment which the organization claimed to be attacking. The Association had committed treason against the Movement, they argued, by colluding with the enemy. Even NSA's dissenting positions *vis à vis* U.S. foreign policy—against nuclear testing in 1961; for the admission of Communist China to the United Nations; against the Indochina War—fit into the CIA's strategy. By supporting moderate dissenters, the Left argued, the agency was attempting to defuse more militant alternatives, both at home and abroad. Internationally, they maintained, the CIA often "hedged its bets," covertly backing "responsible" opposition to a government that the U.S. supported as insurance against strained relations with the country in the event of an opposition victory. Either way, NSA leaders were, at best, pawns in the game; at worst, its most sophisticated players.

Yet the real lesson that the country might have learned from the CIA episode had concerned the relationship between old and new guards, insurgents and elites in a democracy. Published reports to the contrary, NSA had *not* been the youth appendage of the ruling class—the vehicle through which the hip, wheeler-dealers of tomorrow learned the tricks of the trade. Ivy League schools and many large state universities had refused to join the organization, in part, for this reason. Affiliation was accomplished either by student-body or student-government referendum. "We don't need it," Ivy League student government representatives would say, implying, "We're above it. We have our *own* ways of bringing improvements to the campus and gaining influence for ourselves." To this day, the *New York Times* publishes the views of the editor of the *Harvard Crimson* as readily as those of the NSA president.

The NSA, in fact, had been a vehicle for political upward mobility. Student governments from small Catholic women's colleges, private liberal-arts institutions, black colleges in the South, constituted over two-thirds of the organization's membership. Most of the large universities whose students affiliated were middle-range in quality and status—a University of Utah or University of Illinois. For activists and student-government representatives at such schools, an NSA summer Congress was a fantastic opportunity. Where else would a junior from Newton College of the Sacred Heart get to argue the "sit-in" movement with Stokely Carmichael, or, for that matter, a junior from Oberlin College gain a national audience of youth leaders for a few speeches on educational change?

Further, the Congress served to "radicalize" people. Even students from out-of-the-way colleges, the first in their families to receive higher education, responded to the ten days of intensive debate on political questions. Often, they merely had been afraid to identify with the Left; no one else on their campus did. Yet at the Congress, there were hundreds of student leaders exploring new alternatives. Why *not* challenge deans and professors? Why *not* support the black power movement? Why *not* tell Lyndon Johnson to go to hell on Vietnam? One after another, the resolutions would pass, astonishing even those who worked for them. People changed. In the early 60's Left-liberal delegates from the University of Michigan, Oberlin, and the University of Chicago,— Tom Hayden, Rennie Davis, Paul Potter, and Bob Ross— began to talk about "participatory democracy"; and in 1967, an erstwhile Republican from Council Bluffs, Iowa (Redlands University, 1965; Harvard Divinity School) emerged as a leader of the Left-liberal "Dump Johnson" movement—Sam Brown.

Yet the Congress was a place to assess the power of the establishment as well. Such discussions would take place around election time. Even representatives who had supported controversial resolutions began to ask, "How did a candidate look?" "Could he raise money?" "Would he project well overseas?" Although the position of National Affairs Vice-President, charged with implementing resolutions on Civil Rights and student power, occasionally went to a radical like Paul Potter in 1960, or myself in 1966, for the officers who had to deal with the bastions of latter-day Federalism —the foundations, the State Department, the business and civic elites—the delegates invariably chose hygienic, somewhat liberal student body presidents from the Midwest or Far West. Invariably, I say, but unenthusiastically as well. The votes often seemed more a responsibility than a choice.

Such dynamics created a context that rendered a new officer particularly susceptible to the arguments for the CIA relationship, however. Shortly after taking office, his immediate predecessor would invite him to dinner at an expensive restaurant in Washington. A couple of "staff members from a few years ago, now employed by the Agency for International Development," would be there, ostensibly to "fill you in on some background concerning the international program." Eventually, they would ask him to sign a security oath—"just a formality; some of the information is confidential." Then, what to his wondering eyes would appear, but, "It makes a lot of sense. We *never* could get the funds to do what we're doing from other sources. They just don't exist."

As, indeed, they did not. Of course, one reason *why* they did not were the CIA subsidies themselves. Even if the international division of Ford or Rockefeller was unaware of the real income of, let us say, the Foundation for Youth and Student Affairs—a CIA conduit—they at least knew of its purposes and its program. "Why not try FYSA?" program officers of the large foundations would suggest when presented with a proposal for an international youth exchange. "They sponsor projects of this kind." Yet the NSA officers never had the perspective to think through the self-fulfilling situation that the CIA had created.

Moreover, there were rebuttals to every argument. At the Congress, delegates who challenged a resolution backed by the CIA had been told, "You don't know enough about this. We have the expertise," in a manner designed perfectly to exploit the fears of the average man in an Enlightenment culture. To a potential candidate whom the NSA establishment feared—I was in this position for two years prior to seeking office—they had said, "You know, this is a pretty complicated operation. Are you sure you can handle it?" Now, to the new officer who questioned the subsidies, they would say, "Which is better? Maintaining our 'purity' and accomplishing nothing, or building an effective international program?" There were private inducements as well—draft deferments, American Express Cards, European trips, even extra stipends to pay off that debt to school. Pretty powerful stuff to young, insecure graduates from small towns in Ohio and Wisconsin—the sons of Depression families.

Philip Sherburne, the NSA president who began severing ties with the CIA in 1966, observed:

> The real tragedy of the relationship was its impact on the foreign policy debate in this country throughout the 50's. Here was an enormous number of talented young people ready to challenge the dominant assumptions of the Cold War—particularly U.S. policy toward a third world—who all got sucked into an exchange program here, a conference there, in the belief that this was the best way to accomplish something, the only way to receive financial support. Maybe going underground was the most appropriate way for liberals to preserve their power in the fifties, but they left no one else room to maneuver.

Yet even Sherburne stopped one step short of one painful truth—no one, including the liberals of the fifties, had any choice in the CIA relationship, if they cared at all about the programs, that they were trying to sponsor. The elites could set the agenda or remove it as they chose.

B. THE MASSACHUSETTS WELFARE RIGHTS ORGANIZATION

Even radicals operating at a local level find it hard not to internalize, eventually, the prevailing values of the system. A case in point is the sad story of the state-wide branch of the National Welfare Rights Organization (NWRO) in Massachusetts.

In its early days the Massachusetts Welfare Rights Organization (MWRO) was the model of a militant poor people's movement. Established in the fall of 1968, within one year its staff had united more than 4,000 welfare recipients in the state of Massachusetts —black, white, and Spanish-speaking—into one democratic organization that boasted over 50 local chapters. Its goals were clear—to insist, contrary to the practices of the Massachusetts Depart-

ment of Public Welfare, that clients receive all benefits to which
they were entitled by law; to demand that welfare mothers gain
a voice in the decision-making process of the department; and to
obtain an "adequate income" of $5,000 (now $6,500) per year for
every family of four in the United States. "Adequate Income
Now!" Poor People's Power!" "Stop the War and Feed the Poor"
—these were the slogans of MWRO, slogans that reached the
newspapers and the NBC evening news on a regular basis.

The staff of MWRO had synthesized elusive techniques of community organizing to a science. To build a new local group, an
organizer would implant himself in an area of the city where a
great many welfare recipients were known to live. There he
would become a resident for several days, familiarizing himself
with the neighborhood, exploring the housing projects, seeking
out people who might serve as local leaders. The next step involved "hitting the doors," that is, going from door to door with
other organizers and indigenous residents, saying, "Hello, my
name is . . . and we're organizing the Grove Hall (a Boston housing
project) Welfare Rights Organization. Might we speak with you for
a moment?" The organizer would put his foot in the door, enter
the living room, and explain that the new organization would aid
the recipient in finding out what she could receive from the department; that it would handle her daily grievances with her social
worker; that she could fight the system more effectively as part of
a powerful movement. The organizer would urge her to attend an
initial meeting from which welfare mothers from all over her
neighborhood would march to the local headquarters of the department to demand furniture, or winter clothes, or some other
benefit about which they had not been informed. After such a
spiel, it was not uncommon for two or three hundred people to
show up at the opening meeting in a city like Boston; for fifty to
sixty to come out for such gatherings in smaller towns like Haverill
or Lowell. The recipients would elect officers, set up a committee
to handle everyday grievances with the Welfare Department, and
march down to the office for the goods. If the social workers
refused to honor their requests, all hell broke loose. More than one
welfare office in Massachusetts found its desks strewn about, its
papers shoved into waste-paper baskets, its chairs overturned, all
because a supervisor had said, "No," to three hundred mothers
who had demanded food for their children.

At its height, the MWRO was among the most exciting groups
in the country—certainly the most effective of those within
NWRO's national network at the time. When Robert Finch, as
Secretary of HEW, spoke to the Harvard Law School, the MWRO
took over the stage to tell its side of the welfare story. On the day
before the October Moratorium against the war in 1969, 150 "la-

dies," as the organizers referred to the mothers on AFDC, marched to the Boston army base with their children to demand that the supplus food be made available to poor people. At a time when black movements were shouting, "Get Whitey!" and poor whites were crying, "Nigger!," in Massachusetts poor blacks and whites were marching under one banner. It was all, as the staff commented frequently, "fairly impressive."

Success of this sort can by mystifying, however. It can persuade a young organizer that movement, tension, and conflict *is* major change, even when the changes from the confrontations are only minor. So it was with welfare rights—the staff became mesmerized by its ability to bring local welfare officers to their knees. If in the beginning the organizers had seen MWRO as a vehicle to fight for fundamental reconstruction of the economic system, whereby demands for adequate income would encourage the recipients to demand justice in the country as a whole, gradually they began to argue that a philosophy of "get it, get it, get it" was sufficient unto itself. Their many months of marching, of going to jail, of patroling the roughest areas of the city had persuaded them not that justice is a demanding god requiring dedicated and per-servering servants, but that there are no gods in a materialistic society except materialism itself. They became not radicals but petulant liberals determined to prove that in a world of cynics, they would hustle with the best of them.

The effect was disastrous.

It skewed the staff's priorities. For all their skill at implementing a few tactics, the organizers were novices at politics writ large. Liberal politics, radical politics—it didn't matter. They just didn't know very much. Nor did they care to know very much. Each staff member was responsible for his local group. That was enough, wasn't it? Somebody else could do all the thinking. Long, analytical meetings that attempted to come to grips with a variety of possible strategies were a waste of time—"Movement bullshit," the organizers called them.

Consequently, they began to place high premiums only on the tangible signs of tactical success. An organizer won points for the number of people he had attracted to an opening meeting; for the crowds that he had gathered at a demonstration; for the total number of benefits that the ladies had received. He placed little value on transferring his own skills to the recipients, on encouraging them to assume responsibility for themselves, on helping the mothers understand the nature of political power in the state, even though these tasks were also critical to the long-term success of poor-peoples' movement.

Privatism undermined the organizers' overall relationship with the recipients. At one staff meeting, for example, the chairwoman of the organization, Mrs. Roberta Grant, commented, "Welfare Rights needs something like the 'Power to the People' slogan of the Panthers, something which will give us the spirit which we used to have in the early days." What she was seeking was a principle, a higher value, a way to express her anger that a country that professed "liberty and justice" could send rockets to the moon while she was sending her children to school without coats. She needed the backing of a common faith, of a doctrine true to her religious heritage and to her belief in the fundamental doctrines of the Declaration of Independence. Yet the organizers, now accustomed to seeing life in terms of "power," "goods and services," "interests" could not understand. They sat dumbfounded, as if somebody had just asked them to write advertisements for a new brand of soap.

The MWRO lost its capacity to make lasting alliances with other groups, the only hope for an organization whose power to achieve change by itself was limited. To be sure, a few members of the staff did concern themselves with the "friends" of welfare rights (a friend being any supporter who wasn't a recipient) and attempted, feebly, at staff meetings to make the case that the organization as a whole had to take its friends more seriously. Yet the organizers did not want friends, or, more precisely, they could not afford to admit that they needed friends. To do so was to admit that *machismo* was insufficient both as a strategy for social change and as a mechanism of psychic protection against personal defeat. If their theology was "get it"; if their liturgy was "Furniture Now!", their program of religious education entailed participation in a three-week training session in organizing; involvement in at least one major confrontation at a local welfare office; and most of all, adoption of a curious rhetoric whereby the adverb "fairly" preceded almost every adjective. ("That's fairly reasonable. "That's fairly impressive." Even, "That's fairly incredible") The verb "win" became a noun, replacing the word "victory." ("It's a win.") The phrase "out there" replaced the rest of the English language. ("What's happening out there?" "It was really a win out there!" "Things are getting fairly rough out there!")

Those who failed to learn this vocabularly or to subject themselves to these mechanistic hazing procedures all presumably existed "out there"—people to be treated with suspicion and disrespect. The category even came to include some who had fought hard for adequate income, though not affiliated directly with the organization; people who had helped MWRO find money for its organizers at times when it was going bankrupt; people who had spent long hours in the welfare department trying to win support from social workers infuriated by demonstrations that had blamed them for the problems of the system as a whole. Even the

Washington office of the NWRO receded into the ominous "out there" when it began to make alliances with the peace movement ("I mean, it's really screwed up," complained Massachusetts staff director Gerry Shea before a spring anti-war mobilization in 1971. "George Wiley's even going to participate in Ralph Abernathy's goddamned *mule* train."). Welfare recipients within the Massachusetts organization who decided, for one reason or another, that the organizers' conception of humanity was, perhaps, not the last word on the subject were disparaged as "hopeless" or "power-hungry." The only "friends" whom the organizers did respect were a few leaders of other interest groups; and they, less because of their commitment to social change, or to adequate income, or to MWRO, than because of their power, which could not be ignored, or because they agreed that power was the art of making do with what was available. It was not long before these "hustlers" had gained a reputation throughout Boston as being an obnoxious bunch of *ersatz* militants with whom one might deal out of concern for welfare recipients, but for no other reason.

Ultimately, their realism turned out to be crackpot realism, of the sort that C. Wright Mills attributed to the generals of the fifties. It took only one serious countermove on the part of the establishment to topple the whole flimsy structure. In November 1969, Governor Francis Sargent, a great Massachusetts humanitarian, announced a program of "flat grants" to welfare recipients whereby the average yearly budget for a family of four would rise slightly from $3,200 per year to $3,750 per year, in exchange for which "special needs" allocations would be cut entirely. No longer could a recipient receive winter clothing for her children, or furniture, or even money during emergencies. There was to be a ceiling placed on the basic necessities of life. Yet the governor's real reason was abundantly clear from his speeches. "We're tired of seeing a minority of recipients gain benefits from the system," he would say, "at the expense of the responsible (did we hear 'silent') majority!" He was determined to destroy Welfare Rights—to force them to fight the system without relying on "special needs" benefits, or not to fight at all.

The organizers were caught. Soon they discovered that the few lobbyists with whom they had cooperated were powerless to override the Governor's plan. Indeed, the leaders of virtually every social-welfare organization in Massachusetts might create a coalition to fight the "flat grant," but since few of them ever had mobilized their own groups in a major cause, it was a paper coalition. Groups that might have helped Welfare Rights in more aggressive ways—peace organizations, organizations or radical professionals—had been so alienated by past dealings with its staff that they wanted nothing to do with it. A few social workers from the Boston area Department of Public Welfare did join the recipients at a last-ditch demonstration at the statehouse against the "flat grant" proposal—three even got arrested with the "ladies"— but most of the organizers could not be bothered with such alien beings intruding upon their turf. The "flat grant" program passed without even a sizable whimper in response, and to this day MWRO has not recovered.

C. MY LIFE IN WASHINGTON, IN BRIEF

Who is to blame, however? Is it the organizers or the system within which they must work?

I offer a last piece of evidence, a personal one.

My decision to seek a position in the national office of the NSA was made only after a long period of time, despite continuing pressure from friends that I do so. In 1964, I undertook a protest candidacy against a somber delegate from U.C.L.A. whom the NSA establishment had designated as their "man of the year," only to withdraw at the last moment when I was convinced that the points that I had wanted to make had been made. In 1965, I waged a holy war throughout the NSA Congress against "these pompous bureaucrats in the national office who spend as much time worrying about the placement of hairs on the top of their heads as they do about the new ideas inside them," again, only to decline my nomination, respectfully, and to thank all those who had shown such confidence in me, etc., etc. I feared, instinctively, that I would lose touch with the social movements with which I had been working, that I would come to imitate the very establishment that we had been fighting.

At some point, I changed my mind. In part, I felt, after a year on NSA's national board, that no job was as mysterious as the national officers made it out to be. (Boy, was I wrong about that!) In part, I decided to run as an experiment. Could a young Jewish radical from Scarsdale, New York, maintain his dignity in the hurly-burly world of the military-industrial-Great-Society complex? Therefore, in 1966, I brought a suit to the National Student Congress; I announced my candidacy for National Affairs vice-president (charged with administering NSA's "domestic" programs); I hustled for votes; and, when my opponent withdrew— to run in order to make a moving withdrawal speech had now become an NSA tradition—I won.

To this day, I am not sure whether my experiment with power succeeded, but I can say this: to the extent that it did, it reflected my biweekly efforts to leave Washington, to return to campuses, to participate in local student uprisings as they were happening, more than any spirit of democracy that prevailed in Washington, D.C. I would spend two weeks at a place like Berkeley, working

closely with the Left in their battles against the Reagan administration, only to return to Washington to figure out how I, as the
officer in charge of NSA's relations with students, could extricate
myself from the international commission's appalling involvement
with the CIA. One year later, as president, I would walk into the
Ford Foundation literally off the streets, direct from participation
in some of the events 'at Columbia University. There I would
complete negotiations on a $315,000 grant designed to encourage
student-initiated projects in educational change. Abrupt shifts of
this sort represented more than the demands of my job; they were
essential to my personal survival.

Why was this the case? Was I pressured by specific people to
"toe the line?" Did I feel that NSA would go bankrupt were I to
deviate too far from the respectable "Progressive" ("Yes, we believe in change, but not violence") line? Did I fear bugs, wire taps,
CIA agents coming after me in the middle of the night with black-
jacks and guns? The answer to these questions was assuredly,
"Yes." but even they were not as much a concern to me as a
process in which I was becoming involved.

You go to Washington as an advocate for a specific constituency.
Soon, you discover that you exist as part of a community of advocates. In higher education, for example, there are at least six major
organizations with offices in the District that represent slices of the
academic world—their private interests, their own approaches to
educational problems. They include the American Association of
University Professors, the National Association of Student Personnel Administrators (Deans of Men), the National Association of
Women's Deans and Counsellors, and no fewer than three organizations representing colleges and universities as institutions: the
Association of American Colleges; the American Council on
Higher Education; and the American Council on Education—the
largest and most influential.

To advocate "student power" in Washington, then, meant to
deal with these groups. I would attend their conferences, prepare
working papers for their manuals, and participate on panels as a
"spokesman" for the "student point of view." For seven months,
I served as NSA's representative on a multi-organizational committee charged with drafting a statement on the rights of students
comparable to the statement on the Academic Freedom of Professors that has protected members of the nation's faculties for many
years. Later, an acquaintance on the staff of the American Council
on Education asked me to speak to a group of relatively conservative university presidents on the problems of institutional racism
in higher education. In short, I was becoming a "regular," almost
as familiar to the establishment in higher education as it was to
itself.

In itself, there was nothing harmful in this. The staffs of the professional organizations in higher education include a few genuinely dedicated people, as concerned about the crisis of our society as anyone else. Some are even prepared to work for fundamental change. Yet, remember, I had come to Washington as a representative of a student revolution that was turning the university, if not the country, on its head. Those of us who met regularly on drafting committees, or who shared the platform at a seemingly endless round of conferences, might have enjoyed each other's company; but we had our differences, and, more important, the people for whom we spoke had *their* differences—serious ones. We could not afford the luxury of agreement, lest one, or all of us, lose contact with people whom we were representing.

Gradually, then—to resolve the tensions that we were experiencing—each of us carved out roles for ourselves not so much as advocates but as mediators between the "boys back home" and the "boys in the District." Now, the boys back home were good people, mind you, by by God, they sure could go at one another, couldn't they? Not like all of us here in the District. But, on the other hand, the boys here in the District tended to get a little out of touch with things back in the hinterlands, and that was something that the boys who *were* back there in the hinterlands just didn't do. Now, wasn't it wonderful that the country had such a rare group of people like us who could talk to both the boys back home and the boys in the District, telling them all to stop fighting with one another because, after all, we were getting along?

Our own little group encompassed only five or six organizations, none of which exercised power in relation to its membership equal, let us say, to the power of a George Meany over the labor movement. Yet if we, as representatives of three distinct segments of higher education, were evolving into a homogeneous clique in the midst of an academic civil war, what must have been happening to comparable cliques of representatives in less divided sectors of our society—between the Department of Agriculture and the American Farm Bureau Federation; between the Food and Drug Administration and the American Pharmaceutical Association; between the Senate Armed Services Committee and the Defense Department?

Get the picture?

Today's social scientists tell us that America is a pluralistic society in which the variety of its interests wield political power through nationally based voluntary associations. These associations, they say, have rendered traditional forms of party organization irrelevant. They have used the need for lines of access between local communities and the national government. They have created alternatives to class conflict by providing opportunities for any group within the "arena" to get what it wants.

Having served as an officer of one such association for two years and observed several others on a local level, I have concluded precisely the opposite. No national organization that I can name fully represents its members. Some do not even *attempt* to represent their members. Moreover, the system places such serious limits on the demands that a group can make that it must throw out most of its fundamental goals—its best goals, at that—even before it reaches a bargaining table. NSA eventually chose to buck the establishment altogether; today, it is virtually bankrupt. In Massachusetts, the Welfare Rights Organization tried to play within the "rules of the game," but as a lobby for welfare recipients, it, too, was squashed.

To gain power in this country you must convert from what you want to believe to what you have to believe. There is nothing pluralistic about it.

III. TECHNOLOGY AND NEW INSTITUTIONS, OR THE COOL SCHOOLS

For a third group, to seek either equality or power within the framework of existing institutions is to invite defeat. They agree, basically, with the substance of the analysis that I provided (in Chapter 4)—that the deficiencies of our system reflect, largely, its absorption in only one task, namely, the extraction of the wealth of nature through the development of an expanding technological machine. They, too, argue that the inequalities between the classes about which the electoral politicians complain are a function of a meritocracy of the "technically" skilled, that it has been the large bureaucracy, the corporation, the civil service that has destroyed the political power of communities. Therefore, they conclude, the only hope for sane men today is the creation of new institutions—counter institutions—that might emphasize what they say are the values that the technological state denies: personal exploration, self-expression, intimacy, and growth.

One need only examine the classifieds of an underground newspaper to see how extensive the movement to create new institutions has become. It includes food stores; health clinics; theatres; law communes; city planning agencies; child-care centers. There are cooperatives of every description—some that support themselves through shared work in the country, others that function simply as centers of living in the city. Every branch of the media has spawned its counterbranch: The underground film challenges Hollywood; the cable television production company awaits the day when it can perform opposite Johnny Carson; and the underground newspaper itself seeks a permanent place as an alternative to the Associated Press and the *New York Times.*

Often, however, the counter institutions find it impossible to rescue themselves from the premises of the system that they are attempting to replace. This has proven particularly true in the field which has spawned the greatest number of new alternatives: education. While the Movements to change existing high schools and colleges have focused attention more and more on the role of education in the society as a whole, the new schools have chosen merely to reform the learning process. The gap between critique and program could not be wider, but even the reformers themselves frequently don't notice.

It is not difficult to get angry at the American educational system. Put yourself in the place of the average high school student. In class, he is given a standard set of assignments, a standard set of tests, of readings. He is asked to learn these, generally by rote. The teacher reiterates the reading in his or her lectures. There is little class discussion, and what discussion there is revolves around questions that only the teacher is entitled to answer. Young people with a desire to ask new questions, to challenge the teacher, to engage in a different kind of discussion, are not encouraged. Often, the high school teacher herself, given her own acceptance of the predominant system of values, cannot cope with serious questions.

So the student tries to find enrichment outside of class. Here, too, he faces difficult choices. If he takes the institution of "school" seriously, he must learn to make do with a student government that has no inherent power, with a student newspaper that is subject to censorship, with student organizations that offer little challenge to creativity, intellect, or ingenuity. He intuitively represses any desire to change his surroundings, and when he asks for the most minimal of changes, he makes sure to be as deferential, humble, and "responsible" as possible. And if he wants to succeed, he learns to accept the school's standards of success. How many high schools can you name that give awards to the most talented musician, to the best writer, to the most committed to social and political action, to the most challenging intellectuals? Not many. The rewards lie in cheerleading, the athletic field, in picking up papers around the hall, and in being a "good guy."

Are colleges any different? Somewhat, but not enough. Young people are demanding help in the search for justice; the university provides none. Its goal, rather, is to encourage students to understand "things as they are"; to help them, in Edgar Friedenberg's formulation, "stand aside from their present experience;" to prepare them to quantify, to order, and to systematize the phenomena of our world in order that they might later exploit its presumed abundance with greater efficiency.

The university's ideal man is, as Friedenberg suggests in another connection,[21] Gene in John Knowles' *A Separate Peace*—that competent analyst of today's problems, tolerant of mild deviation from the norm, skilled in the techniques of scientific investigation, contemplative in spirit and style, moderately liberal in politics, blessed with a balanced temperament in argument, committed to rational persuasion, fully prepared to assume a high position in one of the new industrial state's finest corporations, or in one of its most important government agencies. He is the student-government representative who sees the need for a new department in Afro-American Studies, but not the need to take over a building to get it. He is the professor whose periodic disagreements with the university president do not interfere with a genuine respect for the man and concern for his problems. He's no theorist; as he will tell you. He's a researcher; he's a pragmatist; he's a doer.[22]

The academics tell us that they are committed to truth, but a closer examination reveals that it is only one kind of truth that they respect—the "objective" truth, the truth, as Friedenberg puts, it, that "consists primarily of what all honest and technically qualified observers can agree on":

> *The essence of scientific truth is that it as general as possible. The test of it is that it works in the same way no matter who is looking at it, assuming a certain minimum of intelligence and competence . . . Yet, all this has a Gresham's Law type of effect for empirical knowledge, is in some ways, worse knowledge and cheaper knowledge than the kind it replaces. Its very scorn of inwardness and subjectivity makes it, by definition, finally unconvincing; one is not even allowed to raise the question of conviction about it—to doubt that which has been, for all practical purposes, proved.*

" 'One can be practical even in Hell,' says Lavinia in *The Cocktail Party,*" Friedenberg recalls. "One can be practical *especially* in Hell. Indeed, there is nothing else left to be."

How can an institution that conceives its mission in such a manner possibly assist young people in a search for justice?

The university is unwilling to subject its own behavior to the test of justice. Student movements demand not simply "power" but "power to do what is right." They insist that a commitment to moral excellence govern every area of academic life: research grants, investments, recruitment, relationships with government agencies, extramural housing projects in the ghetto, admissions, curriculum. They find it strange that a college president who lauds student efforts to combat racism in the South becomes furious

when these same students attack as racist, too, a university building program designed to tear down sixteen square blocks of a
low-income area without providing new homes for the people
who live there, or a university portfolio that includes major investments in South Africa. The students feel that if the president is a
morally sensitive man, he will want them to raise these kinds of
considerations since so few people in the university, and even
fewer outside it, seem to be raising them.

Yet the leaders of the academy do not respond. "Why, we've got
a job to do," says the President, "turning out doctors, and lawyers,
and engineers. If we spent all our time in this dialogue business,
we'd never get anything done." "Students don't understand how
to invest money," says the dean, "and we don't have time to train
them." The professors charge that the students are trying to
"politicize" the university; that political conflict will damage the
scholarly pursuits in which the faculty is supposed to be engaged.
Then they write hundreds of scholarly articles on student movements from the beginning of time to prove it! The university begs
for the "tolerance" of its students, but to the undergraduates, it is
the university that has become intolerant—intolerant of conflict,
intolerant of the exacting moral commitments that the young
people have made, intolerant of any idea that cannot be proved
through "empirical" investigation. "Value judgments" in a university are "matters of your own personal opinion," until your personal opinion conflicts with that of the university.

Indeed, the university is not even *structured* to cope with the
compicated problems of justice with which the students are grappling. Look at the system's requirements. The commitment that
an undergraduate is supposed to make is that he will accumulate
between 116 and 128 "hours," divided into 2, 3, or 4 "subject"
units, each of which is subject to the control of a given professor.
The'total of which "hours," when balanced with a concentration
of several units into one "area," is called an education. A university
hardly cares how the student "breaks" his hours up as long as he
has "enough" in his "area," and "enough" to graduate. Neither the
university nor its professors are concerned with what happens to
the student outside of those blocks of time provided the student
keeps to himself and, most important, "away from activities that
disrupt the critical functioning of the university." So where, in the
midst of all this blocking, does a young person find help—either
from his professors, or even from his friends—in exploring the
most difficult questions of all, the questions of dignity and meaning
in human life?

Higher education has disfigured beyond recognition most of the
courses that concern themselves with the problems of justice.
Today, political scientists treat political theory as little more than

a quaint diversion for a few specialists. Only a handful of sociologists like Alvin Gouldner have expressed dismay that the ideas of the "good," the "true," and the "beautiful" are missing from both positivist and Marxist sociological theory. Only the assaults of the New Left have brought a few courses in "ethics" back to the philosophy departments. After all, say the empiricists, can "most qualified observers" agree, beyond any doubt, on the components of a good society? Why, then, even discuss it? Yet these same academics complain that it is the young people who have "lost a sense of history, a respect for the wisdom of the past."

The university has provided only reluctant support, if any at all, to student movements that have addressed themselves to the problems of justice in the society as a whole. Today it is specious of academic leaders to claim for the youth revolt because it is happening on their campuses. Would a czar take credit for the Bolsheviks? The sources of youth revolution did not begin on the campus; they began off the campus, as we have seen, in small communities in the South, in the urban ghettoes of the North, in the earliest marches against the war in Vietnam, which suggested to a new generation that the world was not all that their leaders had made it out to be. When they returned to the university, asking assistance in grappling with the problems that they had encountered, the professors ignored them, saying that their concerns were not relevant to the "true" concerns of the academy; that it was not the "function" of a college to explore "what should be"; that the world of action was somehow less pure, less noble, than the world of thought. Today, to forestall local revolutions, spokesmen for higher education would like to forget these words of the sixties, yet there are too many of us who cannot forget them, who heard them too many times to wish them away.

No, the educational system has failed, from top to bottom. It has not just lost its authority, it has abdicated its authority by turning its back on the virtues upon which authority in a decent society should depend—idealism, loyalty, and social justice. Radicals and reformers have begged the university to exercise this sort of authority, but they have refused. They are too much enmeshed in the "practical" things to care.

What have the various free schools provided as a satisfactory alternative, however?

Again, the answer is mixed. Some schools—particularly at the elementary level—have defined their function as offering new challenges to the young, and to the extent that they do so, they succeed quite well. Others, however, claim that they are combating alienation by releasing their students from the imposed "restraints" of *all* authority. This tends to be the pattern of many free high schools and free universities. It always results in disaster, and for psychological reasons that are easy to understand.

On an elementary school level, the "open classroom" makes an eminent amount of sense. A child's eyes are just coming into focus. He or she is just testing his powers. Every phenomena of the natural and social environment is a source of endless mystery, of endless curiosity. He darts from one object to another, testing himself, flexing his physical and intellectual muscle. The "open classroom" responds to this energy in a way that the traditional classroom, with its enclosed square of desks and chairs, its barren walls, its podium from which a cardboard teacher delivers the "Word" at regular intervals, simply cannot. At one end of a wall, there are plants; at another, there are building blocks; at another, there is a large map of the world. Every crevice seems to beckon with a new surprise. The children respond.

But when educational reformers at the high school and college level attempt to tell students to "do your thing" without further comment, the effect is quite the opposite. "What do you want to talk about today?" the teacher asks. Or, if the course takes place in a free university, "How do we *really* want to develop ourselves today?" The class sits, sullen, not sure of what to say. "Well, I don't know," someone offers. "I sort of thought I'd like to do something about imperialism." More silence. "Yeah, that's groovy," someone else agrees. After a few such sessions, most students conclude that they don't know *what* they want to do, and, lacking assistance from anyone in the class—which, by this time, has broken up into several "independent study" teams on the premise that seven directionless groups are better than one—they don't do anything at all, Then, at the end of the course, the students participate in an evaluation session in which they try to determine what went wrong.

The reason for the failure of this sort of self-direction is simple. A child needs only a minimal amount of external stimulation to exite his interest because to him the world itself is an endless source of fascination. This was the essence of Rousseau's case in *Emile* for taking an infant out in the woods—not that the infant would be "good" but that he would be powerless to achieve everything that he desired. He would try to climb a tree; he would fall. He would run among the rocks; they would skin his knee. Nature would show him that even in "freedom" he was a limited being, subject to the harsh disciplines of a circumscribed universe.

Rousseau understood well, however, that once a child grew older—once he gained a sense of power over the material world —he would need great, exacting challenges in order to feel the same sense of mystery and awe that nature imposed upon his early life. He contended:[23]

> To know good is not to love it. This knowledge is not innate in man; but as soon as his reason leads him to perceive it, his conscience impels him to love it; it is this feeling which is innate. . . . Conscience! Conscience! Divine instinct, immortal voice from heaven; sure guide for a creature ignorant and finite indeed, yet intelligent and free; infallible judge of good and evil, making man like to God! In thee consists the excellence of man's nature and the morality of his actions; apart from thee, I find nothing to myself to raise me above the beasts—nothing but the sad privilege of wandering from error to another, by the help of an unbridled understanding and a reason which knows no principle.

Most dissatisfied students make similar statements. They do not fight all authority, they fight illegitimate authority—authority that demands that they pursue tedious, secondary questions in human affairs as if they were primary, while ignoring the interesting questions altogether. They are, in fact, demanding a higher form of authority. They are asking the assistance of people who are prepared to exercise self-discipline, talent, energy, skill, commitment to the task of uncovering something of the ideal universe about which knowledge of "things as they are" provides no useful answers. Their heroes are not those who come to them with a pitiable plea to "tell us what you want," not those who smother them in sanctimonious appeals to "express yourselves," but those with a vision, a willingness to reveal it, and a strategy by which it might be realized.

Educational reformers often claim that "autonomy" fosters "creativity," but creative artists generally demand higher forms of authority as well. Take, for example, the problems of becoming a jazz musician—an area with which I have some minor familiarity. Jazz is everything that the "free school" proponents say they want to be: improvisatory, soulful, spontaneous, and "expressive of inner being." To listen to Billy Holliday, or to sit through a Bill Evans concert, or to hear any one of several Miles Davis albums is, for those who dig jazz, to undergo a cathartic experience.

But to play jazz, one requires an image of what a good jazz musician is supposed to be. An aspiring jazz musician spends long hours listening to records of other musicians, and he spends long nights "sessioning" with his friends. He imitates an idol, often, until he can evolve a style of his own—just as Dizzy Gillespie, in his early days, borrowed heavily from Roy Eldridge, and Miles Davis borrowed heavily from Charlie Parker. The agony of the medium, in fact, lies in the artist's continuing inability to translate the sounds that weave in and out of his consciousness into real musical notes—an agony that drives him to practice scales, chords, progressions; to learn the structure of music theory; and to play from morning to night. Tell a jazz musician that the free expression of his "soul" has evolved independently of the forces that have excited it, that his music entails little more than a release of "natural feelings" exploding in all directions, and he will tell you that you don't know what you're talking about.

Thus, the free school often responds to this quest for legitimate leadership no more satisfactorily than does the multiversity that leaves students alone to "do what you want, we won't stop you." The reformer's intentions may be honorable—not to impose his "thing" on the fertile minds of youth. Yet if the assumption of the teacher is that each person's private "thing" is exclusively his and that any effort on the part of one person to encourage, to stimulate, even to make demands upon another is necessarily an imposition, then he is making a comment to the students on his own capacity to share dreams, not on their capacity to direct their own lives.

Indeed, we must conclude that the "free university" has not replaced liberalism, it merely has applied its basic proposition—that people are and always shall be independent—to a new area of the human personality, the emotions. In the nineteenth century, John Stuart Mill urged his countrymen to accept free speech not on grounds that censorship destroyed the ability of part of the community to contribute to the community as a whole but on grounds that intellectuals like himself might gain the private freedom to criticize society[24] In the first half of the twentieth century, liberals fought so that private citizens could protect themselves against concentrations of power in the hands of large corporations. Now, as the twentieth century moves toward the twenty-first, a few liberals, in the name of radicalism, have evolved a new right for private men—the right to feel—and they have pledged to battle a corporation system that denies this right.

Like the right to speak, however, and even the right to control your own labor, the right to feel is meaningless unless there are objects within the society to which feelings can be directed. To give people the right to feel in a community that provides no channels through which feelings can gain the stature of creative expressions is to ring the bell for Pavlov's dog without ever feeding him. Poor dog. He just sits there—drooling.

IV. THE DREARY CONCLUSION

It is clear that each of the strategies for coping with America's problems has failed. Electoral politics has not been able to effect a redistribution of the wealth; community organizing has not won the sort of power for people that gives them lasting control over their destinies; counterinstitutions have hardly overthrown technology, or even provided a satisfactory alternative to the system of values that it fosters.

Nor can we say that by rearranging these strategies, the movements would be any more effective in achieving their goals. Neither community organizing nor the construction of counterinstitutions as presently conceived is going to redistribute wealth, at least not on a large scale. On this point, the electoral politicians are absolutely correct. Nor, however, within the existing framework of electoral politics, is running for office going to give people a substantive feeling of power over the direction in which the country is moving, or even over the affairs of their own local communities. There is no reason to assume, finally, that either a candidate for the Seante or a community organizer is going to care much about creating a new life life style to replace corporatism, at least not as an end in itself. Ultimately, one or the other of them, operating within our current system of priorities, is going to have to insist on cooperation with an existing technocratic institution in order to obtain the material rewards that it offers.

Indeed, the attempts that we have seen to combine strategies, or to make one strategy work for all objectives, should warn us of limits of available strategies for reform. Ralph Nader's Center for the Study of Responsive Law is a good example. Nader has done some extraordinarily effective work as the nation's ombundsman for consumer protection. He has challenged government agencies to enforce existing laws with greater precision than anyone in the country. He has provided useful work for hundreds of talented professionals who might otherwise be stuck in the system or, alternatively, outside of the system wondering what to do.

Yet most people observe Nader; they do not participate in his operation. His is, essentially, a giant law firm with a plantiff labeled "the American people," with a defendant called "the federal bureaucracy, and a judge called the "Congress and the Executive Branch of the United States." He has a large legal staff. His research into the legal basis of our complaints is impeccable. He dazzles the judge both with his analysis of the law and with the evidence that it has not been enforced. He reports to us as to his arguments, making it clear that lawyers only can present cases, not make the final decisions. We applaud Mr. Nader; we are thankful for his victories. Then we go back to whatever else we were doing.

A more ambitious attempt to solve all of America's problems is equally inadequate. I am referring to John Gardner's "Common Cause." Gardner's written work, of course, does allude to many of the problems which I have tried to identify in this book, although he and Eric Hoffer seem to be engaged in a competition to produce the best aphorism of the decade. He writes:

> As things stand now, modern man believes—at least with half his mind —that his institutions can accomplish just about anything . . . To my mind there is an appealing (or appalling) innocence to that view. I have had ample opportunity to observe the diverse institutions of this society —the colleges and universities, the military services, the business corporations, foundations, professions, government agencies and so on. And I must report that even excellent institutions run by excellent human beings are inherently sluggish, not hungry for innovation, not quick to respond to human need, not eager to reshape themselves to meet the challenge of the times.

Yet how does one participate in Common Cause? How does it affect the life of either the ghetto resident in Roxbury or the working-man in Gary, Indiana, or the student at the University of Michigan? Does it give anyone a feeling of participation in the effort to rebuild our schools, or to transform our welfare system, or to convert our communities into exciting environments for work and growth? Gardner has developed an analysis of our system that suggests that it needs reconstruction from the bottom up, reflecting a change of attitude and behavior on the part of citizens in all walks of life, involving nothing less than a redefinition of our national purposes. Then he has created a top-down, nonparticipatory, pay-$15-and-watch-me-tell-the-House-of-Representatives-what-it-ought-to-be-doing organization to achieve this objective. Common Cause, doubtless, will perform useful work. It will even given discontented liberals a feeling that they have contributed to something on "the right side of things." Yet it will neither produce the transformation that Gardner himself says he seeks nor will it give the people over a period of time, the feeling that they have found a new vehicle through which to express their discontent. It has developed no mechanisms to achieve this objective; it has no intention of doing so.

A third attempt to create a coherent alternative for America shows limited signs of success, but has yet to prove itself, either: the effort to develop counter communities around university towns like Cambridge and Berkeley that provide centers of living for young radicals as well as a base from which they can organize their assaults on existing institutions. The recent success of a radical slate in elections for the Berkeley City Council tells us that the overall strategy for community control on the West Coast is proceeding apace. In Boston, radicals have begun to take over whole neighborhoods—creating food co-ops, underground newspapers, free stores, hostels, and other new institutions. They have embarked on campaigns that address themselves to the immediate problems the poor people of a city experience: substandard housing, inadequate health facilities, harassment by police, and unequal treatment by the courts.

To the extent that a counter community provides support for a variety of activities, to the extent that it fosters atmosphere within which people can engage in a collective search for justice, it comes closest to meeting the needs that we face in this period than any of the strategies attempted thus far. Unfortunately, much of the imagery surrounding the countercommunity movement, much of its explicit ideology, vitiates its intent.

The communities, for example, see themselves as "new," part of the "vanguard," moving into the future. The assumption is true to the spirit of the Enlightenment, of course, postulating that what is new must be better than what is old. It also meets a basic need in the young people of any generation to feel that their world is somehow ungoverned by the tired principles of the past. In our culture, this instinct is reinforced beyond all reasonable proportions, but one suspects that even in primitive tribes committed to the preservation of the ways of the forefathers, a few people took pride in weaving their baskets just a bit differently from the existing models.

The problem is that the communities are not new. The Puritans shared with one another toward a common pursuit. The American democrats organized Western towns largely on the basis of the principles that the countercommunities today are trying to popularize. The nineteenth-century Utopian Socialist movement—which argued for the creation of agrarian communes throughout the country—was so influential that in 1823, Robert Owen, one of its leading spokesmen, actually addressed both houses of Congress, outlining his plans. (Could you imagine Ray Mungo addressing a joint session of Congress today?) Nathaniel Hawthorne devoted one of his four novels—*The Blithedale Romance*—exclusively to explaining why he did not agree with what Utopians were trying to do. Therefore, the assumption that the "countersocieties" are new simply is wrong and will offend anyone whose ancestors lived in a cooperative, tried to hold together an extended family, or generally tried to preserve the life of the frontier.

When the emphasis on "newness" gives way to a second emphasis, moreover—to creating an "erotic" culture for its own sake—the counterculture becomes downright counterproductive. Again, the thrust is perfectly reasonable, given the premises that govern the country as a whole. If we learn, in a technological age, that the moralities that people hold are inherently private, that the extent to which we are good reflects the ways in which we flaunt our libidinal energies, then a movement that emphasizes its capacity to release emotions and to project flamboyant patterns of dress is merely putting into practice a slightly different version of what other people preach.

Yet for any movement, new or old, to assert that it is "just" because it is learning how to feel is foolish. No one who goes to church will accept such an argument. Whether honest or hypocritical in his beliefs, he will say that justice has to do with deeds not merely thoughts, clothes, and pleasant words. Those who feel that they are "making the system work" on the principles of welfare liberalism would be able, in this case, to present a few cogent arguments as well. They would point out that a cult of "feeling" does nothing to create new wealth, nor does it encourage a rational distribution of existing wealth.

Therefore, when they identify a new style with a new morality, when the new morality becomes morality itself, the countercommunities sacrifice their claim to any higher morality at all. It is sad, in a way, because the instincts that have driven the revolutionaries into new communities have been sound ones. They are undertaking, more than any other group in the middle-class, the sort of commitment that the country will need to revitalize itself. Yet if the process is encouraging, the content often is not. The "countercommunities" have a long way to go before they prove a satisfactory alternative, even for many in the new generation.

The conclusion is unavoidable: The system not only controls those who accept what it is trying to do, it destroys anyone who attempts to oppose it. An electoral reformer begins by calling for a "fundamental reversal of priorities" only to end up by pleading for "stability and mutual understanding." An organizer rallies the people around the flag of justice only to elevate militancy in pursuit of immediate benefits as a moral end in itself. A counterculture that defines itself as "revolutionary" ends up flaunting its ability to feel without reference to the hopes that aroused its feelings in the first place.

No wonder the mass of silent and not-so-silent Americans are unhappy. Here, they are looking for a sense of belonging, for something that will give them a feeling of participation in a collective effort for mutual growth. Here, they feel that the best traditions of their native land are dying. Yet all the movements that might provide more than the bread and circuses of establishment politics have chosen to offer bread and circuses as well. James Baldwin once said that the various sides of a culture mirror one another. At this point, the refracting images are becoming grotesque, like those on the walls of an amusement park. Yet no one seems capable of escaping their logic.

REFERENCES

1. Robert Merton, "Manifest and Latent Functions," *Social Theory and Social Structure* (New York, Free Press, 1957), see especially pp. 61–82.
2. William Riordon, *Plunkitt of Tammany Hall* (New York, E.P. Dutton & Co., Inc., 1963), p. 3.
3. Peter Finley Dunne, "Mr. Dooley on Why Rayformers Fail," in Edward Banfield, *Urban Government* (New York, Free Press, 1969), p. 236.
4. Riordon, *op. cit.*, pp. 47, 25, 47, 50.
5. *Ibid.*, p. 82.
6. *Ibid.*, p. 28.
7. *Ibid.*, p. 31–32.
8. Eric Goldman, *Rendezvous with Destiny* (New York, Vintage, 1955), p. 62.
9. Wilson Carey McWilliams, *The Idea of Fraternity in American Politics*, ms., p. 178.
10. Tom Hayden, *Rebellion and Repression* (New York, Meridian Press, 1969), p. 22.
11. Paul Cowan, *The Making of an Un-American* (New York, Viking, 1970), p. 10.
12. Perry W. Weed, "Second Thoughts on Mayor Daley," *Saturday Review*, April 24, 1971, p. 29.
13. Riordin, *op. cit.*, p. 17.
14. Joseph Lyford, *The Airtight Cage*, reprinted in Banfield, *op. cit.*, p. 402.
15. Theodore Lowi, *The End of Liberalism* (New York, W.W. Norton, 1969), p. 85.
16. Lon Fuller, *The Morality of Law* (New Haven, Yale University Press, 1963), p. 39.
17. Norm Fruchter, "Mississippi: Notes on SNCC," in Massimo Teodori, *The New Left: A Documentary History*, p. 112.
18. James S. Turner, *The Chemical Feast* (New York, Grossman, 1970), pp. 34–35.
19. John C. Esposito, *Vanishing Air* (New York, Grossman, 1970), pp. 120–21.
20. Edward F. Fox, Robert C. Fellmuth, John E. Shulz, *Nader's Raiders* (N.Y., Grove Press, 1970), pp. 57.
21. See Edgar Z. Friedenberg, *The Dignity of Youth and Other Atavisms* (Boston, Beacon, 1965), pp. 5–7.
22. *Ibid.*, "Truth, Upper, Middle, and Lower," pp. 28, 31. See also, Edward Schwartz, "The New University," in Harold Hodgkinson and Myron B. Bloy, Jr., (San Francisco, Jossey-Bass, 1971), pp. 127–152.

23. Jean Jacques Rosseau, *Emile* (Cambridge, England, Everyman, 1966), pp. 254–255.
24. Isaiah Berlin, *Four Essays on Liberty* (London, Oxford University Press, 1969), pp. 196–99.
25. John Gardner, *No Easy Victories* (New York, Harper Colophon Books, 1968), p. 2.

Toward a
Movement
for Justice

6 What, then, is wrong? Do we experience simply a failure of national leadership? Are we victims of the manipulations of an elite? Does our problem lie in a breakdown of our institutions? Are we entering into the final stage of the decay of capitalism, the stage preceding the glorious revolution? I suspect that a case could be made for any one of these theories, and for all of them put together.

Yet our basic problem is more serious, reflecting our view of human nature itself. We are victims of our own tawdry images of man. Look at the choices we face. The establishment says, "Man is basically evil, selfish, private. Government, therefore, must try to buy off every group with goods and services to prevent them from making demands that will disrupt the stability of the system as a whole." The new liberal says, "Man is basically good, but, oh my, why is he behaving so badly toward his fellows? We need a rebirth of love and understanding among our people and leaders who will keep saying so over and over again until it happens." The revolutionary says, "Man is inherently evil in this society, but in a new society that we will create, he will be almost perfect. Therefore, we must destroy all existing institutions so that the inherent virtue of the new order can emerge."

Nor are images that socialism offers us much better. Some socialists do assert the primacy of certain ideals—justice, equality, brotherhood—and they argue that the capitalist system has made it impossible for people to pursue them. Then, however, they ask us to submit to an authoritarian state in which an elite will exercise absolute control until we are "ready" to live by the correct rules. An alternative within socialism, presented by the social democrats, argues exactly the opposite. This is the view that says, in one form or another, "We must respect the natural evolution of history and society in order to remain true to the preferences of human beings as they are. We have faith that history itself will transform people into what we think they ought to be." Usually, proponents of this position spend their time writing long articles describing what is wrong with society, only to balance them with equally long articles attacking those who grow overly "impatient" or militant in their efforts to change it.

Both liberalism and socialism, finally, contend that man's relationship to the economic order—to how a society allocates its scarce resources—is the relationship that governs his life. The establishment tells us that the "people vote their pocketbooks," and as long as a national administration maintains existing levels of purchasing power, it can remain in office. The socialists insist that people "want to control their own work," defined always independently of the assumptions of any specific culture within which "work" is taking place. Therefore, in socialist theory, the revolt of the "working" class against the rulers becomes the ultimate route to salvation, even though the revolution never seems to come, and when it does, it never comes for the right reasons.

For many of the new radical movements, however—of poor people, of "nonideological" young people, of frustrated working people—none of these images seems satisfactory. It is not the "objective economic relationships" between the "forces of production" and the "social relations of production" that determine the interests of a citizen, they say, but the relative importance that specific societies assign to their various goals. In 1957, for example, in response to the launching of Sputnik, the United States decided that its scientists had been undervalued. Therefore, every institution—the schools, the corporations, the government—was asked to place greater emphasis in their programs on the importance of technology to man. To be sure, as part of the campaign, businesses did raise the salaries of their scientists and engineers, but this was only part of it. Everywhere people were asked to determine whether they were doing their part to contribute to the space race with the Soviet Union. It did not take long before those who were not concerned about science became defensive about their unconcern. The standards of citizenship had changed and the private interests of citizens had adjusted accordingly.

Take another example, one that addresses itself directly to the question of materialism, namely, the demands that unions make for higher wages. It is common knowledge that these are never determined purely on the basis of the "objective" needs of the workers. They are determined on the basis of what workers think they deserve. If the firemen have just received raises of $2.10 per hour from a city, the policemen will be sure to demand just as much. The railroad engineers will insist on pay comparable to that received by engineers in other sectors of the transportation industry. If a General Electric executive reports that the profits of its stockholders have remained constant during a given year, the International Electrical Workers' Union makes certain that the profits of its members also have remained constant during the year. Again, the standards of society determine the interests of its private citizens.

Or examine critical passages from three speeches, all central to movements for "economic betterment" in the pasy eighty years: William Jennings Bryan's "Cross of Gold" speech; Eugene V. Debs' appeal for clemency at his trial; Martin Luther King's "I Have a Dream" address to the March on Washington in 1963:

> It is the issue of 1776 over again. Our ancestors, when but three millions in number, had the courage to declare their political independence of every other nation; shall we, their descendents, when we have grown to seventy, declare that we are less independent than our forefathers? No, my friends, that will never be the verdict of our people. (Bryan)[1]

> I am thinking this morning of the men in the mills and factories; of the men in the mines and on the railroads. I am thinking of the women who for a paltry wage are compelled to work out their barren lives; of the little children who in this system are robbed of their childhood and in their tender years are seized in the remorseless grasp of Mammon and forced into the industrial dungeons, there to feed the monster machines while they themselves are being starved and stunted. . . . I see them dwarfed and diseased and their little lives broken and blasted in this high noon of our twentieth century Christian civilization. Money is still so much more important than the flesh and blood of childhood. (Debs)[2]

> Five score years ago, a great American, in whose symbolic shadow we stand today, signed the Emancipation Proclamation. This momentous decree came as a great beacon of light and had been seared in the flames of withering injustice. It came as the joyous daybreak to end the long night of captivity. But one hundred years later, the Negro is still not free . . . (King)[3]

Do these speeches appeal to man the acquisitor? Do they beg us to behave rationally in the face of the injustices of society? Do they ask us to show compassion for one another as an end in itself or to revolt for the sheer glory of revolution? They do none of these things. They ask us, rather, to take a hard look at our commitment to our fundamental principles as a people.

What, then, is the self-interest served by the social dynamic which I have just described? It can be summed up in one word—

"Dignity," the sense of being important to yourself and others; the spirit that enables one to encounter the obstacles of life without being broken; the feeling that one counts for something as a human being. It was dignity that the Puritans sought in attempting to live up to the teachings of the Bible. It was the dignity which the anti-Federalists claimed in arguing:[4]

> The knowledge necessary for a representative of a free people not only comprehends extensive political and commercial information, such as is acquired by men of refined education who have leisure to attain to high degrees of improvement, it should also comprehend that kind of acquaintance with the common concerns and occupations of the people, which men of the middling class of life are in general more competent to than those of the superior class.

It was the dignity of the people that Andrew Jackson affirmed against the supporters of the national bank; as did the Knights of Labor against the factory-owners; the immigrants against the Yankees; the Populists against the monopolists.

Indeed, we can safely say that it was human dignity that our society sacrificed when it decided that wealth and power could buy life, liberty, and the pursuit of happiness. Our common sense tells us that dignity depends on more than this.

We should be clear, however, as to what it does demand; the ways in which modern society fails to meet this demand; and how we often are forced to respond.

Our dignity depends on the quality of relationships that exist throughout society.

We need a sense of fidelity, that is, we need to have confidence that people will keep their promises to one another. We promise each other happiness in marriage, but are our marriages really happy? We expect the respect of our co-workers, but does any one of them give a damn whether we live or die? Do employers value their employees? Do teachers really respect their students? Do Congressmen work toward the best interests of their districts? Does a President honor his pledges to the people? Whenever we ask ourselves these questions, we are fighting to preserve our dignity, our sense that people and institutions to which we have made commitments will fulfill their commitments to us.

We need to be encouraged to fight for the highest goals that we can imagine. "Can I try it?" an excited child asks when he sees a friend unravel a complicated puzzle. "*Make* something of yourself," a college professor tells an undergraduate who is falling behind in his work. "Ask not what your country can do for you, ask what you can do for your country," a President exhorts his people. "Behold a king shall reign in righteousness, and as for princes, they shall rule in justice," says Isaiah to Israel.[5]. It is dignity that is enhanced when a human being seeks a higher goal, for as he aspires to those things that he values, he places more value on himself.

We need to feel that we possess worth simply because of who we are. We are vulnerable; we know that others are vulnerable as well. We expect compassion, a respect for our limitations in the harsh struggle to survive. "Hath not a Jew eyes?" demands Shylock. "Hath not a Jew hands, organs, dimensions, senses, affections, passions? fed with the same food, hurt with the same weapons, subject to the same diseases, healed by the same means, warmed and cooled by the same winter and summer as a Christian is? If you prick us, do we not bleed? If you tickle us, do we not laugh? If you poison us, do we not die?"[6]

A sense of fidelity, a sense of purpose, a sense of compassion— these are the components of dignity.

A system geared solely to corporate production and private consumption is bound to pervert human dignity by the very nature of its goals.

We cannot afford to make binding commitments to other people. We never know when a job might require that we move to a new place. Gradually, tentativeness in all our relationships— with our friends, with our relatives, within our communities— evolves into a national ethic.

Society perverts our idealism as a people. Most of us do remember the ideals of our past, but can we express them in our communities and factories and offices without someone saying, "Be quiet and do as you're told," or, "You expect too much," or, "Isn't the salary we're paying you enough?" When we raise the banner of justice in politics, are we applauded or are we told not to be so "absolutist"? We bemoan the loss of our dreams; then we forget them entirely. Idealism, we say, is no longer "functional" to our everyday survival.

Modern society lacks compassion for what we are. We are assumed to be invulnerable to harm, to defeat, to emotional trauma. Vulnerability is inefficient, after all. It takes time; it creates waste. Therefore, we are told to reveal our weakenesses only in private moments, when no one is around to see them; or we are encouraged to deny them altogether.

Even our efforts to restore dignity to modern society come to seem tawdry and insufficient.

To preserve loyalty, we end up clinging desperately to the people and things we love. We fight for the survival of the "clan" against everything and everyone else, while rationalizing the worst crimes of "our" people as being "no worse than what anyone else does." Whites prevent blacks from entering their neighborhoods. Blacks insulate themselves from society deliberately even after they are presumably free to enter the rat race on equal terms with others. Young people must develop a youth culture to protect themselves against institutions that lack respect for what they are trying to accomplish. Those who support a President adhere blindly to whatever he says. Patriotism becomes a paper flag stuck to the windshield.

We turn compromise with our ideals into a virtue. Parents almost boast to their children of their lack of political involvement. "*We've* got to work," they say. "When *you've* got to go out and earn your own money, then see if you're ready to change the world." Realism becomes heroism—the heroism of the office bureaucrat who, despite his radical leanings, shields his real beliefs from his boss so that he might make enough money to send his kids to college. Masochism becomes a national pastime, as a worker prides himself on being able to endure the hardships of the factory; the liberal agonizes over "all the mistakes that we have made"; and the revolutionary takes enormous risks in the streets in order to prove that he will do anything for his cause.

Since we cannot find pride in our mutual vulnerability as human beings, we gain satisfaction in asserting our invulnerability to the pain we experience. The ghetto resident refuses to acknowledge that he needs anything from anyone else. The unionist whose real purchasing power has dropped every quarter since 1965 insists that he just wants to be left alone. The bureaucrat learns to control himself. The student learns to keep his cool. A man ain't supposed to cry, we say, and a woman ain't supposed to complain, so we bite our lips and pat ourselves on the back for being able to take it.

In short, we are promised fidelity, idealism, compassion. We experience distrust, resignation, indifference. Yet nothing we do seems to make any difference.

The liberals argue that we can regain our dignity merely by acquiring more goods and services from the productive system as it is.

The socialists tell us that we will regain our dignity when we demand collective ownership of the means of production.

Some within the counterculture claim that we have no chance unless we smash the machines and start all over again.

Yet the major ideologies have failed to address themselves to the anxieties of life as we experience it—to our sense that we no longer trust anyone; to our sense that idealism is no longer respectable;

to our sense that we must hide our weaknesses to preserve our integrity.

Surely we need to take a fresh look at ourselves. For millions of Americans in this country, life is coming to seem like an extended nightmare from which we never wake up. Canada and England and Australia are coming to seem more and more attractive places in which to live.

There is only one vision that corresponds to the basic need for human dignity—the ancient vision of justice. It is the just society, the society that attempts to preserve a balance between what a person wants to do, what he can do, and what he has to do, that fosters the dignity of every one of its citizens.

If, therefore, liberalism has turned the religious image of man on its head—saying that ideals are "superstitions" and merely "relative"; that man can be "naturally good" without them; that the mere exercise of reason can lead us out of the wilderness—we must turn liberalism back on *its* head.

To restore the dignity of the people, we must set as the fundamental objective of the next generation nothing less than the acceptance of justice as the standard against which all issues, all institutions, all politics, must be measured.

There is nothing outlandish in this goal. The Declaration of Independence tells us that our forefathers severed their ties with England when King George proved "deaf to the voice of justice." The Preamble to the United States Constitution tells us that our government was established in order to "form a more perfect union" and to "establish justice," We pledge allegiance to a republic that is supposed to stand for "liberty and justice for all."

Isn't it about time that we began to heed the voice of justice ourselves?

A movement for justice would sharpen the focus, strategy, and tactics of the various movements against injustice that currently dominate the scene. It would render explicit the implicit moral basis of the self-interest demands that we make. It would give us a handle upon which to make demands that have thus far have eluded us.

A movement for justice would address itself to all the major issues affecting our society. It would provide a powerful rationale for efforts to change existing institutions. It would establish a sensible framework within which to discuss the reconstruction of our political system. It would bequeath to the New Left a positive answer to the enduring question: "What do you really want?" Let us examine, therefore, how such a movement might function.

I. REDEFINING THE ISSUES

Liberals view issues as isolated problems to be solved as soon as the experts get enough resources to "handle" them.

Socialists see them as examples of contradictions within the economic system, to be "heightened" in accordance with the dialectic of history.

A movement for justice would treat issues neither as problems nor as objective contradictions but as indignities—as examples of the hardships imposed upon people and groups by an unjust society. It would not use morality merely to dress up self-interest demands; it would use campaigns for immediate interests to demonstrate the importance of morality. Such a movement would insist that every step away from oppression marks a deeper commitment to justice as an end in itself.

Any reader to the Old Testament will understand the strategy. It is the one that God employs in dealing with the Jews on their long march from the oppressions of Egypt to the land of Israel. Yaweh understands that human beings want to know, "What's in it for me?" Consequently, He performs miracles regularly—some that rescue the Israelites from danger; others that punish them for bad behavior. To this day, Jews sing a song, "Dayenu" ("It Would Have Been Enough") at the Passover Seder explaining that had God granted only one of the favors that He bestowed on Moses and Joshua in ancient times, it would have been sufficient to win their allegiance. The point is clear: Jews should be eternally grateful to the Lord and attempt to do as He says. Even now, Jews remain among the more liberal voting blocs in the population.

A movement for justice would apply this principle to its own efforts. It would become sensitive to the precise relationship between private indignity and public justice in every one of its campaigns. It would not simply negate the bad. It would affirm the good.

It would affirm fidelity. Every great revolution has been fought, in some measure, to redeem a broken promise. The United States sought independence from Great Britain only after failing to secure the "Rights of Englishmen" by peaceful petition. The French Revolution occurred only after the reforms promised by the *ancien régime* proved ineffective in solving the problems that they were intended to solve. Liberation movements in the Third World today invariably gain greatest support when ruling elites ignore their own guarantees of self-determination and economic improvement to the people. *A movement for justice, then, would use issues to expand the range of social promises that people take seriously.*

In keeping with its concern for idealism, *a movement for justice would view campaigns to combat specific social problems as opportunities to improve the quality of life in society as a whole.* It would try to show the ways in which an injustice harmed the oppressor as well as the oppressed, the perpetrator as well as the victim. It would challenge the apathetic and the indifferent with a new standard of moral commitment. Its proposals would attempt to project an alternative vision of what life ought to be.

Finally, a movement for justice would use issues to show that human beings need help in pursuing their ideals. It would condemn equally those who insist, "You must leave people alone. They cannot be pressured to change," and those who demand catharsis as the only true test of commitment. It would wage war against technocrats who ask "just a little more time to working things out ourselves" and bureaucrats who want to refer everything to committee. *Every issue, in short, would be an argument for the creation of democratic institutions through which the people themselves might be encouraged to fulfill their highest aspirations for themselves and for their communities.*

It is important to see how these general principles might be applied. Let us examine three critical issues about which the New Left has been concerned: poverty, the environment, and peace.

A. POVERTY

At the moment, the National Welfare Rights Organization (NWRO) remains the most effective organization against poverty to have emerged in the past decade, the mistakes of a few organizers in Massachusetts notwithstanding. In fact, it is among the most effective radical movements of any kind in the country. That welfare recipients of all races, colors, and religious beliefs have been able to unite under one banner, to work together with extraordinary solidarity, and to retain their spirit amidst enormous public opposition should be a lesson to anyone who believes that conflicts between low-income whites and blacks are insurmountable, that the *Lumpenproletariat* can never be a force for social change, or that a people's movement for social reconstruction is impossible to build.

Moreover, NWRO understands that justice depends on fidelity, idealism, and a mechanism of support.

It fights to restore the nation's promises, promises that are broken to poor people on a regular basis.

For years, the organization has been battling to persuade the Department of Health, Education, and Welfare to enforce its own regulations requiring states to raise welfare benefits in accordance with increases in the cost of living. At various points, more than

40 states have violated federal regulations in this area with impunity.

NWRO has been attempting to make welfare recipients aware of special benefit programs available to them in many states, even though such states often cut off the programs once poor people learn about them.

The organization is working to ensure that local school districts obey federal laws stipulating that all poor children in schools with lunch programs should receive their lunches at reduced prices.[7]

In general, NWRO has been trying to make poor people aware that they are entitled to public assistance. Only one out of four people eligible for welfare ever receives it.

NWRO is not afraid to project a vision of an ideal solution to the welfare crisis. As one of its pamphlets puts it:

We believe that every man, woman, and child has the right to live.

The Bureau of Labor Statistics of the U.S. Department of Labor says that a family of four needs at least $6,500 a year for the basic necessities of life, not counting medical care. We call upon the Federal Government to guarantee every American this minimum.

Persons eligible for those benefits should be entitled to free medical care, legal services, and day-care facilities of a high quality where they live.

The system should provide a work incentive permitting recipients to keep 50% of earned income, up to 15% of their grant level.

The organization, in short "is challenging the country to change its priorities from an emphasis on death and destruction to an emphasis on life and peace. . . ."

NWRO, finally, realizes that poor people will never obtain justice from this society unless they organize. Says Welfare Rights staff member Tim Sampson:

The name of the game is organization. You can spend years theorizing, drawing up proposals, making speeches to civic groups, but unless you have some organization behind you, you're never going to get anywhere in this country. Organization is what makes it possible for the poor to get themselves out from under the dominance of middle-class liberals and upper-class reformers, and start making a few demands of their own.

Thus, Welfare Rights has put together a network of state-wide welfare rights organizations across the country.

The promise, the ideal, the mechanism of support—all of these have been critical to the functioning of the NWRO and the movement that it has spawned.

Welfare Rights is doing its part to enlist people in the fight against poverty. Would that other groups in the country were nearly as effective. There is little evidence, for example, that rich liberals in the "New Politics" movement will become half as concerned about poor people as they are about peace. They will hardly welcome the tax increases needed to finance as adequate income maintenance program when cuts in military expenditures prove insufficient to pay for it. The National Board of the Urban Coalition has even balked at endorsing a proposal to increase the inheritance tax.

On what basis, then, might a broad campaign for a guaranteed income of $6,500 per year for a family of four be built?

During the New Deal, one simple demand crystallized public anger at social and economic inequality under a system of *laissez-faire* capitalism—"Share the Wealth". It was this slogan that prepared the public for the welfare system as we know it.

The new industrial state does not *have* a welfare system, however. It *is* a welfare system. As a Welfare Rights pamphlet points out, in 1967, 155 Americans enjoyed incomes of over $200,000 without paying one cent of income tax. In this group of "big welfare" recipients, 25 had incomes of over 1 million dollars. In 1968, moreover, the government provided $6 billion in direct subsidies to private industry; 408 farmers received subsidies of more than $100,000 each; and Senator James Eastland, alone, received over $146,000 for not growing cotton on his plantation in Mississippi.[9]

The evidence is clear: The country needs a new campaign—a campaign to "Redistribute the Welfare."

How could such a campaign be useful to building a movement for justice, however?

First, it could remind older Americans of the social promises of their youth, promises of:

Adequate income for the poor. In 1936, one year following passage of the Social Security Act, Harry Hopkins argued[10]:

> *Intelligent people have long since left behind them the notion that under fullest recovery, and even with improved purchasing power, the unemployed will disappear as dramatically as they made their appearance. Even if they did so disappear, there would remain with us the people who cannot work, or should not, and who have no one to support them. . . . These people cannot be left to fumble their way along alone, to be sent from one vacillating agency to another, given something one month and not the next, with almost nothing at all in the future. For them a security program is the only answer.*

Today, a campaign to redistribute the welfare may be their only hope.

A living wage for working people. Whitney Young reported before he died, "In New York City, the highest-cost city in the country, one out of five jobs in the private sector pays less than $80 per week—what the city welfare department estimates to be its average grant for a family of four."[11] A campaign to redistribute the welfare might force the union movement to start organizing the unorganized again.

A progressive social-insurance program. The present social security tax is 4.0% on the first $7,800," Whitney Young pointed out, "so that the poor man pays social security tax on his entire salary, while the president of the company that employs him may only pay the tax on a tenth of his salary."[12] A campaign to redistribute the welfare would demand that this program be financed out of tax revenues.

An equitable system of taxation. Progressive schemes of taxation, in general, are supposed to restore the relative balance between rich and poor that existed in pre-industrial America. As Herman P. Miller and Roger A. Herriot have reported, however[13]:

> *The distribution of incomes in this country has hardly changed one iota since World War II. The top one percent of the families still receive more than the bottom 10%; the top 5% more than the bottom 40%. . . . Overall, the $50,000 family gave the government no higher proportion of its income than the family with one-tenth as much earning power.*

A campaign to redistribute the welfare would be in the forefront of the fight for tax reform.

A campaign to "Redistribute the Welfare" could challenge society to care about all of its people, not just those engaged in the process of industrial production. Its vision might be sufficiently powerful to unite:

Women who complain that it is impossible to find decent jobs at salaries comparable to men.

Consumer groups that fight to restore the power of the buyer against the power of the large corporation.

The elderly whose plight has been ignored by the rest of society.

The veterans of Vietnam who face the indifference, even hostility, of a country that wants to turn its back on sacrifices they have made.

The handicapped who must rely for support on charity drives that treat them more as a class of subhuman freaks—who nonetheless deserve public sympathy—than as human beings who are, as such, deserving of society's respect.

The artists who have never been given a fair shake by this society.
Human service workers who see what is happening to the people whom society has forgotten.

A campaign to "Redistribute the Welfare," finally, could lend itself to a number of ingenious organizing tactics in its behalf.

Supporters could expose government subsidies to the rich, lampooning such benefits whenever they found them. The California Welfare Rights Organization received national publicity recently for naming Ronald Reagan "Welfare Recipient of the Year" following disclosure of his failure to pay state income taxes in 1970.

Radicals in the "New Politics" movement could revive the tradition of sponsoring "People's Banquets" opposite $100-a-plate fund-raising dinners for the major political parties. In 1968, such banquets included only young people and the poor. Today, they might include working people, women, unemployed professionals, and veterans as well.

Radical lawyers could seize the offensive in uncovering fraud in state and local tax laws, just as conservatives now seek to uncover cheating on welfare.

Housewives and welfare mothers could assemble at employment agencies with their children *en masse* to dramatize the need for day-care facilities at or near places of employment for the children of working women.

Government employees, unskilled workers, and even professionals could picket the headquarters of the A.F.L.-C.I.O., demanding that the labor movement organize the unorganized with greater persistence.

Young people could burn their social security cards to protest the way in which social insurance is financed.

Welfare Rights could sponsor Work Incentive Programs for college graduates, veterans, and professionals unable to find jobs—and announce them in all the papers.

Social workers could expose "United Fund" or "Community Chest" drives for what they are—efforts to extract contributions from working people to support programs for the poor (over which the poor exercise no control) in order to appease the consciences of the rich.

In short, a campaign to redistribute welfare could bring working people and middle Americans to see themselves at the cutting edge of effort to restore equality to the United States. Wide disparities of wealth and power between rich and poor are contrary to the American democratic tradition.

They should be given the chance to say so.

B. ECOLOGY

A movement for justice would sharpen the demand for a balanced ecology.

On the surface, the campaign to clean up the environment seems to have arisen simply in response to growing concern over the pollution of the air, the water, and the land. The dynamic is, in fact, more complicated. Americans always have sought a clean environment. Today, over 70 per cent of the population lives in relatively small cities and towns, each of which guards its prerogatives over zoning, land use, and development with a vengeance. If farmers in the nineteenth century hoped to limit the size of communities, to integrate the processes of life and work, to preserve the quality of the frontier, their descendants in the twentieth century have attempted to preserve a comparable balance between cities and suburbs—expecting opportunity and excitement from the one; peace and quiet from the other.

The renewed concern about the environment, then, emerges in response to the realization that the attempt to achieve these objectives has backfired. People sense a wide gap between what they want out of life and what they actually get.

In the city, they can't breathe.They can't drive without getting caught in an hour-long traffic jam. They can't get on a bus without being packed in with hundreds of others like them, hot and tired, without places to sit. They've got to hold their noses in the subways. They can't afford cabs. They have to wait ten minutes for an elevator. The power fails regularly. The telephones don't work. They can't leave their apartments at night for fear of getting robbed. And, if they're poor, they can't get heat in the winter; fresh air in the summer; decent housing, schools, health facilities, transportation, recreation, and jobs throughout the year.

In the suburbs, they have nothing but their TV sets and an occasional party to keep them occupied. They can't walk out into the street and talk to friends as they once did. Their kids are bored stiff, anxious to get to where the "action" is. They face the constant hassle of traveling back and forth from the city. By the time they arrive home, they're so tired that they have no energy to use their leisure time for anything *but* an evening by the TV set.

In general, they feel powerless to do anything to improve the quality of their lives. The slogan "Stop Pollution" is almost symbolic. Beyond its appeal to eliminate debris, it resonates with the sense that people are being strangled wherever they go. They are suffocating. They want somebody to invent a large electric fan that might drive away the various unpleasant odors, sights, and sounds all at once. In the absence of such an invention, they simply move, either to farms in order to capture the flavor of an earlier American dream or to metropolitan areas in places like Colorado and Vermont, which at least provide a satisfactory compromise between old and new.

Unfortunately, escaping to "new towns" or to rural Arcadia promises only short-term relief. Pollution is a function of our national life style, an outgrowth of our belief that expanding production can solve all problems. As long as the country permits the dominance of such an ethic, its environment will be destroyed. Those who try to flee will find themselves outflanked no less effectively than were the farmers and frontiersmen of the Jeffersonian era. Indeed, the exodus to the wilderness could even accelerate the destruction of the land. As we have seen, the early settlers did not forestall development by migrating; they encouraged it. The entrepreneurs followed them across the country, moving into the areas that they had opened for settlement. When the robber barons finally did come to dominate the frontier, the farmers were unable to fight back.

If the environmentalists in this century are to avoid the tragedy of the last one then they must make a concerted effort to organize movements to rebuild the areas in which people currently are living. Citizens must come to believe that they can cooperate with one another in reshaping their surroundings. They must come to feel, as do many young people, that the pursuit of the vision of a balanced and enriched community—the essence of both ecology and justice—can be as exciting and productive as have been efforts in the past thirty years to fulfill the dream of national wealth and power. Such an undertaking would entail more than merely rebuilding cities. It would require a movement to revive the metropolis as a whole.

Three kinds of campaigns seem appropriate: a campaign to control industrial development; a campaign to replace cars with low-cost means of public transportation; and a campaign to persuade suburbanites to see themselves as residents of a region, as well as of their own local communities.

1.INDUSTRIAL DEVELOPMENT

It is in this area that the environmentalists have made their greatest progress. Residents of Greenwich Village have succeeded in blocking the construction of a lower-Manhattan expressway that would have wiped out many adjoining neighborhoods. In Boston, civic groups have protested successfully the installation of a runway in Logan Airport that would have permitted planes to fly directly over nearby residential areas at low altitudes. Efforts to forestall the laying of an oil pipeline in Alaska, to control the drilling of the oil companies in Florida, and to halt the development of the SST are well-known.

Yet if in their efforts to foster humane patterns of development the environmentalists gain a reputation as opponents of all proposals for development, their efforts will backfire. Unionists who lose jobs because of the termination of projects like the SST are hardly going to be sympathetic to the cause of ecology in the long run. Similarly, many residents of New York City are becoming increasingly annoyed that every effort to construct a badly needed power plant in upstate New York has been blocked. To be sure, conflicts of this sort are inevitable during any transition from one system of social objectives to another. Yet the ecologists can contribute to justice by adhering to a few simple rules derived from the framework of justice.

To ensure fidelity:
Rule 1: Demand that corporations make public all plans for industrial development well in advance of their formal initiation.
Often corporations unveil plans for development without giving community and civic organizations sufficient time to react to them effectively. Environmentalists should be pressing for laws that would require corporations to submit regular reports to the Environmental Protection Agency concerning plans for expansion, such reports to be made available to the public.

In the absence of such a procedure, conservation groups themselves might undertake some form of corporate monitoring, scanning the *Wall Street Journal, Fortune,* and *Business Week* for reports on what industry intends to do next and how different areas of the country will be affected.

To foster idealism:
Rule 2: Always use the case against uncontrolled, destructive industrial growth to build the case for a just, ecologically balanced society.
At every hearing on a proposed highway, or airport, or civic center, or munitions plant, someone says, "This community needs this program if it is to retain its position as one of the truly great cities in the country."
Ecologists should never let such arguments pass without rebuttal. They should affirm the positive values they are trying to preserve: the value of open spaces, of clean air, of parks, of places where children can play, of uncongested streets, of trees and flowers. They should talk about the history of the community in question, the hopes of those who settled in it, and the continuing aspirations of those who wish to remain. They should talk about the early American dream, the dream that people might control the quality of their neighborhoods and communities, setting limits

to the expansion of private wealth and power within them.

They should talk about life itself—what it will be like if in its haste to produce, the country devours the very resources that make a humane use of production possible.

To expand the base of support:

Rule 3: Consider who will foot the bill.

Automobile companies have announced that the consumer will foot the bill for the addition of safety features and anti-pollution devices demanded by consumer groups and environmentalists. If the environmentalists permit every industry to impose a hidden anti-pollution sales tax in the form of higher prices, then the consumers will turn against them. To prevent this, they should be demanding that stockholders accept responsibility for ensuring that their companies are adhering to acceptable standards of health and safety—even if it means lower profit. Ralph Nader's "Campaign to Make GM Responsible" and Saul Alinsky's "Proxies for People" corporate proxy campaigns are obviously two of the most important innovations that should be expanded and strengthened in coming years.

Rule 4: Always be sensitive to the problems generated by ecological unemployment.

Ecological unemployment is joblessness encouraged by the termination of programs deemed harmful to the environment.

An environmentalist who lacks concern for ecological unemployment is no better than a corporation executive who lacks concern for technological unemployment.

In his recent campaign for the Senate in Connecticut, Joe Duffey won the support of a number of local unions, including locals that represented employees of defense plants, despite his advocacy of substantial cuts in military spending. The reason was simple: He talked about conversion.

To duplicate this success, environmentalists should never advocate "terminating" a program; they always should propose the conversion of an industry from one activity to another.

In general, then, environmentalists should look for the hidden opportunity behind every impending disaster. When urban renewal, or an airport, or a highway, or a new factory threatens to wipe out a large area of a city, the residents grow furious. They become extremely conscious of why they value their neighborhoods, why they want to preserve them, and why they feel that the rule of the corporation is unjust. It is, perhaps, the only time when environmentalists who are sensitive to the range of a community needs can gain wide and attentive audiences. They should use the time wisely.

2.From Cars to Public Transportation

Efforts to control industrial development would represent only the first step in a campaign to revive the metropolis. Its second step would be to encourage a lifestyle built around public transportation rather than the automobile:

The reasons are obvious: The automobile congests cities, forcing developers to destroy parks in order to make room for parking lots. It pollutes cities, filling the air with gasoline fumes. It means bedlam wherever people go. It is a killer, among the biggest killers in the country. It is the nation's Number 1 item of conspicuous consumption. Its cost and upkeep are a constant drain on a family's income.

The automobile simply is an inefficient and destructive form of transportation whose use survives in the country only because the people don't know how to fight for an alternative.

Not that alternatives have never been proposed. In *Beyond the Automobile: Reshaping the Transportation Environment* [14]Tabor R. Stone argues forcefully that the nation's widely scattered system of highways and roads—a "random route system," as he describes it—has become woefully inadequate to meet transportation needs. A brief chart that he presents speaks for itself:

The American Transit Association Has Produced the Following Estimates of Carrying Capacities of Single Lanes, Per Hour

Passengers in autos on surface streets	*1,575*
Passengers in autos on elevated highways	*2,025*
Passengers in buses on surface streets	*9,000*
Passengers in streetcars on surface streets	*13,500*
Passengers in streetcars on subways	*20,000*
Passengers in local subway trains	*40,000*
Passengers in express subway trains	*60,000*

From evidence of this nature, Stone concludes that the country must develop the following to meet its transportation needs in the future:

1. A high-speed nonstop rail system between cities;
2. A network of buses and/or subways between cities and suburbs;
3. A system of small buses or mini-trains to commute from homes and offices to bus depots.[15]

Funds are available for such undertakings. State legislatures could use money collected in toll booths to build public transportation systems instead of highways.

The problem lies in organizing a coalition to challenge the automobile companies, the construction companies, and the construction unions that have opposed change in this area.

How might the political forces be coalesced? Again, the framework of justice—the promise, the ideal, and the mechanism of support—suggests several possibilities.

Automobile companies have promised customers safe, convenient, and comfortable transportation to and from work. Obviously, this promise has not been kept. A campaign for public transportation should dramatize the inconveniences:

Drivers should be given a bumper sticker reading, "Aren't you sick of this traffic, too? Support public transportation," for display on their back fenders.

Environmentalists should distribute leaflets to cars at congested intersections reading, "Wouldn't an air-conditioned, clean subway be better than this?"

Student ecology groups in cities should distribute leaflets in public parking lots reading, "You are paying $———per day to park your car here. You would pay only $———per day for public transportation. Support public transportation."

Suburban ecology organizations should urge community newspapers to print articles on the hazards of commuting by car. Petitions for adequate train service to and from the city should circulate throughout the suburbs.

Ecology action organizations should pressure advertising agencies and television networks to sponsor public-service commercials on behalf of public transportation comparable to the American Cancer Society's advertisements against smoking. Automobiles, too, are hazardous to our health.

Stimulating public imagination as to what an ideal transportation system might do for a city should not be difficult. Some cities have already taken small steps in this direction. These should be continued, expanded, and used as part of an overall campaign. For example:

Whenever a city closes off a downtown thoroughfare to traffic —as did New York—it should be sure to record public reactions for use in later efforts to broaden the program.

When a city introduces modern subways or buses to its system —as Boston has—it should purchase advertisements in each subway car pointing out that with decent public transportation all subways and buses could be as comfortable.

Ecology action groups in several cities have sent station wagons throughout metropolitan areas, picking up and delivering hitch-hikers for nothing. Similar services should operate at supermarkets for housewives who have chosen not to bring their cars, or for poor people who do not own them. Drivers can use the opportunity to talk about public transportation with passengers.

National ecology organizations should develop a regular newsletter for distribution to local affiliates, to community newspapers, and to the major networks describing the latest experiments in public transportation. Community organizations concerned with environment should insist that at least one reporter on every local newspaper be willing and able to report on new developments in transportation.

All of these tactics will fail, however, unless environmentalists can build coalitions of disparate organizations to engage in lobbying and political education on behalf of public transportation. Such coalitions might include:

Women's organizations. Housewives lose their cars when their husbands drive to work. Or they have to drive their husbands to the station in the morning. Or they have to drive their small children to school. Wouldn't decent public transportation in cities and suburbs make life somewhat easier for them?

Organizations of and for the elderly. Often the elderly can neither afford automobiles nor drive them. In many cities, public transportation already has become one of their major demands.

Poor people's movements. Welfare recipients, for example, often must return from supermarkets in taxicabs for want of bus lines between shopping centers and their apartments.

High school student governments. At suburban high schools particularly, the use of the parking lot becomes a major political issue between seniors and juniors. Might it not be possible for young people to explore why they need cars in the first place?

The Brotherhood of Teamsters. A truck driver might find his job more pleasant without millions of cars blocking his way.

Railroad and subway workers' unions. Public transportation would mean jobs, prestige, and influence at the bargaining table.

Associations of city planners, architects, and radical engineers. As a matter of principle.

Churches. As a matter of high principle.

The list could go on, but it needn't. It is clear that an impressive number of organizations might unite on behalf of public transportation if the environmentalists were to take the initiative in bringing them together. Such a coalition might be incorporated into a broader coalition to revive the metropolis. The important point is that people cannot hope to make urban living bearable until those who are sick of traffic, noise, and pollution decide to fight for an alternative.

3. Toward a Metropolitan Renaissance

The ultimate goal of a campaign to save metropolitan areas, however, must be to persuade suburbanites to share responsibility for preserving the health of the entire region in which they live. Only a strategy designed to achieve this objective makes sense. The alternative—attempting to bring the middle class back into the city at the expense of ethnic neighborhoods in order to raise the tax base—ends up creating as many problems as it solves. Already, the incidence of drug use among the children of dispossessed immigrant families is staggering.

The suburbanite works in the city; he should support it. Once again, the framework of justice—the promise, the ideal, the mechanism of support—can be put to good use in the effort.

To remind commuters of the promise of the city:
Posters should be put in all commuter trains reading, "If the company where you work moved out of the city, would you move with them? How would your family feel about it? Where you work; where you live—the two go together. Support the City."

Restaurants patronized heavily by suburbanites—coffee shops in the business district as well as ethnic restaurants of various kinds —should give customers a card with their checks reading, "The meal which you have just eaten was made possible by the City of —— Are you giving it your support?"

Museums, theaters, downtown movie houses, night clubs, sporting events, should hand out a similar card.

Stars of local athletic teams should be enlisted in the campaign. One does not need to think very hard to imagine what would happen if the general manager of the New York Mets were to say, "Our guys are getting tired of playing ball for a bunch of people in Westchester County who don't give a damn about the City of New York. Unless the State Legislature comes up with a tax bill that gives this city some cash, and the City itself starts getting tough with pay-nothing commuters, we're going to look elsewhere for a franchise."

Urban movements should protest at civic centers that attract upper-class suburbanites, such as museums and concert halls.

To encourage commuters to consider what decent urban living might be like:
During National Environment Week, or on some comparable occasion, every office and factory in a city should spend part of the

day discussing ways in which the metropolis might be revived. The mayor's office itself might make space available for public meetings and debates.

The city should sponsor "happenings" and concerts in its parks —à la public concerts in Central Park—designed specifically to build support for metropolitan taxation.

Immigrant neighborhoods should receive funds to present festivals showcasing traditional music, art, and food, to impress upon residents of the entire metropolitan area what would be lost were such neighborhoods to vanish.

Advertisements to "save the city" should show the familiar attractions—landmarks, places of historical interest, entertainment centers—that have become inaccessible to suburbanites because of urban deterioration.

Urban movements should urge residents throughout a city to get together, neighborhood by neighborhood, to determine their immediate needs. Planners then could try to integrate the suggestions into a coherent model of a livable city, to be publicized in local magazines and newspapers.

Finally, to build regional coalitions that might fight for metropolitan survival:

Efforts should be made to expand the constituency of people who think in regional, rather than purely local terms, by encouraging social, civic, and fraternal groups to meet regularly on a regional basis. High school athletic leagues might be a start.

Churches within the same denomination should periodically attempt to bring congregations from different local communities together for joint services.

Whenever a poor peoples' movement stages a protest in its own neighborhood, middle-class supporters should stage a parallel demonstration in the suburbs to emphasize the interrelatedness of the problems.

As with the European Common Market, joint efforts on the part of the local communities to administer basic metropolitan services might foster cooperation on other matters as well. Campaigns for public transportation and improved sanitation systems should see themselves as first steps in the process.

Regional "People's Coalitions to Revive the Metropolis" should get together throughout the country, focusing attention on the basic needs of cities and suburbs and sustaining public pressure on all fronts until they are met.

Urban life has spawned many problems—crime, narcotics, racial tensions, a generalized sense of helplessness and despair. Some say that these conditions will never be improved until poor people move into the suburbs; others argue that their solution must await the return of the middle class to the city.

Yet if the cities themselves have become unlivable; if the suburbs are beginning to seem more like strategic enclaves against hell than a new paradise; if developers are destroying the country's last remaining natural resources in their desire to let people escape farther and farther into the countryside, then only a movement to revive the metropolis will restore confidence in the promise of a healthy balance between conditions of living and of work, lack of which drove people to the suburbs in the first place.

The earliest community-action programs of the sixties were developed not simply because they promised to rebuild communities but because they promised to provide constructive alternatives to juvenile delinquency. The Black Muslims have shown remarkable success in rehabilitating drug users and criminals by encouraging their followers to work together to make their communities what they ought to be.

How long will it be before the rest of the country gets the message?

C. PEACE

As with the nation, so with the world. The search for justice is central to the search for peace. Indeed, the conflict between hawks and doves merely transposes the debate between the corporate establishment and the radicals onto an international plane.

If the establishment attempts merely to preserve stability between private groups at home, the hawk seeks merely to preserve stability between nations abroad. The hawk insists that the maintenance of a balance of nuclear terror between the great powers and the imposition of peace settlements by the great powers upon smaller nations must be the central elements of any foreign policy that hopes to respond realistically to the world as it is. If such a balance is preserved, they argue, over a period of time agreements might be negotiated that eventually will pave the way to peace.

To the peace movement, however, the central crisis in the world is the disparity of wealth and power between rich and poor nations, and a strategy for peace that ignores this crisis does so at its own peril. No longer, radicals say, will oppressed peoples accept a role as the bloodied pawns of a global chess game between large nations. They did not invent the bomb. Why should they be the ones to pay the price for its existence? Why should it be their farms, their villages, their countries, that are destroyed?

The United States has had its Dominican Republic and its Indochina; the Soviet Union has had its Hungary, Czechoslovakia, and Poland; even a smaller nation, Nigeria, has had its Biafra. These crises will continue, says the peace movement, until the great powers learn the lesson that their histories should have taught them: Stability without justice breeds only revolution and war.

In one of a number of brilliant articles in his *Between Capitalism and Socialism*, Robert Heilbroner suggests with considerable insight what an appropriate American policy toward the Third World ought to be:[16]

> *First, it would call for an immediate halt to military aid to reactionary regimes and for a cessation of clandestine activity against revolutionary movements.*
>
> *Second, it would require an acceptance of some form of revolutionary nationalist socialism as the political and economic order most suited to guide many developing nations in their desperately hard initial stages of change.*
>
> *Third, it would permit the continuation of humanitarian programs of food and medical aid, as well as technical assistance of a nonmilitary kind, for all governments, revolutionary or not, provided that reasonable standards of international behavior were met.*

We might add one more to the list: Fourth, it would permit foreign citizens to sue American corporations in United States Courts for violations of U.S. law in foreign countries—suits to be brought by trade unions, domestic ecology organizations, foreign governments, or the citizens themselves.

Devising proposals, however, is not the problem. Building public support for them is. Citizens understand domestic problems from their own experience. They must accept arguments concerning U.S. involvements abroad on faith. Whether radicals can inspire this faith depends on their ability to "tell it like it is" in a way that makes sense to them. Once again, a sensitivity to the framework of justice—the promise, the ideal, the mechanism of support—is critical.

Attempting to redeem promises is no secret to the anti-war movement. It has derived its greatest strength, in fact, from predicting accurately the disastrous course of the Indochina War at a time when national leaders of both parties were seeing lights at the end of every tunnel. Now, however, it has become fashionable for radicals to debunk all public promises in order to protect themselves against disillusionment. This stance is a big mistake. When a President pledges peace, his word should not be questioned, it should be tested. The radicals should be the ones to emphasize the high promise, to publicize it to the people, to proclaim that they are waiting for the Chief Executive to do as he says. Then, as each month passes without action, the radicals should keep the memory of the promise alive—not to let it pass unnoticed by a public that is all too willing to forget. Gradually, if the President does not keep his word, it will be the radicals who gain a reputation for fidelity and the government whose credibility will be under attack.

All people need to feel idealistic about their country's role in the world; the Left should respect this need. The establishment has made considerable headway in arguing that the United States is the hope of the free world, that countries everywhere are depending on this country to protect them against the evils of Communist aggression. Rather than confronting this argument on its own terms, the radicals should borrow it and phrase it in a new way. They should point out that the united States once was an underdeveloped nation whose name meant justice almost everywhere in the world. Even today, the preamble to the North Vietnamese Constitution includes the opening lines from the Declaration of Independence. Why, then, has the United States itself failed to fulfill its historical mandate? Why has it reverted to a moral posture that it once tried to avoid: that of justifying great evils in the name of some modest, yet attainable good? Why shouldn't American citizens in the year 1971 have a right to expect decency in their country's relations with other nations of the world, as well as within its own borders? Radicals who pose such questions may not win over the people, but they at least will gain a respectful hearing.

Finally, recognizing human weakness, radicals should never assume that the public understands easily the exact effects of U.S. foreign policy throughout the world. After all, most people do not travel widely. To them, Saigon, Hanoi, Santo Domingo, and Beirut are just names in a newspaper. They are not even sure how to pronounce some of them correctly. The case for justice in foreign policy, then, must be argued in a context that citizens will understand.

Two steps would seem useful:

First, radicals should try to draw concrete parallels between the involvement of American interests abroad and their behavior in the United States. If, for example, a speaker wants to persuade an audience that a large corporation is depriving foreign nations of their right to self-determination, he should be able to say, "In 1970, this corporation was brought before the Environmental Protection Agency for failing to comply with repeated orders to stop polluting the Mississippi. If that's the way the corporation behaves in the United States—in defiance of government regulations—imagine how it must behave overseas in countries where the people have no control over it whatsoever? Let's look at a few examples. . . ."

Second, and most important, radicals should use their own overseas representatives with greater effectiveness. The enormous success of the Vietnam Veterans Against the War in reaching the silent majority suggests an important truth—that Americans still trust experience over statistics, an anecdote over a dissertation. The veteran who can say, "I was there. I was fighting. I have examined what we were doing, and I have concluded that it was wrong," makes more sense to the average citizen than all the tired speeches of university professors put together. The veteran, after all, tends to be "one of us."

An effective follow-up to the creation of the Vietnam Veterans Against the War, then, might be the convocation of a conference of all those who have worked overseas for the United States in the past ten years—Peace Corps volunteers, former employees of AID, refugees from private projects—and who have become disillusioned with U.S. foreign policy. The conference might formulate a few simple demands, comparable to those suggested by Heilbroner, and attempt to develop a program of political education around them. It could establish a counter-State Department to serve as a center of criticism of government policies toward the Third World on a continuing basis. It could publish a list of people available to talk about their experiences overseas and another list of people available to write about them. If convened regularly, such a conference could emerge as a critical force in the foreign-policy debates of the future.

In general, however, the task of the peace movement is the same as that of movements that organize around domestic issues: to explain the way it's supposed to be, the way it can be, and the way it will be if people get themselves together. To say "end imperialism, end militarism, end the war" fulfills only one part of the assignment. The people must know where to begin. The demand that the standard of justice be applied to foreign policy at least tells them that they can face the world in a radically new way, in a way that respects their own collective sense of dignity as well as the dignity of the peoples of the world. If they can grow accustomed to this notion, the rest is certain to follow.

SUMMARY

Three campaigns:

A campaign to redistribute the welfare; a campaign to revive the metropolis; a campaign to redirect foreign policy.

The first would demand that the society distribute its wealth fairly; the second would demand that communities use their resources sensibly; the third would demand that the country treat other nations humanely.

Could a movement fight for any one of these objectives without caring about the success of the others? Could a people understand any one of them without understanding the basis of the others? Could a government acknowledge the morality of any one of them without accepting the moral framework of the others? That's what a movement for justice is all about.

II. CONFRONTING THE INSTITUTIONS

What about predominant institutions, however? How might they be enlisted in a movement for justice?

To pose such a question is to get at the heart of the *malaise* that young people presently experience. They are asked to work in corporations that show little concern for the nature of the goods and services that they produce; in law offices and social-welfare agencies that mediate between private individuals and groups without even attempting to project a vision of common life that might bring them together; in high schools, technical institutes, and colleges that have become little more than appendages to the productive machine. The managers of such institutions do not merely avoid the pursuit of justice; they thwart it. Even as they proclaim that the "system can be made to work," they disparage anyone who raises a question that transcends its values. Then they wonder why students and young professionals and poor people and growing numbers of frustrated middle Americans demand an alternative.

One hundred years ago, farmers and laborers faced a similar problem with the institutions of their society. They, too, were told to work within the system—to give up their farms, their neighborhoods, even their native lands to seek jobs in the factories growing up around them. "Follow us," corporate leaders said, "and there'll be acres of diamonds for all." It was a lie, and the poor people knew it, but they had no choice.

They had no choice, that is, until they built a union movement to fight back.

A new kind of union movement is needed today, one that addresses itself to the promise of modern institutions. Corporate leaders say that technology can guarantee social justice. They claim that employees can share in formulating corporate decisions that affect their lives. A new union movement must hold them to their word.

Consider the following example:

In the winter of 1969, a group of social welfare workers from the

Massachusetts Department of Public Welfare came together to discuss what they could do to contribute to the cause of welfare reform throughout the state. They, like all welfare workers, had been caught in the middle of the welfare crisis. The MWRO had begun to organize recipients to march on local welfare offices for benefits that the system had denied them. The governor, in response, was threatening to cut recipients' "special needs" allocations altogether. The Massachusetts Social Work Guild, the union, was pursuing negotiations on a contract that gave employees lower case loads and a voice in decision-making in the various offices, but no voice over the policies of the system as a whole. In short, for the person who had sought employment in the welfare department to provide decent social service to the poor, there was nothing.

The dissident social workers had to respond. These were not theorists. Many of them had never been involved in politics before. Yet they felt betrayed and exploited, and they wanted to do something about it. Almost by instinct, they began to think in terms of the framework of justice.

First, they related the promise of the Welfare Department to its actual performance. Pat Roderick, the woman who emerged as the group's spokesman, complained:

We're not able to help anyone. Every day we must sit in our offices watching mothers come in and out to whom we simply must say "no." Their problems are not psychological. They don't lack motivation. They need either jobs or income, and the country is not prepared to give them either—at least not on terms which make sense. Yet we're expected to help them cope with their problems. The rich people go back to their nice comfortable homes in Newton while we do their dirty work for them. How long can you live with yourself playing a role like this?

Then the group tried to determine ideally what a social worker should be doing. Since most of the recipients' problems did reflect their lack of economic and political power, the workers concluded quickly that encouraging poor people to get together to demand justice was the critical objective. They realized as well that they had to join recipients in such battles. They had to persuade other welfare workers to fight for social change, and they had to use their knowledge and experience as poverty workers to persuade middle-class liberals in the peace movement that the economic crisis at home was as critical to the survival of the country as ending the Indochina War abroad. Gradually they evolved a conception of the "social worker as organizer" that would replace the notion of the "social worker as counselor." Even those who lacked skills in organizing found themselves asking how they might contribute to the process.

The workers' strategy for building support entailed three basic steps:

1. They constituted themselves as a "client-oriented" caucus within the Massachusetts Social Work Guild to advocate the creation of a coalition between social workers and welfare recipients to fight for adequate income and a basic restructuring of the welfare system.

2. They informed MWRO that they could be counted on for assistance in any way, both within the Welfare Department and outside of it.

3. They initiated discussions with case workers in private social agencies, radical lawyers, and community organizers as to ways in which they could maximize their effectiveness.

And they developed an arsenal of tactics as varied as the crises that prompted them. They circulated petitions throughout the department in support of client demands. Members testified at legislative hearings dealing with welfare reform. When Welfare Rights demonstrated at the statehouse in protest against the governor's proposed "flat grant" program, the caucus joined them, three of their number getting arrested with the recipients at closing time. They took part in union floor fights, becoming identified with campaigns against the authoritarian tactics of the union leadership as well as with efforts on behalf of the poor. They wrote articles for the union newspaper. They ran candidates for union offices, winning shop steward positions, several seats on the union executive committee, and one of two union vice-presidencies. Most important, they began to change the minds of their fellow workers, showing them that they could fight the system instead of accepting blindly everything it did.

Within a year, the Client-Oriented Caucus had transformed itself from a tiny minority on the fringe of the Massachusetts Social Work Guild to the most powerful single force within it.

If a movement for justice is going to succeed, it must generate momentum for the creation of similar caucuses everywhere. To be sure, counterinstitutions such as those created by young lawyers in the past few years can provide opportunities for a few self-sacrificing radicals who wish to pursue social change on their own. Yet a caucus movement is essential for those who cannot afford to work at subsistence wages—college graduates paying back loans for their education; those who have never finished college. Indeed, in many cases, a radical caucus can prove even more effective than its counterpart outside of the system. After all, if management fails to meet its demands, a strike can be called, thereby focusing public attention on what it is trying to accomplish. As an example, the Revolutionary Action Movement of black employees of the Polaroid Corporation gained national publicity lately for trying to change company policy toward South Africa.

What, then, would a coherent strategy for work-place organizing entail? Again, the familiar triad—the promise, the ideal, the mechanism of support—suggests a few alternatives.

Every institution maintains that its work is of critical importance to society; a work-place caucus should take this rhetoric seriously. Perhaps the institution claims that it is serving the poor. Is it? Perhaps it says that it is performing technical services essential to the national security. Is it? Is it really delivering decent health care to patients? Is it really helping young people come to grips with the world around them? Is it really rehabilitating the mentally ill? Is it really selling goods at the lowest price to the consumer? Is it really trying to protect the public against unsafe merchandise and false advertising? Such questions are critical in forcing employes to consider the relationship of their work to the broader community.

In determining which issues around which to organize first, moreover, it would be critical for a caucus to distinguish between the different kind of promises that are made to employees.

First, there is the formal promise that can be fulfilled without difficulty. The employer has neglected to provide employees with group-health insurance forms even though the contract stipulates that he must do so.

Second, there is the informal promise that can be fulfilled without difficulty. The employer will agree to an extra coffee break in the afternoon even though the contract does not require it.

Third, there is the formal promise that an employer will ignore unless a strenuous campaign forces him to do otherwise. A store claims to be selling only high-quality merchandise, but its shelves are filled with commodities known to be harmful to health and public safety.

Finally, there is the informal promise that will require a strenuous campaign before the institution lives up to it. A health clinic promises to give decent treatment to all those who require it even though the clinic lacks resources to do the job.

The organizer's strategy, then, should be to demand adherence to fulfillable promises, while generating discussion among employees about promises that will take more time.

There are any number of ways to foster idealism in employees, that is, to help them formulate proposals that might be brought to a bargaining table. Sometimes, an analysis of the purposes of the institution by itself shows workers how the constitution might be changed. For the Client-Oriented Caucus this certainly was the case. Yet a caucus can draw on a number of outside resources as well: articles in magazines, newspapers, and professional journals about new developments in the field; visits to counterinstitutions that put into practice techniques that the system honors only in theory; experiments within other fields that seem applicable. *Anything* legitimizing change should be brought to the caucus for consideration since—at first, at least—most employees will not have considered the possibilities.

The most important task of a caucus, however, is building a mechanism of support sufficiently powerful to protect workers against getting fired. Here a number of steps would seem useful.

Caucuses should involve employees from all divisions of an office, not simply its professional departments. It is not technical knowledge that determines an employee's commitment to justice, after all, but his or her moral and political beliefs. On this basis, anyone who expresses a willingness to share in the risks of a struggle should be welcome to participate in its planning.

Radical caucuses should try to work within existing unions. However decadent it may be, a union still gives its members a feeling of dignity. The radical who snubs it is snubbing the employees as well, conveying to them that he is somehow above their paltry efforts to survive. For this reason, the caucus should identify completely with all union demands for higher salaries and better working conditions. Later, caucus spokesmen can use union meetings to present proposals of their own.

A caucus should not be afraid to seek help from outsiders. The Client-Oriented Caucus constantly relied on lawyers, other welfare workers, and representatives from community organizations for advice in wrestling with tactical problems stymying them. Often, it was just this sort of advice that made the difference between victory and defeat.

Caucuses should make alliances with groups outside the system. It is doubtful, for example, that social workers in Massachusetts could have created a radical caucus were it not that MWRO was forcing them to take sides between recipients and the department. Similarly, it would be next to impossible for a group of engineers to fight to convert a defense plant to peaceful purposes in the absence of a peace organization advocating the same thing. Teachers should ally with parents and student organizations; doctors and nurses should coordinate strategy with unions lobbying in behalf of decent health-care facilities and national health insurance; employees of offices and stores and factories should unite behind consumer-protection agencies. The rule is self-evident: The broader the alliance pressuring an institution, the greater the chance it will change.

Caucuses should attempt to meet with one another. Management is management in a corporate society. Its techniques to preserve stability, to isolate dissidents, to force employees to give in, are the same all over. If corporate leaders learn from one another, revolutionaries must do likewise.

Finally, critical to the success of the entire caucus movement would be the creation of area centers designed specifically to give support to people engaged in social change on a full-time basis. Such centers might undertake:

Research into the power structure of a region, to be used in connection with movement campaigns.

Historiography of the region so that organizers might familiarize themselves fully with its customs, traditions, and previous struggles for social change.

Vocational Counseling so that new arrivals might determine where they were needed most.

The formation of an organizer's school whereby radicals inside the system could pay experienced community organizers to teach them how to organize.

Publication of a newsletter featuring articles of theory, strategy, and tactics relevant to local movement battles as well as practical information, *e.g.*, which summer programs give funds to movement organizations.

Coordination of campaigns such as those outlined elsewhere in this chapter.

Clearly, then, the creation of radical caucuses everywhere should be a central objective of a movement for justice. The power to paralyze a system is the power to change it. New radicals should direct their efforts accordingly.

III. CANVASSING THE CANDIDATES

Eventually, efforts to organize campaigns around issues and to create radical caucuses within existing institutions would have to be felt by the political system itself. The state is the embodiment of a political community; a reflection of all that is right and wrong with it. If today's state is becoming a monster, it reflects the public values of the system as a whole.

We have seen that even the most idealistic politician is limited in what he can do. He must rely on the support of wealthy contributors to stay in office. More generally, he is circumscribed by the philosophy that liberalism has bequeathed him. For years, liberals tried to bring everyone into the "mainstream of society," that is, into institutions that fostered a continuing spiral of production as an end in itself. Now they wonder why government is powerless to control those same institutions.

What, then, should a radical democrat demand of an electoral politician? On what basis should he offer or withhold his support?

First, he should determine whether the candidate in question understands the highest aspirations of the people to whom he or she is speaking. A politician who spends most of his time reaffirming his faith in the system; who contends that all problems can be solved if only people would learn to lower their voices; who says, "And I think this is what young people are trying to tell us"; who engages in the "who-made-the-first-and-angriest-speech-against-the-war-contest"; who argues that "we should get out of Indochina because of what it's doing to the country," as opposed to what it's doing to Indochina; who cautions against "overpromising" instead of suggesting ways in which high promises can be kept; who flagellates himself and his audience for the "crimes which we have committed"; who insists that someone must "bring us together" without defining the terms of the settlement; or who consistently fails to present arguments in terms that people can understand, should be avoided. A politician who can argue that a bill to bring General Motors under public control is in perfect accord with the American democratic tradition and mean it; who can point to a building in the middle of Memphis and say, "See that. That's where your grandfathers met to work for the election of William Jennings Bryan. If he were alive, *he'd* have something to say about these large corporations that are overpricing the consumer, underpaying the worker, and refusing to pay attention to the overwhelming needs of the people of the United States"; who can show that he realizes how difficult it is to cope with modern society without justifying moral paralysis; who can describe the Vietnamese people as, "no different from you and me. They hate unemployment and inflation too, only they get thrown out of work because Richard Nixon's planes have destroyed their rice paddies, and their prices go up because we still have 100,000 troops spending money over there"—such a candidate should generally be supported.

A radical democrat should ask a candidate to spell out his vision of a decent community and how he plans to move toward it. Does he believe that there are imbalances of wealth and power between rich and poor, whites and blacks, men and women? How does he propose to erase them? Is he prepared to use his influence to persuade suburbanites that the restoration of metropolitan regions is as much in their interests as in the interest of those who live in the city? Will he try to interpret the struggles for self-determination going on in the Third World to his constituents— just as some in the peace movement are trying to do? In general, will he talk to people about the quest for justice and its importance to America in the years ahead?

A radical democrat should insist that the candidate agree to maintain regular contact with movement organizations, to defend radicals under indictment by the government, and to use public power to advance movement objectives. The Democratic Party organization demands loyalty of its representatives; so should the movement. Will the candidate intercede on behalf of radicals who have been fired by employers for organizing in the work place? Will he speak out against the Justice Department's use of the Federal Government to harass the movement in general? Will he ride herd on the Secretary of Health, Education, and Welfare for his failure to enforce provisions in the Food Stamp Bill? Will he demand that a corporation president be subject to criminal prosecution for his failure to obey laws against pollution? Will he support hearings on the charges leveled by the Vietnam Veterans Against the War concerning war crimes in Indochina? Unless a candidate is willing to make these sorts of commitments, his assurances that he "really sympathizes with everything that the movement is trying to do" will not mean too much.

In general, however, radical democrats should view an election year as a glorious time in which to organize. They may not be able to support a candidate, but they certainly can attend his meetings, ask questions, debate his supporters, try to move them to the Left. Even on these occasions, of course, adherence to a few basic principles is necessary:

Never call a candidate a hypocrite. Prove it with reference to his record or to specific inconsistencies in his speeches.

Always treat those working for a candidate with respect. For most of them, the campaign represents a first step toward a continuing involvement in efforts to achieve social change. Since the "Rayformers" really are "mornin' glories—look lively in the mornin' and wither up in a short time, while the regular machines go on flourishin' forever," a coherent movement can win recruits in the aftermath.

Never argue that there is no difference between the two parties. There is a difference. When the Democrats refuse to withdraw from Vietnam, people feel betrayed; when the Republicans refuse, the people feel that the administration is behaving as expected. In general, then, the Democrats generate more activity than the Republicans because they make more promises that they seem to take seriously. Don't knock it.

Yet even within these limitations, the possibilities are endless. After all, at what other time in America are so many people willing to squabble about social problems?

IV. CONCLUSION

Throughout the twentieth century, both liberals and socialists have argued that progress—technical, cultural, historical—will bring justice automatically. Today, most people realize that it ain't necessarily so. We are beginning to understand that justice comes only when a country decides to commit itself to the fulfillment of what it means.

Already, in the past decade, we have witnessed several movements against injustice. "End Racism," "End Imperialism," "End Militarism," and "End Sexism,"—the slogans have become clichés even to those who use them.

A movement for justice—for a society that preserved a balance between its conflicting needs; for a system that created no contradiction between what a person wanted to do, what he could do, and what he had to do; for a nation that fostered the dignity of every one of its citizens—would turn the indictments into a vision.

Such a movement would use issues to dramatize moral conflicts and try to draw the relationships between them.

It would hold every institution accountable to the highest values of the country.

And it would force politicians to take seriously their own professed ideals.

References

1. William Jennings Bryan, "Cross of Gold," in Houston Peterson, *A Treasury of the World's Great Speeches* (New York, Simon & Schuster, 1965), p. 641.
2. Eugene V. Debs, "Appeal for Clemency," *Ibid.*, p. 722.
3. Martin Luther King, Jr., "I Have a Dream," *Ibid.*, p. 832.
4. Melancton Smith, "In the Ratifying Convention of New York," in John D. Lewis, *Anti-Federalist versus Federalist: Selected Documents*, p. 234.
5. Isaiah, 32:1.
6. William Shakespeare, *The Merchant of Venice*, Act III, Scene 1, *11.* 52–57.
7. From NWRO Pamphlet, *School Lunch Program Bill of Rights*, p. 1.
8. From *NWRO Pamphlet, NWRO's Guaranteed Adequate Income Plan*, p. 1.
9. Massachusetts Welfare Rights Organization Pamphlet, *Five Lies About Welfare*, p. 10.
10. Harry L. Hopkins, "The Outlook," reprinted in Ralph E. Pumphrey & Muriel W. Pumphrey, *The Heritage of American Social Work*, (New York, Columbia University Press, 1961), p. 440.
11. Whitney Young, *Beyond Racism* (New York, McGraw-Hill, 1969), p. 170.
12. *Ibid.*, p. 169.
13. Cited in David Broder, "No Doubt About It . . . taxes Must Go Up," *Boston Globe*, Friday June 4, 1971, editorial page.
14. Tabor R. Stone, *Beyond the Automobile: Reshaping the Transportation Environment*, (Engelwood Cliffs, N.J., Prentice-Hall, Inc., 1971) p. 13.
15. *Ibid.*, pp. 68–70.
16. Robert Heilbroner, *Between Capitalism & Socialism* (New York, Vintage, 1970), p. 304.

Epilogue: Will the Revolution Succeed?

7 Yet we must return to the question with which we began: Will the revolution succeed? Will the country accept justice as its major goal? Will the society develop institutions through which citizens can pursue justice on a continuing basis?

It is not inevitable. It will hardly be easy. It will not happen overnight. It will not even happen at any one fixed point in time. Even under the best of circumstances, the pattern, if not the substance, of the past ten years—of idealism followed by disillusionment; of momentum followed by stagnation; of inspiration followed by confusion—is destined to repeat itself over and over again.

Despite these sobering probabilities, however, I believe that the revolution can succeed. People everywhere—in the United States; in the Soviet Union; in Czechoslovakia, Hungary, and Poland; in Indochina and in Chile; in Biafra and East Pakistan—are fed up with the false gods of the twentieth century, gods who have run out of pedestals upon which to stand. They long for a new reason to pursue the perfections that they can imagine. Justice gives them that reason, for it depends not on some new invention in a new world of new men, but on a commitment to build upon the strength of communities as they are.

We must go further, however. The question, "Will the revolution succeed?" implies deeper questions—namely, "Will the revolution be worth the effort? Will we enjoy life more under a commonwealth of justice than under a commonwealth engaged in the pursuit of wealth?"

One is tempted to answer simply, "Yes. Think of the kingdom

of dignity. Surely the chance for such a kingdom is worth the sacrifices necessary to achieve it."

Such a response will no longer do. There have been too many ghastly realities defended in the name of "the glorious future" to justify the resurrection of another one. A movement must offer dignity to those who participate in it, not merely to generations yet unborn. People must sense the nobility of the battle itself.

Past revolutions—those fought in the name of material goods and services alone—handled the problem concretely. The invention of a car, the discovery of a new way to process food, the redistribution of a baron's land provided tangible evidence that the revolutionary was on the right track.

In this respect, today's revolution—aimed at restoring a sense of peace and belonging—is at a disadvantage. Often, people must discover for themselves the rewards that rebuilding an entire society can bring. There is no purely practical way to describe them.

Nonetheless, human beings *have* died for their visions—not merely for their homes but for the memories associated with them; not merely for their cars and washing machines but for the long years of struggling against overwhelming obstacles to obtain them. Of course, as they grow old, they grow tired; but if the movement can remind them of their youth, it can restore their confidence in themselves.

Reviving pleasant memories will not be sufficient, however. A movement for justice must work to rebuild those institutions that foster values as ends in themselves. The process has already begun: the redefinition of the family; the rejuvenation of the church; the transformation of the school. But it has not gone far enough. The new forms must generate new meanings. The new life style must yield new life content. Liberation must lead to fulfillment.

Consider the new extended families that the movement is creating: the collectives, the communes, the urban cooperatives. There is much about them worth supporting. They insist that all members of a household share in its upkeep—a dictum often ignored by men in this society. They grapple seriously with the problems that arise when even a small number of people attempt to function as a coherent group. They operate on the principle that community, like charity, begins at home.

Yet a commune that devotes its time solely to the perfection of the trivial—cooking, cleaning, managing the finances—can become as oppressive as the family that it replaces. Those who join the experiment in order to create a viable alternative to the society soon find themselves entrapped in a web of interpersonal feuds and rivalries. An off-hand comment becomes an excuse for all all-night evaluation. Minor arguments become major crises. Eventually, the commune flies apart.

There is only one kind of commune that helps its members change society—a commune that helps its members challenge society. A movement for justice should say so.

A movement for justice should demand that the church demonstrate its "relevance" to modern life by applying the accumulated wisdom of 6,000 years of religious thought to the world's major moral crises. No book makes the argument for justice and the case against the pursuit of wealth and power better than the Bible. Yet preachers who tell their congregations that they ought to live up to the Scripture because it's really quite simple, you know, and besides, what else do we have; or ministers who think that they can resolve the spiritual crisis of the young by growing their hair long and chanting "Groove on Jesus"; or rabbis who present the moral and ethical teachings of the Old Testament as little more than a collection of rules that decent Jews ought to try to remember once in a while, if only to fight anti-Semitism, are never going to impart the power of the Torah or the inspiration of the Gospel to an errant humanity. A radical theology is the theology of a Dr. Martin Luther King, of a William Sloane Coffin, of an Abraham Heschel, or a Jacques Ellul, or a Daniel Berrigan. It is a theology that takes seriously the demand that modern society transcend its material standards by pointing to the full range of energies that must be devoted to the problem of transcendence itself—not simply faith, but thought, words, expression, and, above all, deeds.

As with the family and church, so with the school. If students are engaged in a search for justice, they should insist that higher education help them in the process. They should support open enrollment not simply because poor people need equality of opportunity, as important a goal as it is, but because academics need a variety of perspectives upon which to base their judgments of right and wrong, truth and untruth. They should contend that a university that cared about justice would organize itself into learning groups, each mandated to pursue a fragment of an unanswerable question. All forms of research—experiential as well as intellectual; creative as well as scholastic—would be relevant. Traditional classrooms would become resource banks to the process of exploration going on inside the groups. Professors would derive their authority not from the letters attached to their names but from their knowledge of what to read and from their greater experience in thinking about fundamental questions seriously. A university-wide representative government would assemble regularly to evaluate whether the institution itself was living up to just standards in its hiring and firing, in its investments, in its research programs, and in its relations with the surrounding community. In time, in fact, the students would get together with the people of the surrounding community to tear down the artificial walls that divide scholar from layman in a technological society.

All of these changes would reinforce the efforts of a movement for justice.

Ultimately, however, the quality of the movement would depend less on its demands than on the spirit of the people within it. This, more than anything else, is what we need to revive.

We need a movement of people who not only can talk about justice but who understand what it means. We need poor people who can wander through neighborhoods and tell you exactly what's been going on in them for the last fifty years. We need internationalists who can grow equally aroused at the treatment of tin miners in Peru as they do at the exploitation of social workers in Boston. We need lawyers who will demand justice from the courts; teachers who will demand dignity from the schools; doctors and nurses who will demand decency from the hospitals and clinics. We need salesgirls who will tell their employers to stop ordering substandard merchandise and factory workers who will tell their bosses to stop polluting Lake Michigan.

We need a movement of citizens in the United States—of people who know both sides of the history of the country, the side that the historians now describe, and the side that our forefathers fought to preserve. We need people whose standard of citizenship goes beyond waving a flag, or marching in a parade on the fourth of July, or voting on election, or writing their Congressmen, or even contributing to political parties and campaigns. We need the kind of citizens who will not permit this country to sell its soul out, to sell the souls of its people out, to sell its Declaration of Independence, its Constitution, and its pledge of allegiance out in the name of a technotronic utopia that lies just around the corner.

We need a movement that will inscribe over every office, factory, church, and school in the nation Joe Hill's dying words to the Wobblies: "Don't Mourn. Organize."

A movement for justice could be that kind of movement. It could restore a sense of common purpose to this country, a feeling that we can come together in pursuit of common goals. It could give us hope that the historic vision of a decentralized America, an egalitarian America, an America which cared about the quality of its communities as much as the quantity of its goods was still worth pursuing. It could give us a chance to be decent again.

Does the idea of that kind of movement turn you on? Does it respond to something in your memory, in your hopes, in your innermost thoughts that has been demanding a response but hearing nothing in return? Does it fit some image that you learned once in a little school somewhere out in Nebraska, or even in a dingy classroom in uptown Manhattan, about what the word "America" was supposed to mean? Does it give you an idea of how far our politicians, our diplomats, our writers, our intellectuals, our corporate bureaucrats, our churchmen, our columnists and pundits, our defenders, and our critics have gone in forgetting everything we really care about?

Do you care about a dream?

What are you waiting for?

Suggested Readings

The footnotes include a number of helpful books, of course. The following are those most useful in understanding the theory, history, and critique of the radical democrat.

BASIC

Alinsky, Saul, *Reveille for Radicals* (New York, Vintage, 1969.)

Bourne, Randolphe, *War and the Intellectuals, Collected Essays; 1915–19* (New York, Harper & Row, 1964).

Green, Philip and Levinson, Sanford, *Power and Community: Dissenting Essays in Political Science* (New York, Vintage, 1970).

Heschel, Abraham, *The Prophets: An Introduction* (New York, Harper & Row, 1969).

McWilliams, Wilson Carey, *The Idea of Fraternity in American Politics* (San Francisco, University of California Press, 1971).

Plato, *Republic* (Any good edition)
     Laws   (Any good edition)

Riordin, William, *Plunkitt of Tammany Hall* (New York, E. P. Dutton & Co., 1963).

Rousseau, Jean Jacques , *Discourse on the Arts and Sciences.*
     Discourse on Inequality.
     Emile.
     Social Contract.

Royce, Josiah, *The Philosophy of Loyalty,* (New York, Macmillan, 1909).

Wolin, Sheldon, *Politics and Vision* (London, George Allen & Unwin, Ltd., 1960).
Wolin, Sheldon and Schaar, John, *The Berkeley Rebellion and Beyond* (New York, New York Review of Books, 1970).

AMERICAN HISTORY

Bowers, Claude G., *Jefferson and Hamilton* (Boston, Houghton-Mifflin, 1966,).
De Tocqueville, Alexis, *Democracy in America, Vols. 1,2* (New York, Vintage, 1945).
Dos Passos, John, *Living Thoughts of Tom Paine* (Greenwich, Conn., Premier, 1961).
Fried, Albert, *The Jeffersonian and Hamiltonian Tradition in American Politics* (New York, Doubleday Anchor Books, 1968).
Goldman, Eric, *Rendezvous with Destiny* (New York, Vintage, 1955).
Grob, William, *Workers and Utopia* (Chicago, Quadrangle, 1961).
Hicks, John D., *The Populist Revolt* (Lincoln, Neb., U. of Nebraska Press, 1959).
Lewis, John D., *Anti-Federalist Versus Federalist: Selected Documents* (San Francisco, Chandler, 1967).
Meyers, Marvin, *The Jacksonian Persuasion: Politics and Belief* (New York, Vintage, 1957).
Miller, Perry, *The New England Mind: The Seventeenth Century* (Boston, Beacon Press, 1954).
　　　　　From Colony to Province (Boston, Beacon, 1961).
Rogin, Micheal, *McCarthy and the Intellectuals* (Cambridge, MIT Press, 1967).
George B. Tindall, *A Populist Reader* (New York, Harper & Row, 1966).
C. Van Woodward, *Origins of the New South* (New Orleans, Louisiana State University Press, 1951).
　　　　　Tom Watson; Agrarian Rebel (New York, Oxford University Press, 1963).

MISCELLANEOUS

Buber, Martin, *Paths in Utopia* (Boston, Beacon, 1950).
Cleaver, Eldridge, *Soul on Ice* (New York, Delta, 1968).
　　　　　Conversation With Eldridge Cleaver with Lee Lockwood, (New York, Delta, 1970).
Ellison, Ralph, *Invisible Man* (New York, Signet, 1947).
　　　　　Shadow and Act (New York, Signet, 1966).
Ellul, Jacques, *The Meaning of the City* (Grand Rapids, Mich., William B. Eerdsman Publishing Co., 1970).
　　　　　The Technological Society (New York, Vintage, 1964).

Friedenberg, Edgar Z., *Coming of Age in America* (New York, Vintage, 1965).

The Dignity of Youth and Other Atavisms (New York, Vintage, 1965).

Grier, William H. and Cobbs, Price M., *The Jesus Bag* (New York, McGraw Hill, 1971).

Hawthorne, Nathaniel, *The Blithedale Romance* (New York, Laurel, 1960).

Heilbroner, Robert L., *Between Capitalism and Socialism* (New York, Vintage, 1970).

Lowi, Theodore, *The End of Liberalism* (New York, W. W. Norton, 1970).

Schaar, John, *Escape From Authority: The Perspectives of Erich Fromm*, (New York, Harper & Row, 1961).

Simmel George, *The Sociology of Georg Simmel*, Kurt Wolff, ed. (New York, The Free Press, 1950).

Stone, Tabor, *Beyond the Automobile: Reshaping the Transportation Environment* (Englewood-Cliffs, New Jersey, Prentice-Hall, 1971).

Twain, Mark, *On the Damned Human Race* (New York, Hill and Wang, 1963).

Malcolm X, *The Autobiography of Malcolm X* (New York, Grove Press, 1965).